In collaboration with:

ANDREW W. BROWN (deceased)
FORREST A. KINGSBURY
MANDEL SHERMAN, M.D.
RALPH W. TYLER
W. LLOYD WARNER
MILDRED DORR
JOAN MURRAY DUDMAN
RACHEL KESTENBERG
MARCHIA L. MEEKER
DOROTHY NEUBAUER
BERNICE L. NEUGARTEN
FRANZ OPPENHEIMER
AUDREY F. RIEGER
ELEANOR VOLBERDING
NORA L. WECKLER

THE COMMITTEE ON HUMAN DEVELOPMENT
THE UNIVERSITY OF CHICAGO

ADOLESCENT CHARACTER
and PERSONALITY

ADOLESCENT CHARACTER and PERSONALITY

Robert J. Havighurst

THE COMMITTEE ON HUMAN DEVELOPMENT
THE UNIVERSITY OF CHICAGO

Hilda Taba

DIVISION OF EDUCATION
SAN FRANCISCO STATE COLLEGE

SCIENCE EDITIONS, 1963

JOHN WILEY & SONS, INC., NEW YORK

Printed in the United States of America

Contents

Acknowledgments

The members of the group who made these studies attended innumerable committee meetings, criticized the work of others and took criticism of their own work, and wrote and rewrote the chapters to which their names are attached.

A very great debt is owed to the teachers, certain townspeople, and the boys and girls of Prairie City. The teachers supplied data and helped the field workers to obtain data. A number of men and women in the town, including all the clergymen, advised and assisted the field workers. The boys and girls in the sixteen-year-old group took many tests, wrote essays, filled out questionnaires, and talked with the field workers.

In addition to field work done by several people working on these particular studies, the field-work material of several other people was available to us in the preparation of this volume. We are especially indebted to Wilfrid Bailey, Arch Cooper, and August B. Hollingshead in this connection. Field work in the community was started by Mr. Hollingshead, who lived in the community for a year and collected interviews and general statistical data on all high-school-aged adolescents then living there. His findings are published in *Elmtown's Youth: The Impact of Social Classes on Adolescents*, New York, John Wiley & Sons, Inc., 1949 (in press).

This volume and *Elmtown's Youth* may be viewed as companion pieces since they have been based upon research in the same community, and in part on the same boys and girls. They differ in that each volume is focused upon a different facet of adolescent life. This volume is an intensive analysis of character in sixteen-year-old boys and girls. Hollingshead's study is focused on the relationships between the community's class system, the adolescent's family, the functioning of social institutions, and the behavior of adolescents.

Finally, it is a pleasure to acknowledge the work of Dr. Bernice L. Neugarten as editor. Hers was the difficult task of integrating the writings of twelve people.

R. J. H.
H. T.

Chicago, Illinois
January, 1949

Preface

The Committee on Human Development consists of faculty members from various departments of the University of Chicago whose fields of study relate to the development of children and adults. Members of the committee include students of biology, physiology, nutrition, pediatrics, psychiatry, anthropology, sociology, education, and psychology. Certain additional members of the committee are staff members of child-serving agencies in the Chicago area. Therefore the committee represents a comprehensive group of disciplines that are used in the study and understanding of human beings.

The Committee on Human Development of the University of Chicago has two major functions. In the first place, it provides training opportunities for preparing persons to work with children and youth. An adequate background for the understanding of children and youth cannot be provided in a single department. The training program of the Committee on Human Development involves courses drawn both from the biological and from the social sciences.

The second function of the Committee on Human Development is to conduct broad-gauge research relating to the development of human beings. The Committee seeks to make a contribution to the understanding of human development by emphasizing three features in its research. The first is that various aspects of development shall be studied in relation to each other; that is to say, the physiological, the psychological, the social, and the educational aspects of human growth and development shall be studied simultaneously and their interrelations examined. A second feature is the emphasis upon longitudinal investigations; that is, the development of the same individuals is studied over a period of time to trace the changes accompanying growth. The third feature of the Committee's research is unique. The Committee seeks to describe and to measure the social environment together with changes in environment and to relate these factors to human development. This enables the investigators to see more clearly the influence of significant environmental factors upon children and adults.

Although the Committee on Human Development is conducting a number of studies at various places and under various auspices, such as the investigation of child development among Indian tribes, in cooperation with the United States Office of Indian Affairs, and the study of cultural factors in intelligence testing, its chief program of investigation is a community study. In order to investigate the factors in human development and the related environmental conditions it is necessary to have a fairly self-contained community of moderate size. The Committee uses as its laboratory a small city that is quite typical of midwestern communities. It has been working in this community for several years and expects to continue its studies there for a long period of time in order that it may have an adequate set of data from which to draw significant conclusions about human development.

One phase of this program of community research is the study of character development. This investigation is supported by the Lilly Endowment, Incorporated. The Committee is deeply grateful to Mr. Eli Lilly for his continuing contributions to this study. The present volume is a preliminary report growing out of an investigation of the youth in the midwestern community who were sixteen years old at the time the study was begun. It is hoped that this book will be of value to persons who work with youth and that it may provide some suggestive findings for research workers in this field. An investigation of character development in a younger group of children is also under way, and further reports of the study of character development are expected to be published from time to time.

Ralph W. Tyler, *Chairman*
The Committee on Human Development

Chicago, Illinois
January, 1949

Overview of the Studies

The Problem of Studying Character

Persons with good character make a society good, and, in the long run, they lead the most satisfying lives. The importance of character is so generally understood and accepted that character is ranked by most people as of first importance in the child's education. In a recent national poll,[1] 34 per cent of the persons interviewed said that character education was the most important aspect of education, a proportion just equal to those who placed the mastery of the three R's in first place. Among people who had a college education, 51 per cent gave character education first place.

Character is influenced by many things. A long time ago Theophrastus, the Greek philosopher, asked: "Why is it that while all Greece lies under the same sky and all the Greeks are educated alike, it has befallen us to have characters variously constituted?" His question has been repeated many times by many people, and we are asking it once more. What things account for differences and similarities in character?

DEFINITION OF CHARACTER

Character is a word with many meanings. It is used here in the current sense of "moral character." Thus, for the purposes of these studies, character is that part of personality which is most subject to social approval. For example, honesty, but not humor, is part of character. An honest person is highly approved by our society, while a dishonest person is disapproved, and may even be put in jail. But a person with a strong sense of humor, though he may be said to have a more pleasing personality, is not therefore said to have a better character.

[1] Published by the National Opinion Research Center, University of Denver, June 10, 1944.

3

It is necessary to make this distinction between character and personality quite carefully. The two terms have been used synonymously, particularly by European writers. Not only have psychologists used the word "character" in more than one sense; the word also has a variety of meanings in everyday usage.

Thirty-four representative adults in a typical midwestern community were asked what they understood by the term "character." Their answers were exceedingly diverse. One person said that character is reliability, be it good or bad. "Thus Hitler has character because he is what he is all the time." Another said: "Character is what you really are." Another said that character is the person's inner convictions. Still another definition was, "Character is a man's attitude toward God and man." Another was: "Character is how you act unconsciously or naturally, or when you believe yourself to be unobserved."

When asked to name traits of character, these people mentioned a total of twenty-five characteristics, the ones most frequently named being honesty, responsibility, kindness, and moral courage.

This concept of character as a composite of moral traits is useful for purposes of scientific study. It enables the scientist to study character by studying psychological traits and their relationships. A psychological trait is a scientific fiction—a name for a discernible segment of a person's behavior. Although a psychological trait is not thought of as an inherited or unchangeable element of personality, in the sense that eye color is an inherited and unchangeable biological trait, it is, nevertheless, a regular, predictable way of behaving. For example, it is possible to say something about a person's "honesty" when his behavior is observed in relation to other people's property, in relation to his own promises, and in relation to his accounts of past happenings. He is more or less honest, or honest in some circumstances and dishonest in others.

Character was defined in this sense as a composite of moral traits. No preliminary assumptions were made about the relations between traits. That is, it was not assumed that an honest individual is necessarily courageous, loyal, and reliable or that a dishonest person is necessarily cowardly, disloyal, or unreliable.

Five traits were selected as representative of the traits which make up moral character. They were *honesty*, *responsibility*, *loyalty*, *moral courage*, and *friendliness*. The first four are usually conceived as central character traits, while friendliness is on the borderline between those traits which are generally thought of as moral traits and others which are not usually judged in moral terms. If a person's behavior in terms of all five traits is described and summarized, the result should be a fairly good representation of his moral character.

The next step was to secure definitions of traits in terms of observable behavior of boys and girls. Just what does it mean, for example, to say that a boy or girl of high-school age is loyal? What is loyal behavior in an adolescent?

Operational definitions of the five character traits were agreed upon by the authors. For example:

Loyalty means to make sacrifices for an institution, a group of people, or an individual with whom the subject feels identified, or with whom the subject feels some common bond. It means to act for the best interests of such an institution, group of people, or individual, even at the cost of personal embarrassment or hardship.

Examples: *Loyalty.* Takes the part of friends in controversies. Will not speak ill of friends and will not permit others to speak ill of friends. Keeps on cheering for the team when it is losing. Attends school games and other events faithfully. When given a minor part in a play or on a committee, works faithfully at it. Attends church, Sunday school, etc., in bad weather. *Disloyalty.* Says unfriendly things about friends behind their backs. Refuses to support team when it is losing. Is active in organizations only when rewarded by prestige or other compensation. Allows personal feelings about other boys and girls to determine attitudes toward school activities in which they participate. Will not stand up for a friend when friend is criticized.

The definitions were used as a guide in devising various research instruments.

PRELIMINARY GENERALIZATIONS ABOUT CHARACTER

The research group shared a set of basic postulates about character development which should be made explicit at the outset of this volume.

Factors Influencing Character

An individual's behavior is a product both of the social environment in which he has lived and of his own personal make-up. The social environment—home, church, school, neighborhood, age group, community—establishes a code for good conduct.

Through these agencies the code is communicated to individuals and in a sense is forced upon them; through these channels a person learns what is expected of him; and through them he is rewarded or punished to the degree to which he lives up to expectations.

The make-up of the individual—his personal characteristics, intelligence, goals, drives, interests, adjustment patterns—constitutes the second general influence on his character development. Although to some extent personal make-up is determined by heredity, to a very great extent these personal qualities are the results of earlier social experiences.

The moral character of the individual is always the result of what he already is as a person combined with the play of social forces upon him.

It is important to note that there is no clear demarcation between that which lies "within" the person and that which lies in the social context around him. Values and codes which were first imposed by society are eventually adopted by an individual as his own.

How Character Develops

These studies are based upon the postulate that character, to a very great extent, is *learned* behavior. It is learned in three general ways.

1. Character is learned through reward and punishment. Moral behavior is especially amenable to the influence of the social environment because it is constantly subject to approval or disapproval. First in the home, then in the school, in the play group, and in the community at large, a person is constantly being rewarded for learning certain moral values and habits and punished whenever he exhibits immoral habits and values. His rewards may be tangible, but more often they take the form of social approval. His punishments may be corporal, but they are no less effective when they take the form of social disapproval.

2. Character is learned through unconscious imitation. By the time a child is a few years old he has formed the habit of imitating people who have prestige in his sight. The first objects of imitation for him are his parents and others in his family.[2] Figuring in the process is a kind of "anticipated reward." The child discovers that he is rewarded very often for behaving like his father or his

[2] The psychological basis for this imitation is described by Neal Miller and John Dollard, *Social Learning and Imitation*. New Haven: Yale University Press, 1941.

older brother. He imitates various kinds of behavior—gait, posture, and speech forms, as well as moral behavior. The habit of imitation carries over outside the family, and the child imitates popular age mates, teachers, and romantic characters in the movies or the comic books.

Somewhat allied to the process of imitation is the process of building an "ideal self" which serves as an object of imitation. The "ideal self" probably begins with the image of one of the parents; it grows to include certain attributes of other family members, adults outside the family, glamorous characters from the movies, comic books, and newspaper headlines, and historical and literary figures, until the image which emerges is a composite of many persons.

3. Character develops through reflective thinking. Moral behavior may also be learned through thinking about moral situations, tracing various kinds of behavior through to their probable consequences, and reaching conclusions which may govern future behavior. If this process is practiced often enough, with guidance which safeguards accuracy of reasoning, it results in a number of general moral principles which may be applied in future situations. In a changing society which constantly poses new moral problems for the individual, it is obviously of great importance that a person have generalized moral principles and that he be able to apply them wisely in specific instances.

The Two Levels of Character

There are two levels of good character. On the popular level moral conduct is controlled by praise and reward from the immediate social environment. A person lives up to the moral expectations of those with whom he rubs elbows. At the second level moral conduct is controlled by ideals; in the pursuit of a moral ideal the person may displease his associates and be blamed and punished for it.

The statesman who said: "I would rather be right than be president," proceeded on the principle that general popularity and approval might be gained only at the cost of compromise with his moral ideals. The memory of Christ, Socrates, and other martyrs reminds us that social approval by one's contemporaries is not the mark of highest character.

On the contrary the highest moral behavior is often unpopular. It is, as William James said, "action in the line of the greatest resistance. . . . The most characteristically and peculiarly moral judgments that a man is ever called on to make are in unprecedented cases and lonely emergencies, where no popular rhetorical maxim can avail, and the hidden oracle alone can speak; and it speaks often in favor of conduct quite unusual, and suicidal as far as gaining popular approbation goes." [3]

The second level is the level of conscience, of moral principle, and of moral choice. A minister was speaking of character at this level when he defined it as "that which causes a person to react as he does to questions of moral choice. Good character is to be guided by high moral principles and not by one's personal convenience or comfort."

The child begins on the first of the two levels. He learns to behave morally in response to reward and punishment from his family and from others with whom he associates. Gradually he develops moral ideals and principles and a moral conscience to enforce those ideals. At the same time he develops intellectually to a point where he can apply his moral principles and ideals to new situations. Thus the second level of character is built upon the first.

Some persons always remain on the lower level of character development. They are honest, responsible, loyal, and kind in the ways which are favored by the people around them.

Other persons develop the more heroic aspect of character. Their honesty, responsibility, loyalty, and moral courage are motivated by moral principles and activated by conscience. They will risk the displeasure of the people around them to pursue their ideals. This latter group probably has greater stability and consistency of conduct because it acts upon inner principles and inner convictions.

While these studies deal mainly with character on the first level, implications for the development of character on the second level have been pointed out wherever possible.

HOW TO MEASURE CHARACTER

Once character had been defined as a composite of moral traits and once five of the traits had been selected as representative of moral character, the first problem to arise was that of *measuring* the degree to which an individual possesses the traits in question.

[3] William James, *Principles of Psychology*, Vol. II, pp. 549, 672.

It was necessary to find something about an individual which would serve as an index of his honesty, responsibility, moral courage, loyalty, and friendliness.

Two possible indices of character were considered—behavior and reputation. The behavior of a person can be observed in many different situations, and from these observations he can be given a score for each of the character traits. Or he can be given scores on the basis of what other people say about his honesty, responsibility, moral courage, loyalty, and friendliness.

The difficulties of observation are immediately apparent. It would be practically impossible to observe the normal everyday behavior of a hundred boys and girls for a sufficient period of time to get reliable information regarding their moral behavior. Instead, it would be necessary to create a number of test situations designed to gauge a person's honesty, responsibility, and so on, and to observe the behavior of the subjects in the test situations. In other words, it would be necessary to devise *performance* tests of the character traits.

This was the procedure followed in the Character Education Inquiry [4] made some years earlier. In the inquiry, Hartshorne and May and their associates devised a number of ingenious test situations to test honesty and cooperativeness. For example, they invented situations to test for cheating in school work, cheating on puzzles, cheating in games, and stealing money.

Good as the tests might be, and the Character Education Inquiry Tests were good, observation of behavior in test situations must always be a doubtful substitute for observation of everyday behavior. The great variety of everyday situations cannot be duplicated in a small number of tests, and there is always the question whether the test situation is lifelike enough to motivate the subject to behave as he would in real life.

In the light of these considerations, it seemed desirable to use reputation as an index of character. A person's reputation is based primarily upon long observation of his behavior by his associates. Although not trained to record and interpret their observations objectively, a person's associates have the advantage over pro-

[4] Hugh Hartshorne, Mark A. May, and others, *Studies in the Nature of Character:* I. *Studies in Deceit;* II. *Studies in Service and Self-Control;* III. *Studies in the Organization of Character.* New York: The Macmillan Co., 1930. Comparisons between the studies reported here and the Hartshorne and May studies are given in greater detail in Chapter 27.

fessional observers that they have observed the person in real life and over a long period of time. If the individual's reputation can be obtained from people who have a variety of points of observation, reputation should be a good index of character. At the end of their studies Hartshorne and May came to the conclusion that reputation might be as good an index of character as performance on a battery of tests.[5]

There are, of course, certain objections to using reputation as an index of character. (1) Some aspects of an individual's personality which are not character traits may cast a halo over the individual's true character and thus give him a character reputation which he does not deserve. For example, the fact that a given family occupies a high social position in the community may result in undeservedly high character reputations for its children; or the individual who belongs to a particular racial or ethnic group may share the reputation of that group current in the community, whether or not the generalized reputation is true of the individual himself. This is the familiar problem of stereotypes, which may affect the validity of reputational ratings. (2) Some character traits may cast a halo over others and thus give a person a reputation for all character traits which he deserves only for certain ones. For example, a high degree of friendliness may give a person a reputation for honesty and responsibility which he does not deserve.

On the other hand, reputation may be defended (1) as giving a very good measure of character on the level of conformity to the expectations of society. (2) When reputational ratings are obtained from a variety of persons, there is the further advantage that the judgment of the individual's character is based upon more points of view than would be possible under any procedure of direct observation.

For the purposes of these studies, then, reputational ratings were used as the principal means of measuring character. Ratings were secured from the individual's age mates, his teachers, Sunday-school teacher, school principal, scout leader, and employer.

[5] "When enough opinions (about the character of a subject) can be gathered with reasonable care and from contrasted sources—as from pupils, teachers, and parents—the resulting score becomes a fair substitute for an elaborate and expensive program of objective testing." Hartshorne and May, *op. cit.*, III. *Studies in the Organization of Character*, p. 369.

QUESTIONS TO BE STUDIED

Provided with a procedure for measuring moral reputation and with definitions of the character traits to be studied, the research group formulated a set of questions about character development, which they undertook to investigate.

The principal questions were these:

1. To what extent is character development influenced by the value systems of the social groups to which the individual belongs, or to which he relates himself positively or negatively?

The values held by the family, by the dominant groups and institutions in the community, and by persons in positions of authority and high status constitute the "moral climate" in which a young person grows up. These groups and persons are in a position to punish undesirable conduct and to reward desirable conduct, and their expectations have much to do with the standards of behavior developed by the individual.

It seemed important therefore to examine the values, expectations, and codes of conduct maintained by the subjects and families, their respective churches, their friends, their school, and their community.

2. How is character development influenced by the quality of emotional relations with parents? with adults? and with age mates?

The quality of a person's emotional relationships is important in determining how he reacts to family members and others and what he accepts and what he rejects of their moral codes. The affectional relations in the family are particularly important because the groundwork of moral education lies in the internalization of the moral commands and attitudes of parents. This incorporation is more likely to take place if there is a positive affectional relationship between parents and children than if there is a lack of respect and love. Similarly, young people often pick out adults as ideal persons, identify themselves with them, and imitate them. Association with peers is a source from which a large part of the meaning of moral courage, loyalty, and honesty is derived.

Consequently, it was decided to investigate the quality of family relations for each subject. It also seemed advisable to find out what types of adults serve as models for boys and girls of various ages and for boys and girls from different social backgrounds.

Furthermore, some picture was needed of the individual's relationships with his peers.

3. To what extent is the individual's character influenced by his values, interests, and goals?

How an individual behaves with regard to honesty, responsibility, moral courage, etc., is influenced by what he himself believes about the value of these traits. A person may value duty and responsibility directly, or he may conduct himself dutifully and responsibly because he wants to win the respect of the group which values duty and responsibility. It seemed important to study what boys and girls believe about moral values, how consistent or mature these beliefs are, and what relationship there is between what they believe and how they behave.

4. To what degree is character development influenced by the individual's ability to intellectualize problems of conduct?

Wise control of conduct is possible to the extent that the individual understands why certain acts are desirable and others undesirable; to the extent that he foresees the consequences of his acts; and to the extent that he becomes aware of certain general moral principles, standards, and values and their relationship to conduct; in other words, to the extent that he formulates a rationale for his conduct and guides his behavior accordingly.

It was necessary therefore to find out how adequately young people can think through various problems of conduct, can resolve conflicts in values, beliefs, and desires, and how consistently they apply whatever principles and beliefs they hold.

5. To what extent is character development influenced by other personality factors of an individual, namely, his drives, his physical make-up, his intelligence, his dispositions toward other people, and his self-adjustment?

The individual's own personality sets the tone for his relationships to his environment. Special talent, intelligence, and sociability influence his status in the group. His own impulses, wishes, and drives determine the extent to which he must exercise self-discipline to make a place for himself. His security and self-assurance color his moral actions.

Therefore, data were needed on all these aspects of the subject's personal make-up.

These questions formed the basis of the studies to be reported in the following sections of this book.

2

The Community Setting

From what has been said about the importance of social environment in the formation of character, it is clear that the writers wished to study not only individual boys and girls but also the community in which they live. It was important to select a community which was in most respects typical of many others, so that the findings of these studies could be generalized.

GENERAL CHARACTERISTICS OF PRAIRIE CITY [1]

The community to be called Prairie City is small enough to be studied intensively, and at the same time it is typical in size and complexity of the many small cities of the Middle West.

According to the U. S. census there are about 250 small cities with populations between five and ten thousand located in the twelve north central states, from Ohio to Missouri and from North Dakota to Kansas. One hundred and eight of these cities are the largest centers in counties which are agricultural-industrial. This type of county has between 25 and 50 per cent of its gainfully employed males in agriculture, and the remainder are in industry, business, and other occupations.

Prairie City, the county seat of Prairie County, is one of these 108 cities. There are communities of twenty to thirty thousand population in the adjacent counties, and there is a metropolitan area within a hundred miles. The total population of this community is about ten thousand, of whom six thousand live within the city limits and four thousand in the surrounding rural territory.

[1] "Prairie City" is a fictitious name, used to conceal the identity of the community and the individuals studied.

Prairie City was chosen for study after a survey had been made of the census data on all the small cities of this type within 200 miles of Chicago and after Prairie City and other cities had been visited. These preliminary studies showed Prairie City to be typical of small midwestern cities according to a number of significant census criteria.

The town is about a hundred years old. Its population grew rapidly until 1900, and since then it has remained relatively stable; it has not changed as much as 10 per cent in any decade since 1900.

The city has shared in the development of the Middle West from a simple agricultural society to a complex industrial-agricultural society. The community is now economically dependent equally upon agriculture, manufacturing, and retail sales. It has a favorable location on railway and waterway lines and serves as an important shipping point for the surrounding region. Census data show that the proportion of people paying an income tax is about the same as in other small cities.

A community like Prairie City tends to be relatively complete and "self-sufficient." Lying outside a metropolitan area, it has an independent social life; there is no college, university, or state institution in the community, nor is it a health or summer resort. Its local autonomy and coherence are therefore undisturbed.

Approximately 90 per cent of its inhabitants are native born; there are two distinguishable ethnic groups—a substantial group of Norwegians and a small Polish group. There is one Negro family and one Chinese. Thus Prairie City has the usual American diversity, though it is not as highly diversified as most of the large cities.

Although the community is simple enough and unified enough so that the scientist can describe its social structure after a relatively short period of study, at the same time it offers "everything" in American life—factories, a complete school system, library, movies and other commercial recreation, banks, hospitals, and specialized medical service. Although it is small enough so that a boy or girl can grow up and be acquainted with "almost everybody in town," it gives a youth enough experience with modern industry and society to enable him to step into the more complex metropolitan world and act with vigor.

Like the other communities of its type, Prairie City is a vital source of new life for the metropolitan areas of this country. The great cities, which fall considerably short of reproducing their populations, continue to draw from smaller communities. Thus the welfare of the great cities, as well as small, depends to a considerable extent on the quality of the children who are reared in Prairie City and its kindred communities.

SOCIAL STRUCTURE OF PRAIRIE CITY

The people of Prairie City like to think of each other as equal in some respects and unequal in others. They are equal in the sight of the law and equal in the sight of God, yet no one in Prairie City feels that all people are equally good morally, intellectually, or socially. Every father would prefer that his daughter marry into certain families rather than into certain others. No one would just as soon sit down to dinner with the squatter down in the river bottom as with the president of the bank.

The social differences which exist in Prairie City form the basis for a social hierarchy. The people in Prairie City place themselves and others on a social scale, some high, some in the middle, and some low. They say that "the C's are at the top" or that "the D family is really low. Not one of them has ever amounted to anything" or "the P family are solid people. We should have more like them." There is a considerable amount of agreement among the residents of Prairie City as to the structure of the society in which they live. Some persons in the community who are especially observing can line up several hundred families into a hierarchy from the top to the bottom of the local society.

It must be emphasized that the residents of a community create the social hierarchy; the social scientist merely maps the structure as he finds it.

In general, he uses two methods:

First, he talks with a number of people about the social structure and finds out from them what families they think are at the top, bottom, and at various levels in between. After getting the opinions of many people in the community, the scientist compares their testimony and follows the consensus of their opinions. Thus he constructs a scale from the social top to the social bottom of the community.

Second, he collects evidence about "social participation," that is, membership and participation in formal and informal groups, such as church, lodge, club, bridge club, and informal social cliques.

Social participation is the principal method for locating an individual on the social scale. A person is classed with the people who are his friends, whom he entertains in his home, and whom he calls by their first names. His income, education, occupation, and other socio-economic characteristics are related to his social position, for reasons that are obvious; but these factors are taken as secondary rather than primary evidence of his social position.[2]

Social mobility, or movement up or down from one class to another, is quite frequent in the social system of such communities as Prairie City. In fact, to most people the democratic ideal of equality of opportunity really means equal opportunity to rise in the social scale. It will be seen that desire for upward social mobility is an important element in the formation of character for a number of the boys and girls in these studies.

On the basis of information obtained in the ways just described, it was found that the families of Prairie City fall into five major groups or "social classes."[3] A social class is a group of people who think of themselves as belonging to the same social level and who generally are willing to associate intimately with one another—to visit each other in their homes, to dine with one another, to have their families intermarry, and so on.

It is worth while to study the social structure of Prairie City and to locate the families of the subjects on the social scale because various social classes have different ideas of what is right and wrong, interesting and boring, important and unimportant. Therefore there may be differences among the social classes in moral character.

[2] A more complete account of the methods used in studying the social structure of Prairie City is given in Chapter 21, including a discussion of the relations of social status to economic status.

[3] The method of studying the social structure of a modern community is described in W. Lloyd Warner and Paul S. Lunt, Yankee City Series: I. *The Social Life of a Modern Community;* II. *The Status System of a Modern Community.* New Haven: Yale University Press, 1941, 1942.

Also, W. L. Warner, Marchia L. Meeker, and Kenneth Eells, *The Measurement of Social Status.* Chicago: Science Research Associates, 1948.

For a description of the relation between the school system and the social structure of a community, see W. L. Warner, R. J. Havighurst, and M. B. Loeb, *Who Shall Be Educated?* New York: Harper & Brothers, 1944.

The following sketches tell something about the kinds of people who make up the various social classes in Prairie City.

The *upper class*, group U, is at the top of the social hierarchy. This is a small group, consisting of about 2 per cent of the people in the town. They are said by others in Prairie City to be "the top crowd," "the aristocrats," "the four hundred," "the money crowd." There is a small group of families who are referred to as "the old families" or "the landed gentry," who have been in the community for several generations and whose wealth lies largely in land. There is another group who have come to Prairie City more recently and who own the principal industries. Together these two groups make up the upper class. They are important in community affairs but seldom appear personally at meetings. They give financial support to the church and to other civic institutions but take little active part in them.

Members of the upper class live in the best houses in town, in two particular neighborhoods. They have a good deal of social intercourse with people in the nearest metropolitan area. They have the reputation of being somewhat free in their morals, but this reputation does not affect their position as "the best people."

The *upper-middle class*, or group UM, consists for the most part of professional men and their families, officials of the industries, the larger or "better" business men, and a few leading farmers. Members of this group are the active community leaders. They are members of the Rotary Club, the school board, and are officers of the women's clubs; they hold the important political offices and are leaders in their churches. They are "the people you go to if you want to get anything done," "the pillars of the church"; they have a reputation for high moral standards and take a great deal of civic pride in the community. Six to eight per cent of Prairie City families fall in this class.

The upper-middle-class families have higher-than-average incomes, live in big houses, and include the individuals of highest educational attainments. Together with the upper class, these people are "above the common man" of Prairie City.

The *lower-middle class* is the "average man" of Prairie City. This group constitutes the bulk of the membership in the various associations, the rank and file of the churches, fraternal orders, and political organizations. These are the people whose bridge parties, bunco clubs, and "get togethers" fill the society columns of the local newspaper. Thirty-five to forty per cent of the residents of Prairie City belong in this class.

The members of group LM are small business men, clerical workers, lesser professional men, foremen, skilled tradesmen, and farm owners. They live in small, well-kept houses or in large, older houses; their homes are to be found all over town, except in certain poorer districts.

The *upper-lower class*, group UL, is the large group which is too busy trying to make a living to have much time for active participation in the social organizations of the town. They are the "poor but respectable" people, making their living as semiskilled workers, laborers, and tenant farmers. They are "the little people," "the people who never give anybody any trouble." In numbers they make up about 40 per cent of the population. Their families are large, and they furnish about half of the children of the community.

Members of the upper-lower class have little organized social life. They are not as active in the card clubs, sewing clubs, and church auxiliaries as are the lower-middle class. They are distributed among most of the churches, but two revivalistic churches are made up almost entirely of members of this group. They live in what are generally known as the poorer neighborhoods—around the edges of town and in some of the poorer commercial buildings. The Polish group in Prairie City belong mainly to this class.

The lower-middle and upper-lower classes make up the overwhelming majority, the "common man" of Prairie City. The dividing line between these two groups is less clearly defined than the line between any other two classes. Movement from one class to the other is frequent. The Norwegians, the largest ethnic group, belong mainly to these groups.

The *lower-lower class*, group LL, is the bottom of the social heap. Some people are there because of extreme poverty or the stigma of belonging to a recent immigrant group. But most of this group are placed there because of "non-respectability." They are considered by the rest of the community to be dirty, shiftless, dishonest, and of low morals. The people in other classes refer to them as "those river rats" and "damned Yellow Hammers." But the members of the lower-lower class think of themselves as "just as good as anybody else." They refuse to admit that there is anything wrong with their way of life. There are several families in this group who boast of fine Scotch and English names and a lineage of several generations in Prairie City. These families have a non-respectable reputation of long standing.

In the lower-lower class there are always some families who are quite respectable, but who by accidents of marriage or because they live in the "wrong places" are associating with lower-lowers. These tend to be the families who are upward mobile, and they may rise into the upper-lower class within a generation.

The LL group has the lowest income, least education, and its members live in dilapidated shacks on the river bottom or beyond the abandoned tannery or above the poorest stores in the business section. Their names appear most often on the police records. They are a considerable distance below the upper-lower group in the social scale, and it is not easy for them to climb out of their present status. Several of the young people in these families are climbing up the social ladder, however, as later chapters will show. About 12 or 15 per cent of the families in Prairie City fall into this group.

3

Subjects and Procedures

The subjects of these studies consist of all the boys and girls in the Prairie City area who became ten years old in the calendar year 1942 and all those who became sixteen. Research on the ten-year-old group is still in progress and will be reported in a later volume. Research on the sixteen-year-olds had to be terminated as more and more of the group entered the armed services or left the community to work in defense industries. This volume concerns itself, therefore, with the sixteen-year-old group; it will be followed in due time by a report on the younger group which will add to the findings of this report.

There were 144 individuals in the sixteen-year-old group; 68 boys and 76 girls. Of this group 114 were in school in September, 1942, and 99 remained in school in June, 1943.

TABLE 1   SOCIAL CLASS, PLACE OF RESIDENCE, AND SCHOOL ATTENDANCE OF SIXTEEN-YEAR-OLD SUBJECTS

	Boys							Girls							Total
	U	UM	LM	UL	LL	?	Total	U	UM	LM	UL	LL	?	Total	
Urban															
In school	2	3	11	13	2	1	32	—	3	19	18	6	—	46	78
Out of school	—	—	1	17	4	—	22	—	—	3	7	5	1	16	38
Rural															
In school	—	1	6	2	—	—	9	—	1	4	6	1	—	12	21
Out of school	—	—	—	4	1	—	5	—	—	1	1	—	—	2	7
Total															
In school	2	4	17	15	2	1	41	—	4	23	24	7	—	58	99
Out of school	—	—	1	21	5	—	27	—	—	4	8	5	1	18	45
Total	2	4	18	36	7	1	68	—	4	27	32	12	1	76	144

Table 1 shows the distribution by social class and urban or rural residence of those in and out of school. There were 116 boys and girls from Prairie City, 28 from the rural area.

There were two ethnic groups, the Norwegians and the Poles, with thirty-two and eight representatives respectively. All eight of the Polish group were urban. This group consisted of five girls, all in school, and three boys, one of whom was in school. Six were in Class UL and two in Class LL.

TABLE 2   SOCIAL CLASS, PLACE OF RESIDENCE, AND SCHOOL ATTENDANCE OF NORWEGIAN SUBJECTS

Class	Boys					Girls					Total
	UM	LM	UL	LL	Total	UM	LM	UL	LL	Total	
Urban											
In school	—	1	4	2	7	—	5	4	—	9	16
Out of school	—	—	2	—	2	—	1	1	—	2	4
Rural											
In school	—	4	—	—	4	1	3	2	—	6	10
Out of school	—	—	1	—	1	—	—	1	—	1	2
Total Group											
In school	—	5	4	2	11	1	8	6	—	15	26
Out of school	—	—	3	—	3	—	1	2	—	3	6
Total	0	5	7	2	14	1	9	8	0	18	32

Data on the Norwegian group are given in Table 2. This group covers a wide range in social class but does not extend into Class U.

There were a number of boys and girls about whom there is relatively little information. These were the ones who had dropped out of school. Since most of the observation and testing was done in school and since high-school teachers gave much of the information on the reputation of the subjects, those who were out of school were studied less intensively. The thirty who were out of school at the beginning of the school year are largely unknown to the investigators. The fifteen who dropped out during the year are better known, and there is a good deal of information on a few of them. Information is quite complete on about 95 of the 144 subjects.

In terms of social class groups, information is complete on nearly all members of the U, UM, and LM classes. Although the number of subjects in the two upper classes is small, it constitutes the total membership of their respective groups, and there is no question of their being a "representative sample." On the two lower classes, information is much less complete. Those on whom the data are least adequate are the boys and girls who had dropped out of school. Their omission from the studies leaves a serious gap. It should not be assumed that what is shown to be true of the UL and LL subjects for whom data were available is necessarily true of all UL and LL sixteen-year-olds in Prairie City.

RESEARCH PROCEDURES

There are, in general, two possible approaches to the study of moral character: one may be called the statistical approach; the other, the study of individuals.

The statistical approach involves the isolation of factors in the social environment, or factors in the personalities of subjects, which may be presumed to affect character development, and the determination of the statistical relation of each of these factors, in turn, to "good" or "bad" character. Examples of this approach are studies of the relation of intelligence to character, of social position to character, or of church membership to character. The results of such studies apply to the group of subjects as a whole but not necessarily to every individual within the group. A finding such as the one that high intelligence goes with high reputation will apply to most of the members of the group; it may or may not be true for a given individual.

The study of individuals, on the other hand, requires the assembling of as much pertinent data as possible on a series of individuals, the making of case studies designed to explore the interaction of social and personal factors as they operate in the character formation of each individual, and the formation of generalizations which emerge from such case studies.

Both approaches were planned and carried on simultaneously. The same set of basic data was used for both.

The group studies were planned by a committee consisting of all the authors. Separate studies were made by individual authors or pairs of authors, but these were all designed in relation to each other and as integral parts of the over-all research program. All the data collected were available to every member of the committee. When a new research instrument was needed, as was necessary in several cases, the committee helped to provide ideas and to criticize tentative forms.

Arrangements were made in Prairie City to secure the necessary data. Tests and other instruments were administered by field workers who lived in Prairie City but who came to Chicago regularly for meetings with the research committee.

To make the individual case studies, the Clinical Conference Group, consisting of seven of the authors, was formed. Each member of this group became expert in interpreting data from one or more sources, and the seven persons met together regularly to integrate and interpret data for each of the individuals being studied.

Part II of this book deals with the statistical, or group, studies. Each chapter in Part II reports a separate study, together with the results obtained.

Part III deals with the study of individual cases. It includes a series of case histories, followed by the generalizations which emerged regarding character and personality.

Part IV consists of a general summary and interpretation of all the findings of the studies and recommendations for a community program of character development.

Part V contains the more technical and statistical details of the research methods. This material has been placed last in the interests of the general reader, who is probably more concerned with findings than with problems of method. The reader who is particularly interested in research techniques may, however, wish to read this section before reading Parts II and III.

The research instruments were both numerous and varied. Although each technique will be described in detail in later chapters, it may help to orient the reader if they are listed here according to the three general areas in which data were obtained.

1. *Data on Character Reputation*
    The *Check List,* used for rating sixteen-year-olds. Ratings were furnished by school teachers, employers, Scout leaders, and Sunday-school teachers.
    The *Character-Sketch Matching Instrument,* for rating by adults.
    The *Guess-Who Test,* for data from age mates on character reputation.
    The *Portrait-Guess-Who,* a variation of the Guess-Who Test.

2. *Data on Social Contexts*

   Social-status classification, giving the social-class position of the family.

   The *Index of Social Characteristics*, a socio-economic index.

   The *Family-Relations Questionnaire*, to get information on emotional relationships in the family.

   Interviews, with teachers and townspeople.

   Records of membership, in churches and other organizations.

   The *Adult-Guess-Who Test*, to get the names of local adults who have good reputations in the eyes of the sixteen-year-old group.

   A *sociometric test*, of the Moreno type, to discover the popularity status of each subject with his age mates.

3. *Data on Individual Characteristics*

   Essays on life ideals, written by the subjects.

   Student Beliefs, an attitude questionnaire about moral beliefs.

   Life Problems, a "life-situation test" to get data on ability to apply moral principles to conduct.

   The *Moral Ideology Test*, a questionnaire to elicit student ideas of good and bad behavior.

   The *Emotional Response Test*, a questionnaire to find out what experiences have strong emotional values for students.

   The *Mooney Problem Check List*, to get data on personal adjustment.

   The *California Personality Inventory*, to get data on personal adjustment.

   Interviews with the subjects and with teachers, ministers, and others concerning the sixteen-year-olds.

   Intelligence tests, the Stanford-Binet and the performance part of the Wechsler-Bellevue Test of Adult Intelligence.

   School marks.

   Interest inventories, the PEA 8.2a and 8.2b Inventories, to get information about adjustment to school and about personality factors.

   Rorschach Ink-Blot Test, to get data about personality make-up.

   Stories from pictures, a test of the thematic-apperception type, to get data about personality factors.

PART 2

Group Studies

Community Factors in Relation to

Character Formation

The chapters constituting Part 2 of this book vary considerably in style, content, and the nature of their contributions to the study of character development. Some chapters are primarily explorations in method; some are most valuable in delineating areas for further research; others contain implications for educational practice.

Chapter 4 discusses, in terms of Prairie City, some of the background factors present in all communities which play a role in character formation and which are often overlooked in studies of character. The values dominant in the peer culture and the adolescent's adjustment to his peers are examples of such factors.

The material in this chapter should prove of interest to teachers and other group workers in drawing attention to some of the less-formal, less-often-recognized social influences which mold character. It should also be of interest to research workers in suggesting areas to be investigated in any study of character development.

This chapter deals with some of the community aspects which must be taken into account in any consideration of the factors influencing character. Much of this material will be important in understanding the chapters to follow, for it describes the moral setting in which Prairie City boys and girls live.

The chapter is divided into five parts, each of which describes one feature of the community background: the values held by various groups in the community, the social life of adolescents, the quality of the home life of people in the community, character-forming organizations, and recreation places frequented by young people.

The first three topics will be discussed on the basis of information gathered in the course of three years of study of the community's social organization.[1]

[1] The basic data for this discussion are contained in a number of field reports in the files of the Committee on Human Development, The University of Chicago.

VALUES OF VARIOUS GROUPS IN THE COMMUNITY

The child learns values from two general sources: from the adults who have prestige in his eyes and from his own age group. Some of the values which the boy or girl learns are community wide. They are held by all persons, regardless of social or economic status. Such variations as occur in these values are individual and not the result of systematic group differences. Other values learned by children are characteristic of smaller groups within the community, such as social classes, churches, ethnic groups, and the age group to which the boy or girl belongs.

Values of the Community as a Whole

The community values the general moral virtues of honesty, responsibility, loyalty, and kindliness, though these virtues are interpreted differently by different groups in the community. For example, loyalty to one's own family is valued by everybody, but loyalty to the community is a value limited largely to middle-class people. Projects for community betterment, for making Prairie City "the finest little city in the Corn Belt," enlist the active support of middle-class people but fail to stir the interest of the lower classes.

Prairie City is socially and politically conservative. It changes its mind slowly and holds to the ideals that have served it in the past. Above all, it holds to the doctrine that the individual should be responsible for his own economic security.

At the same time one of the traditional American ideals seems to be losing ground in Prairie City. This is the ideal of progress— the goal of making the community bigger and better. Instead of working toward this goal, most people in Prairie City feel that inscrutable external forces will have their way, regardless of what individuals do. Consequently, the community makes no effort to expand. For example, when all the vacant houses in Prairie City were filled as a result of a war boom in a neighboring town, it was proposed that Prairie City apply for federal funds to construct several hundred new houses. But there was very little public sentiment for the proposal. None but a few merchants pushed the idea actively. Some people feared that a post-war business recession would leave houses empty and that an increase of population would leave just so many more families to "go on relief" when the boom was over.

People are not optimistic about life growing better in Prairie City. The memory of the depression of the 1930's is vivid, and World War II created a pessimistic uncertainty about the future. Thus, while the individual is expected to make the most of his abilities, the people doubt that this will result in better economic and social conditions.

Nevertheless, people do not let their uncertainty about the future mar their enjoyment of the present. They prefer present comfort to the promise of future wealth and power. They want the joys of this world, the solid joys, and they are more interested in the comfort that material wealth can provide than in the power it can bestow upon its owner. For this reason they value leisure. When the duck-hunting season opens, for example, men of all economic levels leave their businesses and their work and go hunting for a few days. Fishing is popular too, and men and boys will take a day off any time to fish in near-by lakes and rivers.

We see this desire for material comfort and stability reflected in the following excerpts from essays written by sixteen-year-olds on the subject, "The Person I Would Like to Be Like."

I would like to be about 23 years old. At that age I would probably know something about what my future occupation would be. I would be more or less settled in life as an adult and my worries and anticipation of what I was to do for a living would be over. I would like to do manual labor on a project of my own or for someone else. I like work where I would be able to decide things for myself. If I wanted to go somewhere, I would like to go without my work always hampering me from doing it.

When I become an adult I would like very much to own a little business of some kind, grocery store, sporting store, something on that order. After I have established a good profitable business I would like to settle down and get married. Have two or three children. Then spend the rest of my days making my family happy.

These boys at sixteen want security rather than adventure. They will be content with modest achievements. The following two essays, written by middle-class boys who expect to be engineers, show a surprising lack of the youthful enthusiasm and the aggressive drive for achievement which have long been considered American characteristics.

The clothes I have would be good and not worn out. I would not be fat. My profession would be such as to provide me with enough money for a home of my own, a car, a wife, etc. My profession would probably be electrical engineering or some other sort of engineering. The town I live in would not be too big, and not too small. I would travel quite a bit. I would do some hunting, play golf, probably gamble some. I would know how to fly if at all possible, and I'd own my own plane.

Suppose I am thirty-five years old. I would like to be an engineer at some plant. I would be making a good income, enough to have a small home of my own, in a town of about 5,000 population, and enough to support a small family and be able to save enough to go on a vacation every year and to have some of the things I have always looked forward to having. I should like to be very healthy and have an electric tool shop in the basement as well as a boat in the river and short enough hours at work so I could use some of these privileges. Maybe I would be more satisfied if I owned a business of my own, small or large; it makes no difference.

The following essays, written by girls, express similar values. All three girls are thinking of settling down in Prairie City to a comfortable, industrious, but not ambitious, life.

When I become an adult I would like to be an understanding person, also a very patient one. I would like to be a person that gets up in the morning at regular hours and that gets her housework done in the morning without fooling around and stopping to monkey with every little thing. Also I would like to be respected enough to have discipline in the home among the children. I also would like to be an economizing person and not to waste money. I would like to be able to cook good meals and know quite a little about sewing, canning and other things useful in the home. I want to be a person that people like if I want to have many friends. I also want a home where religion is stressed and where everyone works for the good of each other.

I would like to be a combination of several people I know. I would like to be a beauty operator when I get out of school. I would like to have the appearance of someone "neat" all of the time. I would like to have character like that of Greer Garson in her pictures. She is a movie actress but I would like to be the character that she usually plays in her pictures, kind-hearted, always smiling, and helpful to others when they need help. For recreation I would like to do things around the home or to do any kind of recreation with other people if it were at all possible.

When I am 21 I would like to be well liked by everyone. Have a nice disposition and be easy to get along with. I would like to have a nice complexion, straight teeth, and nice hair. I want to be a typist or a secretary, make a good salary and live comfortably. I want to be able to dance well, play tennis and all sorts of sports. I would like to know about the world of today and of tomorrow, so I will be an interesting person to talk to.

The impression one obtains from all the essays is that their authors are down-to-earth and unimaginative—none of these young people wants to save the world or to set it on fire.

Religion is a basic element of Prairie City culture although many people do not take active part in the churches. When a Prairie City resident says he lives in "God's country," he believes he is speaking the literal truth. The general attitude is that the churches are good for the community. For the church goers, religion nearly always takes an active form—the churches exist for service. Contemplative religion does not flourish.

Human nature is considered rational and responsible. A person is responsible for using his will power to control his impulses; if he behaves immorally, it is his own fault. Moral character, therefore, is generally thought to be the responsibility of the individual and of his family. Most people in Prairie City would say for instance that delinquency is a sign that something is wrong with the delinquent individual. Few persons would stop to question whether or not juvenile delinquency is also a sign that something is wrong with the community. On the other hand, the leaders in the community are beginning to think of the social environment of boys and girls as having something to do with their character development. An indication of this is the fact that a recreation center for young people was recently established under the sponsorship of the Rotary and Lions clubs.

Values Held by the Various Social Classes

The various social classes of Prairie City have somewhat different sets of values.

Members of the *upper class* place importance on their family's past history. They like to talk about the preceding generations. They like to spend money on things which will not produce a profit, such as objects of art, fine horses, fine houses, and philanthropy. Prairie City's upper class is not so clearly marked off from the upper-middle class as is the case in older cities in the East and South. Hence the characteristic upper-class values are not much in evidence, and the community is dominated more by the values of the upper-middle class.

The *upper-middle* class set great store by civic virtue. For them a man's duty to God is his duty to the community. They may even let their responsibilities as parents be subordinated to their responsibilities as citizens, by giving time to community affairs which they might otherwise give to their children. They are great believers in education and in education as the solution of social problems. Their children are leaders in the high school and nearly all go to college.

A leading upper-class man defined the virtues of the upper-middle class when, in speaking about the father of one of the sixteen-year-olds, he said:

> He is one of the finest men we have in town. He has an excellent community attitude. Of course, maybe I judge people too much by their community attitudes, but if people are really interested in their children and interested in the community institutions and working together, I don't give a damn about their social standing.

The values which the upper-middle class instill in their children are self-reliance, initiative, loyalty, good manners, and responsibility to the community. The vices against which they train their children are stealing and destruction of property, sexual immorality, bad manners, and carelessness in dress and speech.

In the upper-middle class certain of the general moral virtues held as values by the entire community have taken on specific forms which differentiate them from the same moral virtues in other social classes. For example, honesty is accepted as a virtue by all classes, but in the upper-middle class it is a generalized virtue. One is expected to be honest toward all people; and honest in matters of property, of truth telling, and of keeping promises. In the lower class, honesty is limited to dealings within the family and within a small neighborhood group. The average lower-class person does not feel compelled to tell the truth to everybody, to be careful of the property of everyone, or to keep his promises to everyone.

The *lower-middle* and *upper-lower* classes are very much alike in their values. They stress respectability, thrift, loyalty, responsibility to family and church, and fidelity in marriage. The church is important in the lives of these people. It is, for them, what the community is for the upper-middle class. It is the scene of most of their social life and the theater of their efforts toward moral improvement of society. The lower-middle people are the most active and faithful church workers, while the upper-lower group follow their lead.

Moral and religious beliefs vary somewhat from one church to another within the lower-middle and upper-lower classes. The Lutherans, for example, teach against dancing, smoking, card playing, and movie going. Their argument against these practices is that, although they are not sins in themselves, they lead to sin.

The lower-class members of a church tend more toward other-worldliness—the belief that they will be rewarded in the next life for good works and sacrifice and suffering in this life. They also set great store by personal religious conversion and the personal experience of salvation.

Education has a different value for this group than it has for the upper-middle class. The majority accept school simply as a means of getting children ready for adulthood. Education, for them, is necessary for individual vocational success. The socially mobile minority of this group—those who are trying to "improve their station in life"—look on college as a means for getting their children ahead in the world, but the majority think of high-school graduation as the highest educational goal. In contrast to these attitudes, the upper-middle class thinks of college as necessary to give their children their own status, and they put great trust in education and research as a means of solving social and economic problems.

The *lower-lower* class are thought to be immoral, by those above them on the social scale. The members of this class are arrested more frequently than those of any other group. Their violations of the code of sexual morality are, if not more frequent, at least more widely known and more flagrant than those of other groups. On the other hand, there are some thoroughly respectable families in this social group who, because of being "foreigners" or because of poverty, are placed in the lowest class.

The principal values held by the lower-lower class center about food, leisure, and family solidarity. The moral virtues of honesty, responsibility, and loyalty are restricted to a small sphere of action that includes the family and a few neighbors or friends.

It seems probable that at least some of the moral ideals held up to children of the lower-lower class are different from those taught to children in the other classes. Stealing is more apt to be over-looked or condoned. Church influence is absent or weak. The moral teaching of the school is not so strongly reinforced by the home, and children of this class tend to drop out of school at an earlier age than children of other social classes. Lower-class children are taught to fight. They experience more open exhibition of aggression in their homes, where the father may beat the mother, the children are whipped frequently, and the child's own aggressive impulses are not much restrained by his parents.

Similarly, lower-class children suffer less restraint on sex play and sex exploration than do middle-class children.

As a generalization it might be said that lower-class children have fewer and less rigid controls on the free play of their impulses, while middle-class children are made to inhibit their impulses through the watchfulness of their parents and the ever-present question in their own minds, "What will people think?"

Lower-class life in Prairie City differs in one important way from lower-class life in a metropolis. The great city presents the disturbing phenomenon of "disorganized areas" in which, from the middle-class viewpoint, social values have gone awry. In these areas it is normal for a child to steal, to lie to the authorities, and to be sexually delinquent. In fact, delinquency is normal, and only those children who deviate from the normal have a chance of adopting middle-class values. This phenomenon of a "delinquency culture" is possible because of the geographical fragmentation of the city, which forces thousands of lower-class people to live together, with their own schools and places of recreation, and which effectively prevents their children from having contact with children from other social classes.

In Prairie City there is very little segregation by social class, and there is no "disorganized area." The people of the lower-lower class live in a fringe around the town, as well as in the poorer parts of the business district. Their children are found in all the elementary schools. Thus they are exposed in the school and on the playground to middle-class influences among their own age group. There are no delinquent groups in Prairie City, though of course some groups of young people have lower reputations than others. Among the sixteen-year-old group there was no history of gang delinquency.

The differences in moral values among the various social classes are probably greater in practice than in words. People all up and down the social scale in Prairie City tend to agree verbally with an official moral ideology, from which their actual moral behavior departs in various ways. For example, upper-class parents undoubtedly tell their children that gambling is wrong, although adults in this class do gamble. Parents of the lower-lower class tell their children that stealing is wrong but do not punish stealing consistently and may themselves set an example of stealing.

The official value system and moral ideology of Prairie City is that of the middle class. This was found to be true when boys and girls were given a test called the Moral Ideology Test in which they were asked to name examples of good behavior and bad behavior. There were few differences between children of the different social classes.[2]

VALUES OF THE ADOLESCENT CULTURE

Recent studies of adolescents have emphasized the fact that boys and girls in their teens have a culture of their own with moral standards and with moral pressures behind those standards. This culture has been called the "adolescent peer culture." [3] Boys and girls, desiring the approval of their age mates, follow the fashions of the peer culture in morals, dress, and speech; and the moral standards and practices of the adolescent peer culture are probably an important factor in character formation.

The principal values of the adolescent peer culture in Prairie City are social participation, group loyalty, and individual achievement and responsibility. As a means of social participation, such social skills as dancing are desirable, as well as a supply of spending money and good clothes. Group loyalty takes the form principally of loyalty to the high school and its activities, but church youth groups and the informal cliques of the adolescent social world also command loyalty. Individual achievement and responsibility mean, for most young people, doing well in school, getting a part-time job, and being a responsible member of several clubs or other organizations.

The high school is the principal locus of the adolescent peer culture. School dances, athletic contests, hay rides, and club activities, as well as study halls and classrooms, are the places where boys and girls learn how to behave socially and morally as young men and women. When a community recreation center

[2] Bernice L. Neugarten, "Family Social Position and the Social Development of the Child," Ph.D. Dissertation, University of Chicago Library, 1943.

[3] National Society for the Study of Education, *Forty-Third Yearbook*, Part I, *Adolescence*, Chap. 12. Chicago: Department of Education, University of Chicago, 1944.

was opened for the use of young people, it was placed under the supervision of the high-school Student Council and became an adjunct of the school program.

The moral standards of the adolescent peer culture are largely middle-class standards set by the high school, which is, in turn, run by people with middle-class values. The teachers are nearly all middle-class people and so are the parents who are most active in school affairs. Finally, the dominant adolescent group in the high school is composed mainly of middle-class girls and boys.

During the period of these studies, the adolescent peer culture of Prairie City was dominated by one clique of girls, who formed themselves into a secret society. This clique was composed of girls from upper-middle-class families and the few upper-class girls in school, together with a few popular girls from lower-status families. These girls elected their candidates to school offices and also set the social pace. There was no comparable group of boys. The leaders among the boys tended to cooperate with this group of girls. The teachers gave this girls' clique their tacit support, since it included the "best" girls in the school.

Thus the two most powerful groups in the school, the teachers and the leading clique among the adolescents, worked pretty much together in setting standards. Most of the students followed their lead. Only in the sphere of relations between boys and girls was there any considerable conflict between teachers and parents, on the one hand, and adolescents, on the other hand.

To achieve success in the adolescent peer culture, a boy or girl must stay in school, be a reasonably good student, take part in school activities, and go to the school dances and parties. In the process of adjusting successfully in these ways, he would be learning middle-class morality. The majority of young people attempted to fit themselves into this situation.

There were three groups which did not adjust well to the dominant adolescent peer culture as it operated in the high school. Failure to adjust meant for each group that it adopted a code of morals which deviated from the accepted code of the school.

One of these groups was the Lutherans. As will be explained in a later chapter, the Lutherans are largely a Norwegian group who try to keep themselves apart from the rest of the community. Since they oppose dancing and motion pictures, their young people cannot participate freely with the dominant group. The Lutheran

Church has an extensive young people's program, including parties at the church on the nights when the school holds dances. Thus a rival peer culture has been established by the Lutherans, with a somewhat different set of moral standards from that of the group that centers in the high school. This does not work out as well as the leaders of the Norwegian group would like, for it causes a good deal of conflict in the lives of the young people as they feel the pressure of the dominant peer culture. Some of them leave the church, at least temporarily.

One of the young people who had dropped out of the Lutheran social group had this to say:

> Those Lutheran kids gang together, except for me. They stick together just like glue. I was ostracized from them because I danced and went to shows and played bridge. They're against everything. In fact, every time we had a dance at the high school, they threw some kind of a party at the church and tried to make the kids come. Those that didn't were ostracized.

The character reputation of the Norwegian group does not suffer from their lack of adjustment to the dominant peer culture. This is easily understood, for they deviate from the accepted pattern toward the side of more rigorous morality. Furthermore, their academic adjustment in the school is satisfactory, and they participate freely in athletics and other activities which are not frowned on by the church. If anything, membership in the Norwegian group is an advantage, as far as moral reputation is concerned.

The second deviant group consisted of a number of high-school students who felt that they were "out of things" socially. They came mostly from upper-lower-class families. Perhaps because the dominant social group consisted of girls, the most vocal of this deviant group also were girls. They openly flouted school regulations, made no effort in their studies, refused to attend the school dances, and went with boys who had dropped out of school or lived out of town.

One of the leaders of this group was a girl who will be called Esther. She was the third child in a large family. Her father was a factory worker with a good reputation. Esther had been an inconspicuous student in school and seemed to be getting along all right until her junior year, when she was sixteen. About this time a number of things went wrong for her. During the summer she had begun to go out at night with boys. She had a job at this time in a soda fountain which was a favorite meeting place for boys and girls of lower-class families and also for young men who lived in the surrounding country. Her parents became alarmed at reports they heard about her and ruled that she must be home by ten o'clock in the evening and that she was not to go automobile riding with boys. She resented these restrictions and complained that she was being treated like a baby.

When school started for her junior year, Esther made an attempt to win social prestige by competing for the post of cheer leader. There were three girls to be chosen. The ruling clique put up three candidates who practiced together and learned from each other. Esther and another girl who tried out for the position were left alone, without aid and encouragement from anyone. The three who had the backing of the ruling clique won the positions, and Esther became bitter about it. Shortly afterward she and some of her friends began "skipping school," which was a serious offense in Prairie City. After one flagrant case of "skipping," the mothers of several of the girls were called to the school. These mothers were worried about their daughters but were inclined to blame the school for what they called "playing favorites" and discriminating against their daughters.

Interviews by a field worker with Esther at about this time showed something of her situation and her reactions to it. The field worker, in this case a man, said to her:

"Well now, Esther, could you tell me how you feel about school cutting, and why you did it? I just want to have some idea of how you feel about the school situation, the cutting, and so on."

"Well, I'll tell you, Mr. S——," she said, "the way a lot of us girls are treated here, you can't blame us for the way we feel. Frankly, for a lot of us, there's nothing here but just coming to classes, and listening to the teacher, and reciting our lessons, and studying, and going home again. We're just pushed out of things. There are a group of girls here who think they're higher than us, and they look down on us. I won't mention any names, but they're a group of girls from the wealthier families. They have a club that's supposed to be outside the school, but it's really in the school. They can do things that we can't afford, and they hog all the offices and are in all the activities. They just won't pay any attention to us. I've almost quit going to church because some of this same group go to the church I used to go to, and there's only one girl besides myself who goes there that's not in that group. They snub us, and they won't talk to us. Now, I know that we're not rich. Dad's only a factory worker, and we can't afford to do a lot of things, but we'd like to be in the school activities and the school games, go to the dances, and things like that. But they just make us feel like we're not wanted. I went to some of the activities when I first started high school, but they just ignored us. Last year I was in two clubs, but this year I'm not in anything. If we go to the high-school dances, nobody will dance with us. They just dance among themselves and have a good time, and we're just nobody. Well, why come to school? We're made to feel out of place, and that's just the way it is."

"Well," said S——, "do you go with boys in the high school?"

"No, I don't go with boys in the high school. I just don't care to. I'd like to go with some of them, but most of the boys that I'd want to go with, they wouldn't ask me. I guess they just don't want to go with me. This year I've been going with a boy that works over at the ammunition plant [in a near-by town]."

"What's his name?"

"His name is Joe."

"What's his last name?"

"Well, I don't know just how to spell it. I know it starts with K-r-a-k-o, but I don't know the rest of it."

"Did he go to Prairie City High?"

"No, he never went to high school. His family just moved over into the neighborhood last year."

"I've been in the doghouse so long now I don't know whether I'll ever get out." Esther changed the subject.

"Well, what would you like to do in school?" asked S——.

"I'd like to have an office, just a secretary of a club, or something like that. I like to do things, and I just want to have fun like the rest of these girls do."

Esther is one of a group of about ten girls in her class who feel this way about the social life of the school and have said so in interviews with field workers. Several boys have made similar comments, though somewhat less articulate.

Esther and her friends are caught in a vicious circle. Since they are not accepted in the social life of the adolescent peer culture, they make a life for themselves with other adolescents who are not accepted. This gives them a bad reputation, and they have more difficulty than ever in their relations with their school mates. School becomes a prison, and, when they try to escape from it, the school authorities come down on them heavily and bring their parents into the situation. The parents alternately punish their children and accuse the school authorities of favoritism.

The character reputations of Esther and others in this group are low—probably lower than their behavior actually warrants. But their situation is a bad one and may influence their characters negatively. They need, obviously, a more wholesome situation, one which offers greater possibilities for satisfaction of their social needs.

The feelings of the majority of high-school students toward this deviant group and the resultant attitudes of the deviant group are brought out in a study by Neugarten.[4] She studied how high-school students were rated by their fellow students on popularity and other personality traits. The dominant clique of girls all came out with high favorable scores though they were rated unfavorably by members of the deviant group. On the other hand, Esther and her friends were mentioned frequently on unfavorable items. With a few exceptions, the upper- and upper-middle-class boys and girls received the most favorable ratings; the upper-lower- and lower-lower-class youth received unfavorable ratings.

The third deviant group consisted of those who had dropped out of school. These boys and girls were almost completely outside the dominant adolescent peer culture, except for a few who participated in the young-people's organizations of the churches. This group had a loose, ill-organized culture of their own, with its locus in certain recreational places of questionable repute, such as a skating rink, the bowling alley, and two or three small eating places. Here they came in contact with the unadjusted high-school students who hovered between the two cultures.

The out-of-school group had poor reputations among the teachers and students in the high school, as well as in the community at large. The values of this group were quite different from the values of the school group. They did not care about education. They had no desire for social participation outside their own group. Their vocational expectations were lower. Their moral standards were said to be lower, by the dominant group. They probably were somewhat freer in their sexual behavior than would be approved by middle-class standards.

There were several out-of-school youth with very good reputations, and everybody recognized that they did not belong to this out-of-school peer culture. They had to stop school for economic reasons or because they were needed to care for invalid persons at home. They tended to seek association with other adolescents in church groups.

To summarize what has been found about the social life of Prairie City adolescents as a factor in character formation, the dominant peer culture encourages conformity to middle-class

[4] Bernice L. Neugarten, "Family Social Position and the Social Development of the Child," Ph.D. Dissertation, University of Chicago Library, 1943.

values and morals; boys and girls who do not adjust well to the dominant peer culture are subject to somewhat deviate character-forming influences. The Norwegian Lutheran group has a peer culture which encourages a rigorous, puritanical morality. The out-of-school group has a peer culture which encourages a moral code that is undesirable judged by middle-class standards. Within the school, but on the fringe of the dominant peer culture, is an unadjusted group which is hostile to the school and the things the school stands for and which leans toward the peer culture of the out-of-school group.

MORAL QUALITY OF HOME LIFE

Undoubtedly the most important single influence on character is the home. Consequently, it is necessary in a study of character formation to evaluate the moral influence of the home upon different individuals and different groups of individuals.

The following description of home life in Prairie City is based on the observations of field workers; it needs to be supplemented by more detailed information and analysis in subsequent work in Prairie City.

There is something of a contrast between middle- and lower-class family life. The middle-class family has allies in the school, church, and youth organizations. The lower-class family takes a relatively greater responsibility for training its children and relies less upon the assistance of outside institutions.

The child of a middle-class family spends relatively more time than does the lower-class child in activities of the Boy and Girl Scouts, in school activities, in the public library, and in the church (with the exception, in the last instance, of the lower-class Lutheran child). The child of a lower-class family spends more time with his parents. His parents do not belong to many associations, nor do they have many things to do in their leisure time that take them out of their homes. Furthermore, since families are larger in the lower classes, there is more chance for a lower-class child to find playmates in his own home. This does not necessarily mean that the lower-class parent plays a more important role in the character formation of the child than does the middle-class parent. It may be that middle-class parents give more thought to the training of their children, and, with fewer children in the family, they may be able to give more attention to the individual child. Lower-class parents may be too busy or too careless to put forth much effort on the moral training of their children, even though they spend much of their time in the company of their children. The lower-class parent transmits his moral values to his child in an effective manner; but this is probably due to the fact that the lower-class child is subjected to a minimum of pressure from the dominant middle-class, child-caring institutions in the community.

The middle-class family is supplemented by the school, church, and character-building organizations which reinforce middle-class values. Thus the middle-class child finds little or no conflict between the standards of his home and the expectations of his teachers, Sunday school, and club leaders. The lower-class child faces such a conflict but usually resolves it by participating in few activities outside the home.

CHARACTER-FORMING ORGANIZATIONS

Prairie City has a full complement of organizations designed to improve the character of boys and girls. For the most part Prairie City residents regard the influence of these agencies as good, although enthusiasm is frequently tempered by awareness of factors that limit the influence of a given organization.

The Boy Scouts, Girl Scouts, and Camp Fire Girls are generally approved. However, these organizations tend to draw very largely from middle-class families when perhaps the lower-class children need them more. For example, the following comments by people in the community were made about the Boy Scouts: "Unfortunately, that group doesn't reach the children that need it most." . . . "It has the weakness that it reaches those who would be reached in the home anyway."

Concerning the girls' organizations, one person said: "Probably the Girl Scouts have done pretty well as a character-building agency, but both the Girl Scouts and the Camp Fire Girls have drawn social and religious lines a little close, and that has hampered their work somewhat."

While extracurricular school activities in general are considered good influences for high-school people, the activity that has attracted most attention is music. The high-school band is a very popular organization. The following are typical comments by Prairie City people: "That is a very fine influence, and the director is a splendid influence, too." . . . "The music program touches a lot of young people in Prairie City, and there is a fine spirit of good fellowship and working together."

One person spoke approvingly of the extracurricular activities themselves but critically of the fact that participation was limited to too small a number: "Those things are good, but I criticize them from the standpoint that they don't reach a lot of the youngsters. They are quite selective."

The men's service clubs are interested in character formation. They have tried to accomplish something in the way of dealing with the problem of juvenile delinquency. One club has a special committee for boys' work. The other club has been responsible for the recreation center.

The recreation center was established during the course of these studies. Its purpose was to provide under good auspices a social center for teen-age youth. Though financed by adults, the operation of the center was a responsibility of the high-school Student Council. The boys and girls who frequented the recreation center tended to be the ones who were best adjusted to the social life of the high school. Relatively few out-of-school youth attended. One local resident commented as follows: "Well, it's done a fairly good job, but it doesn't reach the ones that you want to reach." The center was closed after less than a year of operation.

RECREATION PLACES FREQUENTED BY YOUNG PEOPLE

Perhaps fully as effective in character formation as the so-called "character-building" organizations are the commercial recreational places frequented by young people. These are the swimming pool, the pool hall, the roller-skating rink, the bowling alley, the movies, and the taverns.

The public swimming pool is generally approved. This is an open-air pool, available only during the summer. "I think our swimming pool provides the right kind of recreation and guidance." . . . "It is very valuable for young people, well supervised and well directed."

It is interesting to note the attitudes of Prairie City people toward the pool hall in their town. In most towns a pool hall has a poor reputation as a "hangout" for young men; but such is not the case here. People will not go so far as to say that the pool hall is a good influence, but they almost invariably point out that it is not a harmful influence and that it is well supervised. The following comment is a typical one: "I don't think that the pool hall is a bad influence here. It certainly has a very good reputation. The boys think a great deal of the man who operates the place, and, the way it is run, I don't think it is a bad influence at all."

There are mixed feelings about the skating rinks. There are two rinks: one in the municipal park and one over a store downtown. People agree that skating is a desirable form of entertainment, but some are skeptical of the way in which the rinks are run: "That's probably a combination of both good and bad. Skating itself, under the right supervision, is certainly good recreation. They have well-supervised high-school parties at the rink downtown, and I think that is a good social function. But the general run of youngsters who hang around there night after night do considerable drinking, I know." . . . "The rink in the park is a grand place, very clean and well run. They don't allow any drinking there." . . . "I guess the rink downtown is not very good. People speak of it as a 'hole.' "

The bowling alley has a variable reputation also. "In some ways it is fine, and in other ways it is not, but I think it is pretty well run. They don't permit drinking on the premises, and that is a considerable help." . . . "I don't believe they serve alcoholic drinks there so probably that wouldn't be a bad influence. It may even be a good one." . . . "I enjoy bowling, but I'm not inclined to think too well of our bowling alley here."

Motion pictures are a pervasive influence. Except for those whose parents forbid movie going on religious grounds, nearly every boy and girl goes regularly, and averages about two shows a week. There is no question that the movies play an important role in determining superficial behavior patterns of adolescents such as choice of clothes and hair styles. To what extent the movies influence character development remains a moot question.

The middle-class people of Prairie City deplore undesirable movies but do little to influence the type of pictures shown. "In this community they are decidedly bad, just decidedly. So many of the young people go regardless of what's being shown, and it seems to me they must waste a lot of good time. I enjoy good movies, but we don't get many of them here." . . . "Some of the shows are simply terrible. I think we are cursed with poor pictures here in this community." . . . "Movies may be both good and bad in their influence, but here we are likely to get about ten bad ones to one good one." . . . "It's partly the parents' fault. Parents appear to be complacent rather than critical, and it seems to me that any mother would have to be critical of some of the things that are brought in to be shown to children." . . . "I wouldn't say that movies are an absolutely negative influence, but I don't think they have much to contribute by and large. At best perhaps they are a neutral influence, but certainly they have contributed to poor living standards. They have tended to give people an idea of money as the chief value in life, and I think our young people definitely reflect that fact."

The people who were interviewed were unanimous in their opinion that the taverns had a definitely harmful influence on the young people who frequent them, but judgments varied as to how many young people were actually affected. One person said: "Taverns are not a problem here in town. Kids are afraid to go into them here. When they go to places of that kind they stay away from this town and go where they won't be recognized." Another person said: "There is some drinking. No question about that, I know. Some of the tavern keepers are no help. There are some that 'cheat,' and there are various ways in which it is done." Another said: "I know that a great many high-school people go to taverns. The law is certainly not very well enforced so far as age is concerned." Still another person made this comment: "I hear people say that very many of our young people do go to these places, but as far as I'm concerned it is just hearsay. I think quite probably some of the girls have tried it out, and personally I think that's rather a natural reaction. They want to see what it is like."

CONCLUSION

Through the home, school, church, youth organizations, recreational agencies, and the informal "peer culture" of the children's own world, values and moral standards are taught to boys and girls by their parents, teachers and other adults in positions of prestige, and by leaders of their own age groups. In Prairie City some values are community wide, and some are held mainly by members of a particular social class or of a particular church group.

Boys and girls tend to learn the values and standards of their own homes, churches, and social classes. But the adolescent peer culture of the high school is a pervasive middle-class influence, affecting all boys and girls who go to high school. In general, the school teaches middle-class values.

There are three deviant groups of adolescents in Prairie City who are learning values and standards which deviate from the middle-class forms. The Lutherans are learning a more rigorous, puritanical morality. Most of the out-of-school group are learning a morality which is generally stigmatized as "lower class," and some of the lower-class boys and girls who are in high school but not well adjusted to its social life are becoming discontented and hostile toward middle-class values.

The "character-building" youth organizations teach middle-class values and appeal mainly to middle-class youth, though they also succeed in serving a minority of lower-class youth.

The commercial recreation places vary in their moral influence. Several are very well managed from the point of view of middle-class people and are quite generally approved. Others are less well managed, and their owners are indifferent to their character-forming influence.

5

Social Class and School Adjustment in Relation to Character Reputation

This chapter deals with one of the significant problems of the research, namely, to what extent the character reputation of adolescents is a reflection of their social-class status. Both statistical and case-history data are presented to support the conclusion that it is not social position itself, but the degree of conformity to school expectations, which seems to determine the character reputation of Prairie City sixteen-year-olds.

These findings carry implications for theories of character formation, as well as implications for educational practice. The findings indicate, first, that character reputation is very closely related to the individual's success in adjusting to the dominant social situation and, second, that for most adolescents—at least in communities like Prairie City—the dominant social situation is the school. The implication therefore emerges that the high school, finding itself in a crucial role in regard to character development, must strive to meet the needs of all young people. It must, in other words, do all it can to facilitate good school adjustment for an ever-increasing number of its entering students.

Human behavior, including those aspects we call character, is influenced by the social milieu within which the individual develops. This is particularly true of moral behavior or character since the latter is constantly subject to approval or disapproval by the members of the social groups with which the individual comes in contact. If the behavior is approved by the particular group, it is reinforced by a system of rewards; if disapproved, it is inhibited by a system of punishments. What behavior will be rewarded and what will be punished will depend upon the moral values of the particular group in which the individual is participating.

Of the many groups in which the individual participates, the home or family is generally recognized as the one most influential in affecting his behavior. It has also been recognized that families differ in respect to the systems of moral values they try to enforce on their children and in the stringency of their methods of enforcement. Recent studies [1] have suggested that these differences in moral codes tend to bear some relation to the social position of the family. Those families whose position is at the bottom of the social hierarchy tend to have as one of their distinguishing features a system of moral values which not only differs from that of, but which is also frowned upon by, those who are above them in the social hierarchy. Or, if these people accept the moral values of the more privileged classes, they are more lax in their enforcement. Their rewards are less certain, and their punishments are less consistent, and consequently their children are less likely to conform to the standards of the middle and upper classes. One would anticipate a relationship between the character of sixteen-year-old youths and the social class of their parents.

The methods for determining the character of the sixteen-year-olds and the social class of their parents are discussed in detail elsewhere.[2] For this study, the subject's reputation among adults and age mates on five traits, honesty, moral courage, friendliness, loyalty, and responsibility, was used as the criterion of character. Subjects were assigned to one of five social classes on the basis of information known about their families: to the upper, upper-middle, lower-middle, upper-lower, or lower-lower class.

THE RELATION BETWEEN SOCIAL CLASS AND CHARACTER REPUTATION

Social class position was found to be related positively to each of the five character traits. In descending order of relationship, the traits are: honesty, loyalty, responsibility, moral courage, friendliness. The relationships, expressed in quantitative terms,[3] were

[1] Allison Davis, Burleigh B. Gardner, and Mary R. Gardner, *Deep South*, Chaps. III–IV. Chicago: University of Chicago Press, 1941.

Allison Davis, "Socialization and Adolescent Personality," *Forty-Third Yearbook*, Part I, *Adolescence*, National Society for the Study of Education, 1944.

Clifford Shaw, Henry D. McKay, and James F. McDonald, *Brothers in Crime*. Chicago: University of Chicago Press, 1932.

[2] See Chapters 19 and 20.

[3] Tetrachoric coefficients of correlation were, respectively, 0.57, 0.54, 0.52, 0.49, and 0.40. Tetrachoric r for social class and the average score for all five traits was 0.52.

very similar for the first four traits; for friendliness, the relationship was somewhat lower.

The data show that subjects in the upper social classes tended to be rated above the average in all five traits; those in the lower classes, to be rated below the average.

Since the relationships between social class and each of the character traits are so similar, it might reasonably be supposed that some general behavioral or some general reputational factor plays a major role in determining the individual's reputation for any one trait.[4] For example, the judgments made about honesty may have been determined less by specific observations of honest and dishonest acts than by the general impression of the ratee on the rater.

The fact that a lower relationship was obtained between friendliness and social class than between any other trait and social class may be due to at least two factors: (1) Friendliness may actually be less related to social class than any of the other traits. (2) Friendliness may be a more visible trait than the others. Thus in rating individuals on friendliness the rater may depend more upon his actual observations than when he rates individuals on the other traits. In other words, ratings on friendliness may be less affected by the general impression of the ratee on the rater than are ratings on other traits.

The remainder of this chapter will be devoted to a search for a general factor which may account for the data secured.

SOCIAL CLASS STEREOTYPES AS A FACTOR IN REPUTATION

The relationships found between social class and reputation might be the result of stereotypes people have about the behavior of individuals in different social classes, rather than the result of objective observations of actual behavior. Those sixteen-year-olds in classes U and UM may be rated high in character because of the high status enjoyed by their parents in the community, while

---

[4] This assumption is more directly supported by the fact that there is a high positive correlation between the separate trait scores. See Chapter 20 for these data.

those in the UL and LL classes might be rated low in character because of the low reputation of their parents in the community.

However, if stereotypes about the behavior of people in different social classes are the chief factors contributing to the relationship

TABLE 3   CHARACTER REPUTATION SCORES IN RELATION TO SOCIAL CLASS

Social Class	Trait					Number of Cases
	Honesty	Moral Courage	Friend-liness	Loyalty	Respon-sibility	
U, UM	22.5 *	22.8	22.7	23.4	23.0	10
LM	20.8	20.8	20.7	21.4	21.0	41
UL	18.4	19.2	18.7	18.7	18.9	50
LL	19.5 †	20.2	18.7	19.0	19.1	11
Average	20.0	20.2	19.8	20.2	20.0	

* These scores represent the mean for the group. Scores are expressed in D units, where the distribution has a mean of 20 and a standard deviation of 4.

† Differences on character reputation scores for the four social-class groups have been tested for statistical significance. Inspection of the critical ratios shows that, on all five traits, the U, UM group is significantly higher than the other groups; on all five traits the LM group is significantly higher than the UL group but not significantly higher than the LL group although the tendency is consistently in that direction. There is a consistent trend downward in character reputation as we go from U, UM to LM to UL, but the LL group does not follow this same pattern.

between character reputation and social class, one might expect a higher relationship than was actually found. Moreover, the character reputation of those in the LL class should be consistently lower than those in the UL class, since one of the chief differences between the two classes is in reputation. (Members of the UL class are characteristically regarded as "the poor but honest, hard-working people," while those in the LL class are "the shiftless no-goods.")   However, Table 3 shows that the average reputation for the LL group is higher than that of the UL group.

In interpreting the ratings given group LL, it is important to remember that only part of the total group LL were included in the analysis.   These were the members of the group who remained in school.   Six members of group LL were out of school.   They were not rated by enough judges to warrant inclusion of their scores in the table.   Since such scores as they did obtain tended to be much lower than those of the group who were in school, it may be surmised that the LL subjects in school are a select group.   Perhaps they are the socially mobile members of their class, who, by continuing their education and by taking on the behavior of people in more favored classes, are trying to improve their social status. If this is true, one would expect that these LL sixteen-year-olds in school would not share the reputation of typical lower-lower-class persons.

The fact that even a few members of the LL group were rated high in character indicates that the stereotypes about their class are not applied indiscriminately.   Presumably, the discriminations made by the raters are based to a considerable extent upon observed behavior.

Furthermore, if the character reputations of sixteen-year-olds are based largely upon stereotypes existing among raters rather than upon actual behavior, one would expect to find considerable consistency in the way in which the members of each social class are rated.   This can perhaps best be studied by comparing the amount of variability in the character reputation scores of each class group.   Data on variability are presented in Table 4.

Table 4 shows that variability increases as social status decreases.   In other words, the consistency with which the members of the U, UM group are rated is very high; and the consistency becomes less as one goes from the LM to the UL to the LL group.

Hence, if stereotypes about social classes enter into the determination of the character reputation of the subjects, they are more influential in determining the scores of the members of the upper class than they are in determining the scores of those in the lower classes.

From the data presented in this section, the hypothesis that

TABLE 4   VARIABILITY OF REPUTATION SCORES FOR EACH SOCIAL CLASS *

Social Class	Trait					Number of Cases
	Honesty	Moral Courage	Friend-liness	Loyalty	Respon-sibility	
U, UM	2.3	1.5	1.4	0.7	1.8	10
LM	11.2	8.2	4.9	7.0	11.1	41
UL	14.5	9.7	8.4	11.7	13.4	50
LL	16.5	8.2	16.8	14.7	12.1	11

* Variability is expressed here in terms of variance (the square of the standard deviation). Since the variance of the entire group of subjects on any given trait is approximately 16 (4 D units equal 1 S.D.), any subgroup will have a variance approaching that of the total group if its variance scores approximate 16. If the variance of a subgroup is much less than 16, it indicates that the scores of members of the subgroup are bunched together. For example, the small variance scores of the U, UM group are due to the fact that the scores of the persons in this group are all above the mean for the entire group. On the other hand, the LL group, with only 11 members, has scores distributed over the entire range of scores.

character reputation of sixteen-year-olds is largely determined by stereotypes regarding social status seems inadequate to account for the findings.

CONFORMITY TO SCHOOL EXPECTATIONS AS A FACTOR IN CHARACTER REPUTATION

An alternative hypothesis which seemed substantiated by the findings is that the character reputation of subjects is determined primarily by the degree to which their actual behavior conforms to the middle-class standards of the school. If the individual fits into the life of the school, if he strives for the goals set up explicitly or implicitly by the school, his reputation for character will be high. If he does not conform to school standards or subscribe to school ideologies his reputation for character will be low.

In terms of this hypothesis, the UM group may be more homogeneous in character reputation because the behavior of this group is in line with the middle-class behavior demanded by the school. Upper-middle-class boys and girls may conform to school expectations because of the consistent reinforcement of middle-class standards and goals by all the character-building agencies with which they come in contact—their homes, their play groups, their schools, their churches, and so on. Many of the values that are important in maintaining the position of their families in society are the values which the school stresses, namely, higher education, the adherence to the "social amenities," leadership, and responsibility in dealing with others. These values will be more likely to have immediate significance for children of the middle classes than for children of the lower classes; and the former will adopt the appropriate behavior patterns with comparative ease. Another factor in the success with which upper-middle-class children conform to school expectations may be that teachers and other school personnel are predisposed in their favor because of the influential social status of the families of these children.

The variability in character ratings of the lower-class youth, on the other hand, may reflect the fact that some lower-class homes reinforce the values of the school and other middle-class agencies, whereas other lower-class homes do not. In the former instance, the child is more likely to conform to the standards of the school and hence to have a high reputation for character; in the latter instance, the child is more likely to accept the values of his family, and hence his behavior will not conform to the middle-class expectations of the school. Even in cases where the home supports the school values, many of the other character-forming associations which affect the lower-class child may be in conflict with them. Moreover, in almost all families of low social status, the value of an education and other factors stressed in the school environment are not impressed upon children in their immediate daily life. Even if the parents do stress these values verbally, it is more difficult for their children to see their significance and thus more difficult for them to accept. It is probable that the character-forming influences are never as unanimous in their effects upon lower-class as they are upon middle-class youths.

There is some evidence available to support the hypothesis stated above. This evidence involves one assumption which should be made explicit, namely, that conformity to school expectations is reflected in school achievement, the latter being measured by academic grades. The relation between academic grades and conformity to school standards is both direct and indirect. Academic grades are a direct measure of the success with which the adolescent is meeting the demands of the school. On the other hand, there are a host of subtle factors which influence teachers in the assignment of grades, among them the student's demeanor in class, his interest in higher education, his participation in school activities, and so on. All these are, in turn, indices of the degree to which the student accepts the values and ideologies of the school.

Proceeding on the above assumption, the contention that the reputed character of sixteen-year-olds is determined largely by the degree of conformity to school standards is substantiated by the fact that there is a high relationship between school achievement and character reputation and a comparatively low relationship between school achievement and social class.[5] Furthermore, the relation between intelligence and character reputation is lower than the relation between school achievement and reputation.[6]

The degree to which school achievement overshadows intelligence and social class in influencing character reputation is shown in Table 5.

Inspection of Table 5 shows that all those who are above the median in character reputation, regardless of social class, tend to do about equally well at school in spite of differences in intelligence.

If it can be assumed that intelligence-test scores measure capacity and that school achievement measures the effectiveness with which that capacity is being used, the following interpretation seems plausible: In view of the fact that their capacity is less, those lower-class youths who are successful in conforming to middle-class goals, as shown in their relatively high school achieve-

[5] School achievement was measured by the average of the academic grades earned by the student in the present and preceding school years.

The product-moment correlation between achievement and character reputation was 0.74 ± 0.04, while that between achievement and the index of social characteristics was 0.32 ± 0.11.

[6] Intelligence was measured by IQ scores on the Revised Stanford-Binet, Form L.

The product-moment correlation between intelligence and character reputation was 0.49 ± 0.07, while that between intelligence and the index of social characteristics was 0.52 ± 0.07.

ment and high character reputation, are exerting greater effort to attain these goals than are middle- and upper-class youths.

But a smaller proportion of lower-class youths are making that effort. Going down the social scale we find fewer and fewer members of each class who are above the median in character reputation

TABLE 5   SOCIAL CLASS, SCHOOL ACHIEVEMENT, AND INTELLIGENCE IN RELATION TO CHARACTER REPUTATION

Character Reputation	Social Class	School Achievement (Mean)	Binet IQ (Mean)
Above median	U, UM		
	N = 9 (100%)	87.0 *	127.4
	LM		
	N = 18 (56%)	84.9	117.2
	UL and LL		
	N = 14 (38%)	85.0	112.0
Below median	LM		
	N = 14 (44%)	76.9	111.2
	UL and LL		
	N = 23 (62%)	77.7	107.0

* Comparison of the probable errors of the average scores for school achievement with the probable errors of the average scores for intelligence indicates that the differences in achievement between those above and below the median in character reputation are significant, whereas the differences in *intelligence* between the two groups are not.

and achievement. To be sure, if the LL group had been separated from the UL group in this analysis, the percentage of LL's below the median in character reputation would not have been lower than the percentage of UL's. But this atypicality in trend can be accounted for by the fact that a large number of the sixteen-year-olds who had dropped out of school, and hence were not included in the table, belonged to the LL class. The character-reputation scores they received were extremely low. Those individuals, it would seem, did not feel that school was worth even the effort of attendance.

ANALYSIS OF CASE HISTORIES

If the hypothesis is accepted that conformity to school expectations is a principal factor in character reputation, the further hypothesis may be advanced that conformity to school standards depends in large measure on the extent to which the goals and values of the school are reinforced by the child's family. This is supported by evidence from case-history material. Although the data on family relationships are not complete, the information at hand shows significant trends.

The U, UM Group

It has already been pointed out that the nine members of the U, UM group were, in general, conforming satisfactorily to the school situation, and all had high reputation scores. The case-history material on their families shows that in all cases the parents accepted the value of higher education. One or both parents of the youths in this group had college educations themselves and felt that a similar education was important for their children.

None of the nine subjects was openly rebelling against his family or the standards implicit in his life. In three cases where the parents were reported to have loose moral standards, the children were reported to disapprove of their parents' behavior and to be particularly conscientious in their school work. In one of these cases, the son, in contrast to the parents, became an active member of a church. The other two boys had intimate friends from the LM, UL, and LL groups, but these friends were outstanding members of their social classes in terms of values dominant in the school.

Only one of the youths in the U, UM groups was not working hard at academic subjects and fell just below the mean of the total group of sixteen-year-olds in school achievement. This boy was a star athlete and received considerable recognition in extracurricular pursuits. He was accepting the school values in their broader aspects but was using his energy largely in the non-academic areas, with the result that his school work suffered slightly.

The LM Group

Of the LM group the eighteen individuals with high reputation had parents or guardians who were highly respected in the community. There were two striking features which seemed characteristic of this group: one was the particularly active participation of the families in church affairs; the other, the very close identification of the children with their parents.

In only one case was there any evidence of resentment against the home. This was the case of an orphan girl who was being reared by a very strict relative. She was reported to be independent in all her dealings with adults, and she resented the controls this relative had over her. Although she was said to have associated with girls of bad reputation in the community, she herself was striving for upward mobility, and she specifically stated that the school was a vitally important means to the attainment of her goals. In spite of her somewhat dubious associations, she had a high character reputation.

Of the eighteen LM individuals with high reputations, five had achievement scores below the general median for the entire age group. Three of these five, in spite of their below-average achievement during 1942–1943, were reported by the teachers to be good students. In fact, the one receiving the lowest grade was described as bright, conscientious, and serious. These favorable comments indicate that the individuals in question were conforming on the whole to the patterns of behavior expected of them by the school, even though their academic achievement was below average. The other two in this group lived on farms. They received very good grades in homemaking and agriculture but fell down slightly on the more-academic subjects. The families of all five individuals were highly respected in the community.

In general, the case-history material shows that the parents in this group set relatively high moral and educational goals for their children, and the family relationships were such that the children accepted these goals without question.

Of the fourteen youths in the LM class who were below average in reputation, six were reported to have parents who had little control over their children or who were very undemanding and exerted little discipline. These parents were not enforcing the middle-class standards of the school. Two of these six adolescents were boys whose parents were actively striving for upward mobility, but both boys overtly rejected their families and rebelled against any disciplinary measures their parents tried to enforce. All six youths seemed content to remain in a lower-middle-class position; at least, the desire for higher education did not figure in their ambitions. None was successfully meeting the standards of the school. Three had regular jobs outside the school; all three received high character ratings by their employers. Apparently they were making a good adjustment in the work situation, in spite of the poor adjustment to school.

In five cases of the fourteen, there was insufficient evidence on the role of the family. Three of the five families were rural. The children of the other two had low scores on the Family Relationships Questionnaire, which is indirect evidence that they were not getting along well with their parents.[7] It suggests that, if these parents were attempting to reinforce middle-class standards, their children were not susceptible to the pressure.

The remaining three individuals in the LM class with low reputations were reported to have respectable families, but no information was available on the values which were stressed in their homes. Two of the children were described as "nonentities" in school. Two filled in the Family Relationships Questionnaire; one received a high score on it, the other, a very low score.

The UL and LL Groups

Of the fourteen individuals in the UL and LL social classes who were above average in reputation, ten were reported to have parents who were anxious for them to stay in school. Although all these families were poor, many were said to have clean, well-kept homes and neatly dressed, well-groomed children. In many instances, the families were said to have strict moral and religious standards.

Three of these ten youths had achievement scores only slightly below the general median. All three received favorable mention from teachers for their academic work, and in the previous year they had received considerably higher grades.

For two individuals, both rural girls of Scandinavian background, there was no information available on parental ambitions and familial relationships. In both instances, however, the parents had well-kept farms and were respected in the community, indicating their acceptance of middle-class standards.

Among the fourteen members of this group, there were only two, a boy and a girl, whose parents were known not to be rein-

[7] See Chapter 21 on family relationships.

forcing the standards of the school. In both cases, the reputation of the parents in the community was extremely low. Both young people were reported to be considerably upset by their inferior social position and to be striving for upward mobility through education. Although the school achievement scores of both were slightly below average, they were achieving considerably beyond the level one would expect on the basis of their intelligence-test scores. The girl was said to be very resentful of her status and envious of those above her. She adhered to a strict moral and ethical code. The boy had strong feelings of inferiority and was quite depressed. He ignored other members of his social class and used his abilities in athletics to gain recognition from young people of higher social status than his own.

All the lower-class individuals of good reputation for whom there are sufficient data to warrant an interpretation seem to be striving for upward mobility. In the majority of cases the parents are seeking higher social status for their children and are reinforcing the middle-class standards of the school. For their children, conformity to school practices and acceptance of school ideology is not difficult, and they are adjusting without much psychological strain. For the two persons who are striving for mobility without the support of their parents, the struggle to overcome the handicaps of their lower-class backgrounds leads to considerable psychological disturbance. They are succeeding in their efforts to conform to the behavior expected of them in school, but it is at considerable cost to their mental equanimity.

Of the twenty-three lower-class youths whose character reputation was below the median, twelve were reported to have parents who were uninterested in the school and who gave their children little direction or guidance. These parents were content with their position in society, and it may be inferred that most of their children were accepting the standards and values of their parents. At least, they were not striving for advancement through the medium of the school. In only one case, that of a girl, was there any evidence of interest in social mobility. The girl had stated that she would like to be a nurse but that her parents had objected to the amount of schooling involved and wanted her to get a job. This girl's school achievement was just above the median for the sixteen-year-olds. However, her reputation for associating with "undesirable" people was widespread, and she did not participate in any of the social activities of the school. Of the other eleven in this group, no pertinent family information was available for nine cases. The remaining two were girls whose parents were interested in having them finish high school. In one case, only the mother was interested; the father was a man of low reputation who was away from home a great deal. The daughter's friends were not in school, and she had married a working man while she was still in high school. Although her adjustment to school was none too good, reports indicated that she had made a good adjustment to married life and to her non-school environment.

The other girl, whose parents were interested in her completing high school, belonged to an immigrant group; she was inconspicuous and relatively unknown to her school associates. Although her intelligence score was low, she was doing good work in school. Since she was so little known, it may be that existing stereotypes about her ethnic group determined her reputation ratings more than her actual behavior.

With the possible exception of the case last described and of two cases for whom no information was available, none of the lower-class individuals with low reputations seems to be striving for social mobility through education. One of the boys in this group was working regularly when not in school, and he received a high character rating from his employer. Like those boys in the LM group whose reputation for character among their school associates was low, he is adjusting adequately to the work situation. It is quite possible that all four of these boys may achieve higher social status by exerting their efforts in the business or industrial world, rather than in school work.

In general, the case-history material corroborates the hypothesis that the degree to which an individual conforms to the standards of the school and subscribes to school ideologies determines his character reputation. The material also substantiates the inference that, if the home reinforces these values and ideologies, the child will be more likely to accept them and will receive a high character rating by his classmates and by school authorities. All families of sixteen-year-olds in the U, UM group reinforce the values stressed by the school. In the LM, UL, and LL classes, progressively smaller proportions of the families reinforce school ideologies. Correlated with these phenomena is the fact that the proportion of sixteen-year-olds with high reputations in the school situation decreases as one descends the social scale.

SUMMARY

Returning to the original finding that reputation is positively related to social-class position, this relationship can be interpreted in something of the following terms: The adolescent's character reputation is largely determined by the degree of conformity to the school. The school in Prairie City is middle class in its values and ideologies. A large proportion of the boys and girls who come from middle-class homes will conform to the prevailing school pattern; and, as one descends the social scale, this proportion grows smaller. At the same time, there are a few individuals in even the lowest social classes who, striving for social mobility, take on the behavior and value patterns of the middle class, conform to the school, and enjoy favorable reputations.

If this formulation is correct, it explains the facts that, first, there is a correlation between reputation and social class; second, social-class position itself—or stereotypes about social classes—is not the determining factor in the relationship; but, third, that it is conformity to middle-class standards which causes the relationship and which, for most Prairie City adolescents, is synonymous with conformity to school expectations.

6

The Relation of the Church to

Character Formation

The study reported in this chapter is exploratory in nature; results are suggestive rather than definitive. Differences in reputation between the churches reflect not only differences in moral teachings but also differences in the social positions of various churches. The fact of church membership is probably not as important in determining character as is the degree of religious observance and feeling.

It is generally agreed, by middle-class people at any rate, that the church is an important factor in character formation. In order to find out whether this opinion could be supported by objective evidence from Prairie City, several kinds of data pertinent to the problem were assembled.

The data deal with 105 young people, of whom 70 per cent had some church connection. There were another forty subjects in the age-group, but information on them was not complete enough to include them here. Since most of these forty persons were from the upper-lower and lower-lower classes, the chances are that their inclusion would have lowered the proportion of subjects who had church connections.

The percentage distribution of the 105 individuals among the various churches is shown in Table 6.

The relation between church membership and character reputation was complicated by a third factor, that of social position. As shown in the preceding chapter, character reputation is related to social class. Furthermore, the various churches in Prairie City differ in social position.

The distribution of the 105 subjects according to social status is shown in Table 7, where the churches are ranked according to the proportion of the group who fall in the upper half of the social scale. This order of the churches in average social status is ap-

TABLE 6   DISTRIBUTION OF SUBJECTS ACCORDING TO CHURCH AFFILIATION

Church	Percentage of Subjects
Lutheran	19
Federated (Congregational and Presbyterian)	14
Methodist	12
Baptist	11
Catholic	11
Other churches	3
	—
Total church	70
Non-church	30

proximately what would be found if the entire church membership was sorted into social classes.

The Federated Church has the highest social rating, with the largest representation of any church in town in the upper and up-

TABLE 7   DISTRIBUTION OF SUBJECTS BY CHURCH MEMBERSHIP AND SOCIAL STATUS

	U, UM, LM Percentage	UL, LL Percentage
Federated	87	13
Methodist	69	31
Baptist	55	45
Lutheran	45	55
Catholic	17	83
Non-church	29	71

per-middle classes.   But the Federated Church runs through a wide range of social classes and has many members from the lower-middle class.   The Methodist, Baptist, and Lutheran churches may be grouped together as churches of "the common man."   They run from upper-middle down to lower-lower class in composition. The Catholic Church includes members of all classes, but the great majority of its members are lower class. In Prairie City the Catholics are mainly Irish and Polish, with a few families of German descent. The Polish, being recent immigrants, are at the bottom of the social scale, almost all falling into the upper-lower and lower-lower classes.

Two other churches are not represented in Table 7. The Free Methodist Church is confined almost exclusively to the upper-lower class; and the Tabernacle, a fundamentalist group recently established, draws mainly from the upper-lower, with a few lower-lower members.

Character reputation was found to be related to church membership according to the social status of the church; that is, the sixteen-year-olds who belonged to churches of high social status had higher character ratings than the sixteen-year-olds who belonged to churches of low social status. There was one notable exception, to be described in more detail later, the Lutherans.

RELIGIOUS OBSERVANCE AND CHARACTER REPUTATION

Since the social status of the church seemed to be related to the character reputation of its members and thus to obscure any relationship that might exist between religious life and character, it was decided to investigate the relation of religious observance to character reputation within given social classes. It was thought that a relation might exist between quality of religious observance and character, regardless of the type of church. That is, the sincere Lutheran, Catholic, or Methodist, who attends church regularly and has a strong religious attitude, may have a better character reputation than the lax or indifferent church member.

In order to study the relation of religious observance and character reputation, additional information about the church group was needed. Accordingly, the pastor of each church was asked to give his judgment as to the degree and quality of religious observance for each subject associated with his church. In some instances, the information secured from ministers was supplemented by interviews with lay members who were well acquainted with the young people in their church. Opinions of lay members coincided almost exactly with those of ministers.

After this information was secured, the authors rated all subjects with church connections according to a four-point scale. A rating of 1 indicated sincere religious interest and regular attendance at one or more of the following: church, Sunday school, young people's organization. At the opposite end of the scale, a rating of 4 indicated lack of interest and almost no association with the church. The following comments are typical of statements which formed

TABLE 8   RELATION BETWEEN RELIGIOUS OBSERVANCE AND CHARACTER REPUTATION

	Quartile Standing on Character Scores (Honesty and Responsibility)			
	I	II	III	IV
(Lower-middle class)				
High religious observance	2	5	4	12
Low religious observance	3	1	4	—
Non-church	3	2	1	2
(Upper-lower class)				
High religious observance	2	4	2	6
Low religious observance	6	3	4	1
Non-church	10	6	2	2

the basis for rating: "Very active and dependable. Good religious background and faithful in attendance." . . . "Isn't very active. Comes to young people's meeting once in a while." . . . "She is a member, but that's about all you can say. Her parents aren't interested and neither is she."

In order to keep constant the factor of social position, the data are analyzed separately for lower-middle-class subjects and for upper-lower-class subjects. The number of cases in each of the other social classes was too small to allow such analysis.

Table 8 shows the relation between religious observance and reputation on the two traits, honesty and responsibility. Subjects were divided into two groups: those rated 1 or 2 on religious observance constituting the "high" group and those rated 3 or 4 constituting the "low" group.

Table 8 shows that, when social position is kept constant, there is a reliable tendency for those subjects rated high on religious observance to have higher character reputations than those rated low on religious observance, although those subjects with no church affiliation tend to have a lower character reputation than those who are affiliated with a church.

If the assumption is correct that religious observance, as measured here, is a good index of middle-class morality, then these data bear out the hypothesis that conformity to middle-class standards is determining the character reputations of the subjects.

MORAL TEACHINGS OF THE CHURCHES

The fact that character reputations for sixteen-year-olds varied according to the church to which they belonged is probably due not only to social status differences between churches but also to variation between churches in terms of their moral teachings. The moral and religious teachings of seven churches will be described briefly: the Federated, Methodist, Baptist, Catholic, Free Methodist, Lutheran, and Tabernacle.

The Federated Church is the most liberal church in town in terms of doctrinal and moral latitude assumed by its members. When people leave one of the other churches to join the Federated Church, they give as reasons either that their own church was too strict in its doctrine or its moral code or that their friends are in the Federated Church. However, a desire to climb socially is probably the motive in many cases.

The Methodist and Baptist Churches occupy a middle ground in respect to doctrine and moral latitude. Their ministers have been liberal in theology and liberal socially. Although they do not encourage dancing and card playing, they do not prohibit them.

The Free Methodist Church is more rigid and literal in its interpretation of the Bible than are the three already mentioned. It is also stricter with respect to such things as dancing, card playing, and movie going. The Tabernacle group are similar to the Free Methodist group in moral and doctrinal rigidity.

The Catholic Church follows its traditional inflexibility on matters of doctrine, and its traditional liberalism on drinking, smoking, dancing, and card playing.

The Lutherans constitute a distinct group. Most of them are Norwegians, descendants of Norse immigrants who came to this part of the country in the period from 1825 to 1910. The earliest immigrants were followers of the Norwegian religious reformer, Hauge. They were a pietistic, evangelistic sect, with lay preachers. They had little use for the orthodox Lutheran church and its ordained ministers. Although their descendants eventually accepted the orthodox Lutheran ministry, the Prairie City church has a very active group, mainly members of the upper-lower class, who hold their own prayer meetings, believe in their own approach to God, and oppose their minister on certain matters of policy.

The Lutherans form not only a church but also an ethnic group. The Norwegians are proud of their background and confident that their welfare lies in maintaining their own social and moral traditions. Their strict moral views serve to set them apart from the rest of the community. Outsiders are impressed with their success in maintaining their beliefs and standards and handing them down to their children. Yet outsiders are also vexed with their exclusiveness. The following comment illustrates the attitude of many people in Prairie City:

The Lutherans are too narrow. They don't believe in dancing, card playing, or drinking. They don't even believe in movies, and they're a terribly clannish outfit. The whole life of the Lutheran is tied up in his church. It isn't just a religious organization, it's a social and fraternal organization as well.

The Norwegian Lutherans present an exception to the general rule that high social status accompanies high character reputation. Lutheran subjects rank lowest among the four Protestant churches in social status as shown in Table 7, yet their character reputations are as high as or higher than those of subjects from other churches. Table 9 shows how the Lutheran subjects were distributed among the four quartiles of the total group, on each of two scores—the average reputation score on the five traits and the average reputation score on two of the traits, honesty and responsibility.

The Lutherans make an exceptional showing; 70 per cent of the group are in the upper half on average reputation score, and 80 per cent are in the upper half on honesty and responsibility. The latter score is perhaps a better index of moral reputation than is the total reputation score because Lutheran subjects tend to have lower total scores than non-Lutherans by the inclusion of friendliness in the battery of moral traits. This is readily understood. The Lutheran adolescent, because of restrictions placed on him by the church and by his parents, does not participate widely in

TABLE 9 DISTRIBUTION OF CHARACTER REPUTATION SCORES OF LUTHERAN SUBJECTS

	Percentage of the Group in Each Quartile			
	I	II	III	IV
Average reputation score	8	25	40	30
Honesty and responsibility score	5	15	35	45

social activities and has fewer opportunities to be friendly with people outside his own ethnic-religious group.

CONCLUSIONS

This study leads to the conclusion that church membership itself is not an independently powerful influence in the development of character but that church membership is often associated with other factors or constellations of factors that tend to produce good or bad character reputations.

It is obvious, for example, that church attendance is one of the things that communities like Prairie City expect of their "good, respectable people." It is part of the accepted pattern, and most people who value their status in the community do not treat it lightly. Those who disregard church attendance are likely to be people whose position in the community is so secure that it will not suffer by failure to conform to this community expectation, or people whose reputation is irretrievably poor and will not be affected in one way or another by church attendance.

It is to be noted that the "meaning" of church membership, as far as reputation is concerned, varies from one church to another. The people of any given church have certain general characteristics with reference to social position, ethnic make-up, and reputation in the community, and the church tends to take on the characteristics of its collective membership. The individual, in turn, takes on the reputation of the particular church group with which he is associated.

The real effectiveness of any given church in influencing the character of its young people cannot be discerned from the facts reported in this chapter. Only in the case of the Lutheran group is there clear evidence that membership in the church has a favorable effect on character reputation, and even there the supporting influence of the ethnic group must be kept in mind. The true role of any church in the character formation of its members should probably be sought in an intensive study of individuals rather than of groups.

7

The Role of Adults Outside the Family
in Character Formation

This chapter presents findings from two related studies: one dealing with the types of adults mentioned by sixteen-year-olds in essays on "The Person I Would Like to Be Like"; the other dealing with the adults in Prairie City most often mentioned by adolescents as possessing certain admirable traits of personality. The study is exploratory and seeks to approach the general question of how adults outside the family play a role in the character development of boys and girls. The results are suggestive, but they do not actually show how adults outside the family influence character.

The chapter raises the important question of the place of imitation in character formation. It may lead to more intensive study of this question. The chapter is perhaps of most value in what it contributes, both directly and indirectly, to theories of character formation.

Boys and girls form an image of an "ideal self" which acts like a magnet, attracting and directing their behavior. The "ideal self" contains something of the father and the mother, various teachers and youth-group leaders, important people in the local community, heroes read about, and ordinary successful young adults.

The "ideal self" is especially important in directing behavior and shaping character during the years of adolescence when major life decisions must be made and when parental example and precept are no longer accepted with blind faith.

It may be assumed that the "ideal self" develops out of experience with people and reflection upon that experience. Such experience may be direct person-to-person contacts, or it may be limited to observation from afar, to seeing pictures, or to reading about persons of the present or past. These experiences, direct and indirect, are the raw materials out of which the "ideal self" develops.

Imitation of the unconscious type seems to be a basic element in personality and character development.[1] As a child grows up, he imitates all those people who have prestige in his eyes and whose behavior he can observe closely enough to make imitation possible. Since imitation is usually unconscious, the boy or girl cannot always tell us whom he imitates. He cannot, of course, imitate people who are unknown to him. He must have something to imitate, even if it is no more than a photograph or a word picture in a history book. It may be supposed, also, that he will imitate most faithfully and successfully persons who are physically near to him. For example, imitation of a movie actress may be limited to what a girl can observe, such as the actress' hair dress, while the moral behavior of the actress is not so visible and not so much subject to imitation.

Two questions were asked:

1. What persons do sixteen-year-olds want to be like?

2. What adults in Prairie City are most "visible" to sixteen-year-olds?

If it could be determined what adults were visible to boys and girls and what kinds of persons were most attractive to them, the authors of this study were prepared to infer that these persons were entering into the "ideal selves" of the subjects. Boys and girls would imitate these persons, consciously or unconsciously.

WHAT PERSONS DO SIXTEEN-YEAR-OLDS WANT TO BE LIKE?

The sixteen-year-old group was asked to write on the topic, "The Person I Would Like to Be Like." The following classification was developed for persons mentioned in the essays:

1. Parent, brother, sister, other relative.

2. Glamorous adult—one whose appeal is clearly based on romantic and ephemeral qualities, such as a movie actress, a comic strip character (Superman or Flip Corkin), or a military figure who gains publicity by a fortuitous set of circumstances.

3. Hero read about—a character, living or dead, who has some claim to lasting fame, such as Abraham Lincoln, Florence Nightingale, General MacArthur, Madame Chiang Kai-shek.

[1] Neal Miller and John Dollard, *Social Learning and Imitation*. New Haven: Yale University Press, 1941.

4. Friend or acquaintance of approximately the same age.

5. Attractive and visible adult—one who is visible to and admired by the subject.

6. Composite or imaginary character.

The results of analyzing the data on the basis of this classification are shown in Table 10.[2]

TABLE 10   THE PERSON I WOULD LIKE TO BE LIKE: TYPES OF PERSONS SELECTED

Type of Person	Percentage of Mentions
Family member	14
Glamorous adult	5
Hero read about	0
Age mate	3
Attractive, visible adult	15
Composite, imaginary character	57
Not classified	6

We asked the boys and girls writing the essays to indicate, if possible, the age of the person they were describing. The results are shown in Table II.

TABLE 11   THE PERSON I WOULD LIKE TO BE LIKE: AGES OF PERSONS SELECTED

Age of Person	Percentage of Mentions
Under 20	5
20–29	54
30–39	13
40–49	8
Over 50	3
Not given	17

[2] Comparable data were available for ten-year-old subjects of Prairie City. Compared with ten-year-olds, sixteen-year-olds name fewer family members, fewer glamorous adults, and more composite or imaginary characters. Teachers were mentioned only once or twice by either group.

The results suggest that the subjects tend to think of themselves as young adults when asked to imagine themselves being grown up. This may be taken to mean that young adults are more at the focus of attention of adolescents than are older adults.[3]

WHAT ADULTS IN PRAIRIE CITY ARE MOST VISIBLE TO SIXTEEN-YEAR-OLDS?

To throw more light on the formation of the "ideal self," subjects were asked to name adults in the community who fitted certain brief character or personality descriptions. An instrument for this purpose was devised and called "The Adult Guess-Who Test." The instrument was used to find out which adults were actually seen by boys and girls in various desirable roles and which adults therefore were possible subjects for imitation.

The procedure was to draw up a number of thumb-nail character or personality descriptions, such as "Here is someone who does a lot of things for the good of this community"; "Here is someone I admire very much. I want to be like him (her)"; "Here is a person who works hard to make a success of any organization he belongs to";[4] and to ask subjects to fill in the names of Prairie City adults whom they thought fitted each description.

The items on this test were grouped into five groups:

1. Friendly and makes a good appearance (two items).
2. People to be admired and imitated (two items).
3. Helpful to boys and girls (one item).
4. "I am really a great deal like this person" (one item).
5. Respected, responsible citizens (five items).

Results from this test are shown in a series of tables to follow. The five groups of items will be referred to, for abbreviation, as "friendly," "admired," "helpful," "I'm like," and "responsible."

Types of Persons Mentioned

Table 12 shows how the persons mentioned were distributed among family members, teachers, and other adults.[5]

---

[3] Results are substantially the same for ten-year-old subjects. They, too, mention young adults much more frequently than older adults.

[4] The instrument is reproduced in Chapter 22.

[5] On the same instrument, ten-year-old subjects mention family members much more often, and other adults much less often, than do sixteen-year-olds.

It will be noted from this table that, although 7 per cent of all mentions were those of family members, 21 per cent teachers, and 72 per cent other adults, there is considerable variation with the

TABLE 12   TYPES OF PERSONS MENTIONED ON ADULT GUESS-WHO TEST

| Type of Person | Percentage of Mentions | | | | | |
	Friendly	Admired	Helpful	I'm Like	Responsible	Total Mentions
Family member	2	8	2	59	7	7
Teacher	20	13	42	0	23	21
Other adult	78	79	56	41	70	72
Total	100	100	100	100	100	100

nature of the items. For example, no teachers are mentioned on "I am really a great deal like this person"; family members get the majority of mentions on this item.

Ages of Persons Mentioned

The ages of the people mentioned on the Adult Guess-Who are shown in Table 13. Ages were assigned by field workers, who were well enough acquainted with all the persons mentioned to place them in ten-year age-groups. In this table, the items are grouped into four sets, "friendly" and "admired" having been combined. The highest percentage in each column is italicized.

These results indicate that, on items requiring a statement of admiration or emotional attachment, the sixteen-year-olds tend to choose young adults. On items requiring appraisal in the less personal terms of service to the community ("responsible" items), they choose older adults.[6]

[6] Ten-year-old subjects, differing from sixteen-year-olds, mention the age group 30–39 (their parental age group) most frequently on "friendly" and "admired" and on "I'm like." On the other two groups of items, they agree with sixteen-year-olds.

TABLE 13   AGES OF PERSONS MENTIONED ON ADULT GUESS-WHO TEST

Age Group	Percentage of Mentions			
	Friendly, Admired	Helpful	I'm Like	Responsible
Under 20	13	3	18	0
20–29	34	12	26	13
30–39	22	41	25	23
40–49	23	31	12	46
Over 50	8	12	20	20
Totals	100	99	101	102

Social Class of Persons Mentioned

Another question to be raised was how the adults who are most visible to Prairie City boys and girls are distributed according to social class. Table 14 gives the relative frequencies of mention of

TABLE 14   SOCIAL CLASS OF PERSONS MENTIONED ON ADULT GUESS-WHO TEST

Items	Social Class of Adults Mentioned				
	U	UM	LM	UL	LL
Friendly	1100 *	267	89	63	17
Admired	750	250	100	70	25
Helpful	500	750	116	5	0
Responsible	600	850	86	14	1

* Figures are adjusted to equate the number of adults in each social class. Relatives and teachers have been omitted.

adults of the various social classes. The figures in this table have been adjusted to allow for the differences in numbers in the various social classes.

Relatives and teachers have been omitted from the data in this table and in Table 15. Consequently, it was necessary to omit item 4, "I am really a great deal like this person," because the great majority of responses were the names of relatives.

TABLE 15   SOCIAL CLASS OF PERSONS MENTIONED ON ADULT GUESS-WHO TEST IN RELATION TO SOCIAL CLASS OF SUBJECTS

Social Class of Subjects	Social Class of Adults Mentioned				
	U .	UM	LM	UL	LL
	Friendly				
U, UM	2250 *	300	73	23	0
LM	800	283	111	61	8
UL	1000	217	68	93	25
LL	1100	370	100	26	96
	Admired				
U, UM	2050	300	111	0	0
LM	550	183	124	65	8
UL	600	266	73	95	0
LL	1000	167	162	0	0
	Responsible				
U, UM	950	1017	48	2	0
LM	950	917	89	5	8
UL	700	633	100	26	0
LL	0	883	92	30	0

* Figures are adjusted to equate the number of adults in each social class and the number of subjects in each social class. Relatives and teachers have been omitted.

This table shows that upper- and upper-middle-class adults are the most "visible" to sixteen-year-olds. On the items expressing personal admiration, the upper-class group is mentioned most frequently. On items expressing community service and responsibility, the upper-middle class is mentioned more frequently than the upper class.

The relation of the social-class position of adolescents to the social-class position of the adults they mention is shown in Table 15. Here the same procedures have been used as were used in the calculation of Table 14. The number of mentions on the "helpful" items was too small to permit subdivision of the sixteen-year-old group; they have been omitted from this analysis.

Table 15 shows a preference for upper and upper-middle classes on the part of all sixteen-year-old subjects, regardless of their own social class. In addition, sixteen-year-olds show a secondary preference for adults of their own social position. This secondary preference is shown by subjects of lower-middle and upper-lower classes more than by subjects of the lower-lower class. In this connection it should be recalled that only about half of the sixteen-year-olds in the lower-lower class took this test; they were the boys and girls who had remained in school, thus indicating their interest in the values of the social classes above them.

Character Reputation of Adolescents in Relation to Adults Mentioned

To study differences in the adults mentioned by boys and girls of varying character reputations, responses to the Adult Guess-Who for the 25 subjects ranking highest in character reputation and for the 25 ranking lowest were analyzed and compared to the responses made by the total group of subjects. Some differences appeared; but these differences could not be satisfactorily interpreted because each group of 25 included subjects from various social classes. It could not be determined whether deviations were due to social class differences or to some other factor.

Consequently, to hold the class factor constant, lower-middle-class subjects of high and low reputation were compared. Some large differences occurred between these two groups; but, because the number of cases involved was so small, the significance of these differences cannot be determined. It was found, for example, that those subjects with low reputation mentioned upper-class adults less frequently than did subjects with high reputations. The low-reputation group mentioned adults under twenty years of age more frequently, while the high-reputation group mentioned older adults—age group forty to forty-nine—more often. This seems to indicate that the subjects with low reputations associate with young people under twenty, who are not likely to be well established or to have good reputations in the community, while subjects in the high-reputation group use as models the established town leaders who are older and who are members of the higher social classes. Finally, parents were mentioned more often by the high-reputation group; teachers, by the low-reputation group. These findings are merely suggestive and must be interpreted with great caution, for the reasons given.

Individuals Mentioned

Turning now to the individual adults mentioned most frequently by sixteen-year-old subjects, it was found that, of a total of 1,328 mentions, ten persons received 25 per cent of all mentions and twenty persons received 34 per cent of the total. It seems clear that a relatively small number of people in the community are named frequently by sixteen-year-olds. The highest number of mentions for a single person was sixty-six.

Four of the first ten persons and seven of the first twenty were teachers. The first six people who were not on the school staff will be described briefly:

A is a friendly upper-middle-class banker, active in church and in community affairs. B is an active, successful businessman, a "self-made" man. He is a devoted church member and belongs to all the organizations that work for the good of the community. C is a professional man who has succeeded in the world largely by his own efforts. He is well read and intelligent. He has been active in community affairs. These three men received most of their votes on the items having to do with responsible citizenship. They were named as people who hold responsible positions and who work hard to make a success of organizations they belong to.

D is a local politician, a member of the upper-lower class. He is a genial fellow with a glad hand and a ready smile. He was mentioned mainly on the item, "Here is someone who always has a ready smile for everyone." He is the only lower-class person who was mentioned repeatedly. He was mentioned most often by subjects in the upper-lower class. E is an upper-class woman who is mentioned most often on the same item as that for which D is popular. She is a friendly woman, interested in boys and girls, and one who likes to assist in planning good times for young people. F is an outstanding young member of the Lutheran Church, reliable, conscientious, and industrious. He occupies a lower-middle-class position. His home is a rendezvous for young people, for social and religious activities.

The members of the school staff who received the most mentions are those who have administrative responsibility and whose contacts with students tend to be on a personal rather than on a classroom basis. Classroom teachers who received the most mentions are those who are responsible for extracurricular activities which increase their personal contacts with students. Practically all the high-school teachers were mentioned by at least several students.

The fact that a large proportion of the test items deal with social and civic responsibility tended to magnify the number of votes for middle-aged people. Except for several teachers, nearly all of the first twenty people were over thirty years old. However, a number of young adults received from five to fifteen mentions each.

The young adult who was mentioned most frequently is a good-looking young man of the upper class who grew up in the community and plans to make his home there. This young man is mentioned frequently by boys of all social classes as one they admire and one who is friendly and well dressed. Another young man who recently graduated from high school and is now attending college is mentioned frequently. He was very popular in high school and was a good student. His family is upper-middle class. Two young women are mentioned frequently, both of whom grew up in Prairie City and have married and settled there. One is an upper-class girl; the other is a middle-class girl who married an upper-class man.

These four young adults are probably the unconscious subjects of imitation by many boys and girls in Prairie City. Though not as frequently in contact with boys and girls as are the high-school teachers, they join the teachers as key people in their influence on the characters of adolescents. To this group must be added a number not exceeding fifteen or twenty middle-aged men and women who have leading positions in the community and who are symbols of civic morality to the younger generation.

If an individual received frequent mentions on the Adult Guess-Who Test it would seem to be sure evidence that he is visible to young people in the community. To what extent it also signifies imitation by young people is not clear, but the hypothesis appears justified that a rather small number of persons in Prairie City have considerable positive influence on the character development of boys and girls.

CONCLUSIONS

The "ideal self" seems to be increasingly influenced during adolescence by adults outside the family, and especially by attractive and visible young adults. The data indicate that, if imitation takes place, the objects of imitation tend to be attractive young adults and successful middle-aged citizens. They also show that a small number, probably not exceeding 1 per cent of the adult population, are unusually visible to boys and girls and that perhaps these persons play an influential role in the character formation of adolescents in the community.[7]

The data from the essay on "The Person I Would Like to Be Like" suggest that the sixteen-year-old is actively integrating the characteristics of a number of people into a composite "ideal self." This conclusion is at least consistent with, and perhaps to some extent supported by, the fact that on the Adult Guess-Who Test different kinds of people are mentioned as outstanding in the community for different desirable characteristics.

The process which is going on in the sixteen-year-old seems to be very well described by one of them when he writes: "I have created an imaginary hero and attempted to fit my personality into his. I am not sure who this hero is, but part of him is what I consider myself. I imitate myself and extracts of other people."

[7] See Chapter 22 for further discussion of this point.

8

Moral Beliefs and the Ability to Apply
Them in Solving Problems of Conduct

This chapter describes the moral beliefs held by Prairie City sixteen-year-olds
and the relationship between character reputation and moral beliefs. It makes
its contribution to methodology by describing two test instruments devised
for studying the moral beliefs of adolescents.

The last sections of the chapter discuss the sources or driving forces which
cause a person to adopt certain moral beliefs. These sections also include
implications for practice.

As boys and girls grow up, we expect them to formulate an increasingly conscious and rational code of conduct. Through expressions of approval and disapproval from adults, through punishments and rewards, as well as through verbal teaching, young
people are expected gradually to acquire generalized standards and
beliefs about what is desirable, approved, and right and what is
undesirable and wrong.

Moreover, as these beliefs and values mature and crystallize, we
expect young people to make more adequate use of them in thinking through problems of conduct and making decisions. For example, we expect people who believe in honesty and friendliness to
recognize the situations in which these values are involved. Since
in most conduct problems several conflicting values are at stake,
we expect some reasonable evaluation as to the relative importance
of each value.

One of the hypotheses of the study was that overt conduct is at
least in some measure influenced by what people believe about
conduct and how well they can apply what they believe in thinking through the problems of conduct. The first task was therefore
to find out to·what extent persons who had good reputation en-

joyed that reputation because they valued the qualities which make up good character.

The second problem was to find out to what extent good conduct was influenced by the ability to apply moral principles rationally and consistently in making decisions, by the ability to resolve conflicts in values, and by the ability to consider the consequences of various decisions and actions.

Two instruments were developed to obtain information on these points. One, called *Student Beliefs*, is a general questionnaire surveying beliefs closely related to the five character traits. This questionnaire contains general statements of opinion which cover the five character traits and include a variety of relationships with peers, home, school, and employer. Subjects were asked to check each item "agree" (A), "disagree" (D), or "undecided" (U). The following examples illustrate these statements.[1]

15. A person should not feel obliged to be friendly or attentive to persons who have few friends because they do not know how to get along with people. (Friendliness.)

25. Regardless of what happens to you as a result of it you should challenge untrue accounts about another person when you hear them. (Moral courage.)

32. Some matters in life are so important that it would be foolish not to cheat a little to gain them. (Honesty.)

47. A busy person has the right to refuse to do a job which will benefit a club to which he belongs but which will not benefit himself. (Loyalty.)

53. You need not feel under any obligation to do things at school which have not been especially assigned to you by a teacher or a student officer. (Responsibility.)

Another instrument, *Life Problems*, consists of eight problem situations, followed by alternative courses of action and a list of reasons supporting these actions. The reasons represent different values which are often in conflict with each other. Students were asked to choose courses of action and then support these choices with reasons.

The exercise given below illustrates this instrument:

Problem 111

A committee was appointed to take care of the scrap collection in the school. Bob was a member of the committee. His task was that of weighing the scrap. The chairman, who was popular, was careless in his work. Bob found it difficult to do his share well without also doing some of the work the chairman was supposed to do. He spoke about it to the chairman, but the chairman

[1] For a complete copy of the questionnaire *Student Beliefs*, see Chapter 23.

did nothing about it. Many other students defended the chairman because he was so well liked.

What should Bob do? (Check which statement you think is the best.)

_____ A. Do the things that the chairman was supposed to do and say nothing about it.

_____ B. Propose that someone else be appointed as chairman.

_____ C. Do his own job well enough to get by and not worry about the rest.

_____ D. Resign from his job quietly.

Why? (Check in the spaces below the reasons that express *why you believe* the action which you have checked is best.)

Reasons

_____ 1. This job is important enough for Bob to reveal the inefficiency of the chairman, even if that makes Bob unpopular.

_____ 2. Bob's duty is to act as a committee member; he will not be thanked for butting into affairs which are not his business.

_____ 3. People who complain about how things are run are not well liked.

_____ 4. Under the circumstances there is nothing Bob can do about poor leadership except to get out.

_____ 5. Bob has done his duty by doing his own part as well as he can.

_____ 6. By resigning, Bob will avoid being party to a failure.

This chapter deals mainly with the conclusions drawn from the results of these two instruments. The analyses on which these conclusions are based are described in Chapter 23.

WHAT DO YOUNG PEOPLE BELIEVE?

To obtain a picture of what our subjects believed about honesty, responsibility, moral courage, loyalty, and friendliness, responses to items on both instruments were examined for the relative frequency of approval and disapproval of various values; and the distribution of scores and the relationship of the several scores to each other were examined for the relative strength of positive, negative, and uncertain responses. In addition, a detailed study was made of the responses of nineteen individuals, to find patterns of responses which would not be revealed in scores. By these methods it was possible to account for such limitations as may have characterized the instruments and to arrive at fairly dependable interpretations.

Friendliness

The prevailing concept of friendliness is that of being amiable and accommodating to all people, being popular, and having many friends. For example, 75 per cent of the students believe in not saying unkind things, in taking time to cheer up unhappy persons, in making strangers feel at home at a party, and in having many friends.

Whenever there is a conflict between personal friendship and attending to lessons, being honest, or just being busy, attention to friends is usually subordinated. Expressions of common politeness, such as paying attention to people neglected at parties, are accepted more frequently than acts of friendship involving sacrifice of personal values. Few subjects, for example, agreed with such statements as "When you haven't the time to keep up with your lessons and your friends, it is better to neglect your lessons than your friends," or "Keeping friends is so important that it would be foolish not to tell a little fib to accomplish that."

Loyalty to personal friends figures none too strongly and is usually subordinated to other values. Rarely is a boy or girl willing to defend the wrongdoing of a personal friend. On the surface this fact seems to contradict common observations as well as evidence from studies of adolescent gang loyalties. However, considered in the framework of this test and in the context of the community, it seems natural for these students to give precedence to character values other than friendliness—at least intellectually.

Honesty

Of the five traits, standards of honesty are the most widely and unquestioningly accepted. Positive scores in this area are the highest, and negative scores are low.

The concept of honesty is dominated by ideas about the use of property and telling the truth. Such acts as borrowing things without permission and using small sums of the family's money without permission are highly disapproved. Telling the truth to employers, teachers, and parents is uniformly and rigorously accepted. Compromises occur only when telling the truth involves betraying another student, thus suggesting tattling. Usually, also, some compromise is attempted when protecting friends conflicts with being honest and truthful towards school authorities. Rigorous and even extreme standards are used in judging other people's honesty.

Only with reference to responsibility can one detect a similarly strict pattern of moral beliefs.

Loyalty

Beliefs in this area seem to be confused and uncertain. The medians for positive scores are the lowest, and on negative and uncertain scores they are the highest for any of the five traits (see Table 33, Chapter 23). This is partly explained by the fact that several conflicting types of loyalty were included: loyalty to friends, loyalty to family, and loyalty to school and its activities. But it seems evident also that a clear position on issues of loyalty requires greater maturity than is evidenced by sixteen-year-olds.

Loyalty to personal friends is often subordinated to other values. Apparently for Prairie City subjects there is a code of not betraying friends outright, but not a similarly strong code of pleasing or cherishing friends.

Loyalty to school seems to be limited to obeying school rules—attending school parties and school activities is not taken very seriously. A somewhat more positive attitude is expressed in connection with the problem situations. These suggest willingness to contribute to school welfare, willingness to carry on certain activities in spite of the razzing of immediate friends, and willingness to stand up for worth-while causes against the criticism of peers. This suggests that loyalty to school is seen in terms of obvious, concrete actions but that a generalized concept of loyalty to school as an institution is lacking.

Loyalty to leaders is qualified by an unwillingness to support them if one disagrees with them.

The least-developed aspect is loyalty to ideas, principles, and values. A high degree of uncertainty characterizes reactions to all issues involving conflict of several loyalties or conflict of loyalty with other values, such as defending the family against criticism or dropping a friendship if one's reputation is endangered.

Moral Courage

The strongest aspect of moral courage is that of defending and protecting one's own rights and those of others. There is practically a unanimous feeling that one must defend anyone against gossip. Yet doubt and fear are expressed about any opinion or action, no matter how right, which is likely to arouse the displeasure of any person in authority or jeopardize one's popularity with peers. There is hesitancy in raising questions of rightness and wrongness in criticizing peers, for fear of being regarded a prig. Subjects also show unwillingness to undertake action which may be needed for the benefit of a group or project, if that action suggests direct or implied criticism of other students. They seem inclined to leave others' business alone, even though other values may be sacrificed. Following the group, even into wrongdoing, is rather highly approved.

On the whole, rebels show more moral courage than do students who are generally amenable to accepted standards. This suggests that rebels and negatively disposed individuals have greater opportunity to develop moral courage because their personal make-up predisposes them to act in ways which are conducive to moral courage. Individuals with positive moral values, but more submissive dispositions, have fewer opportunities for defending their positive and desirable values.

Responsibility

Standards of responsibility are highly developed, and they are applied under a variety of circumstances. Duties toward school, home, and employment are taken seriously. Punctuality in attending meetings, completing accepted jobs, and aiding the family financially stand high on the list of approved items. Especially rigorous standards are set up for other people, and lenience toward athletes or talented or forgetful people is highly disapproved.

There is a great assurance that the first duty of a student is toward his own success, whether in earning grades or in preparing for life work. Very few of our subjects consider it wise to sacrifice this value to any demands that might be made by the general school welfare. On the whole responsibility toward work outside school is taken more seriously than responsibility toward school work or school activities.

Uncertainties occur most frequently in the case of conflicts between family loyalty, school responsibilities, and friends.

Some Common Characteristics

Accepting familiar stereotypes is one outstanding characteristic of these beliefs. High agreement usually occurs on statements which express the obvious middle-class codes of conduct in stereotyped language requiring little thought or analysis. Thus, politeness characterizes the concept of friendship. Punctuality and completing accepted jobs characterize the concept of responsibility. Such general slogans as "One has to sacrifice fun for honesty in life" or "It is always a good policy to be nice to people" are among the most frequently marked items, as are such repeatedly emphasized verities as the necessity of obeying school rules, no matter what they are, and doing boring jobs if the school needs them, in order to be a good citizen. These slogans are accepted in a general way without question; but exceptions and inconsistencies appear when these values are represented in specific situations.

Individual positions deviating from the generally accepted code are feared and shunned. This is shown by hesitancy in expressing opinions contrary to common beliefs and by approving wrong behavior if most of one's associates are involved in the act. There is a marked tendency to subordinate individually held positions and beliefs to both adult and peer-group opinion, even when one's own positions are considered morally right. Exceptions to this submissiveness to peer-group opinion occur only in cases of conflict between peer opinion and some higher authority, such as the church, parents, or the community code. Peer censure is often subordinated to parental censure.

A third common characteristic is the lack of readiness to face conflicts of choices. The predominant reaction to conflict situations is uncertainty or an attempt at a compromise solution. For example, there is hesitancy in taking positions when loyalty to friends and school work conflict, or when loyalty to family and loyalty to friends are opposed to each other. On the whole, uncertainties or negative responses are frequent on items expressing a conflict of values, whereas positive responses predominate on items stating a straightforward position.

THE RATIONALE OF MORAL BELIEFS

Relationships between the Five Traits

To find out to what extent there was variation from trait to trait and to what extent a general and uniform acceptance of all values prevailed, the scores on Student Beliefs for each trait were studied for their interrelationships. Beliefs about honesty, responsibility, friendliness, moral courage, and loyalty proved to be more related than had been expected. Although the relationships varied from any one pair of traits to another, all were fairly high.[2] Thus those

[2] Intercorrelations between the five traits ranged from 0.41 between friendliness and responsibility to 0.66 between friendliness and loyalty. Coefficients of correlation are shown in Table 35, Chapter 23.

subjects who are high on one trait tend also to be high on others, and vice versa.

Apparently, when the expression of opinion takes place on a comparatively general level, as on the Student Beliefs Questionnaire, moral principles are accepted or rejected rather uniformly; the differences between various traits are not great.

Consistency of Moral Beliefs

Examination of the responses on Student Beliefs revealed marked inconsistencies. For example, although 75 per cent of the students believe that one should not say unkind things to another person, a much more ambivalent reaction occurred on the item "One cannot always be expected to consider whether what one says or does would hurt the feelings of others." Similarly, there is high agreement with the statement that members of clubs and committees should expect help from non-members; yet a large number of subjects maintain that a person has a right to refuse a job for a club when it does not benefit him personally.

Inspection of test items suggests that sixteen-year-olds assent to generalized statements and statements which conform to accepted stereotypes, but reject others which express the value in connection with an unusual detail or take a less-familiar approach to it. The phase "avoid saying unkind things" may be more familiar than "consider whether you hurt other persons' feelings."

The degree to which personal interest is involved seems also to influence responses. Thus subjects tended to agree more often with statements expressing the obligation to help others when these statements omitted any reference to personal difficulties involved in meeting such obligations.

It seemed further that the acceptance or rejection of a value depended in large measure on the situation in which it was presented. For example, loyalty to school as an institution was less frequently expressed than was loyalty to certain specific activities in school. Expression of moral courage also varied depending on whether or not criticism of persons was involved.

Whatever the specific reasons for these inconsistencies, it seems clear that a variety of considerations other than awareness of value principles influence both the expression of moral beliefs and their application.

Extreme vs. Moderate Standards

Another aspect of the rationale of moral beliefs lies in the discrimination between extreme positions and those which conform to reasonable social expectations. Statements on Student Beliefs which express extreme positions were isolated and scored separately. For example, "No one is an honest person unless his statements can always be relied upon" represents an extreme expectation regarding honesty. These statements are referred to as "superitems." No items to which 75 per cent or more of the students agreed were included among the superitems, on the assumption that they expressed commonly accepted stereotypes for our subjects rather than extremes of position.

The relationship between the total score and the score on superitems was quite high.[3] This indicates that many students reacted to the questionnaire without much discrimination between the extreme and the moderate positions. This impression of lack of discrimination was also borne out by the case studies. Over and over again seemingly intelligent and mature students accepted extreme statements about the various character values as readily as they assumed moderate positions.

Moral Beliefs and Their Application to Life Problems

For evidence on the relationship between moral values and their application, scores on Student Beliefs were studied in relation to scores on Life Problems. The degree of relationship proved to be very low.[4] The main reason for the low relationship lies in the fact that in Life Problems several acceptable values were set into conflict with each other, while on Student Beliefs each item represented a single value. Making decisions which involve conflicts of values requires compromises which are not faced when each of these values is considered separately. It is also quite evident that expediency and emotional factors play an important part in making decisions and force individuals to sacrifice some of their abstract beliefs. Thus people who believe in friendliness in general may take exception to this belief when some specific person is involved or when conflicting interests are at stake.

[3] The coefficient of correlation was 0.68.

[4] Coefficients of correlation ranged from -0.13 on friendliness to 0.29 on responsibility. See Table 44, Chapter 23.

The comparison of quartile standings, given below, clarifies the relationship between the two instruments:

> 25 out of 70 students stand in the same quartile on both instruments.
> 11 out of 70 students are one quartile lower on Life Problems.
> 8 out of 70 students are two quartiles lower on Life Problems.
> 4 out of 70 students are three quartiles lower on Life Problems.
> 14 out of 70 students are one quartile lower on Student Beliefs.
> 3 out of 70 students are two quartiles lower on Student Beliefs.
> 5 out of 70 students are three quartiles lower on Student Beliefs.

These data indicate that one-third of the group have the same standing on general beliefs and on application of their beliefs. They are able to reason in terms of whatever values they accept. Another third has a discrepancy amounting to one quartile step.

The main impression derived from studying the cases of extreme discrepancies was that the students who were high on Student Beliefs and low on Life Problems were those who had accepted certain stereotyped slogans but who had not thought through the meaning or implications of these slogans. There was little relationship between what these individuals expressed as their general beliefs and the values which determined their particular decisions. These students also vary in their position regarding the same value if the value is presented in different contexts or involves different emotional components. Several students who were quite positive in their general beliefs reacted negatively to the same values on the Life Problems Test when the situation described touched on any area in which these students showed maladjustment.

RELATIONSHIP BETWEEN REPUTATION AND BELIEFS

The consistency between beliefs and overt conduct was studied by comparing reputational status and status on the Student Beliefs Questionnaire.

> 22 out of 75 students stand in the same quartile on both measures.
> 19 out of 75 students are one quartile lower on Student Beliefs.
> 9 out of 75 students are two quartiles lower on Student Beliefs.
> 10 out of 75 students are one quartile lower on reputation.
> 6 out of 75 students are two quartiles lower on reputation.
> 1 out of 75 students is three quartiles lower on reputation.
> 8 out of 75 students are three quartiles lower on Student Beliefs.

These data reveal that beliefs and reputation agree for about a third of the students. For another third, the standing on beliefs and reputation differs by one quartile.

An examination of the case studies suggested several factors accounting for the discrepancies. Among the students who are high on reputation and low on beliefs, eight in all, some are ambitious and are striving for social mobility. They are afraid of being wrong and have high uncertainty in their beliefs, which reduces their positive scores on the beliefs questionnaire. These same individuals are also anxious to conform overtly in the presence of authority; hence their reputations tend to be exaggerated toward the positive. Others are indifferent to values of any sort and conform to expectations of conduct because of lethargy, rather than because of their moral beliefs. A similar relationship exists in cases of individuals with few conscious moral principles but who behave in the interests of expediency.

Among those subjects whose beliefs are higher than their reputation, some are rebels. They reject any authority, and, although inwardly they accept the sanctions of good conduct, they tend to behave contrary to expectations. Others are maladjusted and insecure in school and in their relationship to adults. Their reputations, therefore, are probably lower than they deserve and probably bear little relationship to their moral convictions.

MORAL BELIEFS AND INTELLIGENCE

It is usually assumed that intelligence has a good deal to do with the adequacy and maturity of moral beliefs. In particular, intelligence might be expected to influence the ability to intellectualize moral problems. But this did not prove to be the case. The relation between the scores on Student Beliefs and the Binet IQ was quite low.[5]

Study of the cases representing high discrepancy suggested that several other factors overshadowed the importance of IQ in determining scores on Student Beliefs. In persons striving for upward social mobility, uncertainty or negativism caused low scores on Student Beliefs. Although these subjects have high intelligence, they earn low scores on the test because they feel unsure about taking positions on moral issues. There are also individuals who re-

[5] The coefficient of correlation was 0.29.

act in an expected and intelligent manner in concrete situations but who show little disposition toward formulating a generalized code of morals.

Motivational patterns also seem to cut across and to modify the effects of intelligence. Two intelligent students who earned low scores on the beliefs test react negatively to most values in the school context.

All who were higher in intelligence than beliefs are either uncertain or give negative answers when confronted with statements or situations involving conflict. Three students with low IQ are anxious to please, respond in an expected manner to an attitude scale, and thus earn high scores on the Student Beliefs.

MOTIVATIONAL SOURCES OF MORAL VALUES

Each person's beliefs and his way of applying them are colored by his particular goals in life. Analyses of the case studies revealed several types of motivation which underlay the formation of moral beliefs and character. They are summarized here because they suggest points at which character development can be influenced.

Ambition and Social Mobility

When moral values are developed as a means for reaching certain personal ambitions and goals, conformity becomes an outstanding characteristic. This is usually accompanied by a high degree of uncertainty about moral principles because of the fear of being wrong, and apparently also because social mobility often involves a "virtuous" pose in conduct without the corresponding conviction in heart. This characteristic naturally varies depending on the nature of the ambition.

One boy, for example, is ambitious to become a minister, which would, for him, constitute a step "up" in the social scale. He conscientiously accepts obligation both in school and at home, and he has a strong sense of duty. He strives always to meet the expectations of moral authority, such as the family and the school, although he places only secondary importance upon affectional relationships and upon peer acceptance.

This type of motivation does not usually lead to an early generalization and abstraction of a code of values. Uncertainty and insecurity in moral beliefs seem to be a natural counterpart of the transition from one social group to another. In some cases of this type there is no evidence of any internalized moral beliefs; right conduct is that behavior which is most suitable for reaching a given goal.

The effectiveness of this type of motivation in building character depends, of course, on the nature of the ambition. If the ambition is consistent with good character, this motivational influence is positive; if not, negative.

Affectional Responsiveness

Another and rather frequent source for developing moral beliefs is the need for affection. The individual may desire primarily the affection of his family, or he may strive for general popularity. Being liked by other people is the important thing; and conduct is adapted to this aim. A concrete, common-sense code of conduct is usually developed. The individual tends to be highly adaptable in whatever milieu he finds himself and to whichever group commands his affection.

Depending on the quality of the group, desirable or undesirable influences are accepted with equal ease. In a stable and compact group life, a consistent moral outlook develops. In a conflicting or changing group, the individual is likely to be vacillating. If there is personal security in relationships with other people, the outcome is likely to be successful conformity. When these relationships are insecure, timidity and submission result. Because personal attachments represent the dominant motivations, these individuals tend to react toward other people and their values uncritically.

Submission to Authority

For some individuals the main source of moral values lies in authority of some kind: community, parents, school, or church. These people are characterized by a timid submission to any authority. When the authority is consistent, their beliefs are consistent. When different authorities, such as home and religion or home and friends, conflict in their demands, these persons tend to become inconsistent in belief and in conduct.

Accepting things without question is a characteristic of these individuals. Because of this attitude, they lack a rational framework for their values. Often they do not see, in concrete situations, the implications of the general precepts they accept. Therefore, there are likely to be differences between what they believe and how they conduct themselves. In the main, they see and appraise their own conduct through the eyes of other people or by some such symbol as "good daughter," "good student," or "good Christian." Since they value a good reputation, they develop conscientiousness and a high sense of responsibility in all situations involving authority, but they lack initiative. Inability to face conflicts in a rational way is also an outstanding characteristic. Lacking a generalized concept of moral values, they have little moral courage and show a high degree of ambivalence whenever personal desires conflict with the dictates of authority.

Impulses and Emotionality

A fourth prevalent source for moral beliefs is represented by personal impulses and emotionality. In a number of case studies an impulse reaction to the desires and drives evoked by concrete situations seemed to be the mainspring of moral conduct. Beliefs developed from this source show little consistency because impulses arising from immediate situations are none too predictable a guide for conduct. Rebellion against authority frequently occurs. The conduct of these persons is undisciplined and their beliefs are immature. They tend to accept good and bad without discrimination and often show a total absence of rational principles.

Rationality and Reflection

Rational consideration of values is another way of developing personal morality. Few adolescents in this group make use of this source for developing a code of conduct. This may be partly caused by general immaturity. Partly, however, the cause lies in the ways character is taught in Prairie City. Moral values are taught by reiterating rules for conduct in specific situations and by appraising specific acts. Rational consideration of the principles of conduct is emphasized infrequently, except by reiteration of generalizations, and these are limited to obvious points, such as obeying school rules, not lying to mother, not stealing, and not cheating in school. There is little opportunity for reflection on such matters as loyalty and moral courage. Speaking one's mind, especially expressing difference with the majority's views, is not encouraged. Certain types of loyalty and moral courage may even be discouraged because their expression tends to be in conflict with the norms of good conduct.

Negativism

For many people, rebellion against any established authority is a real source for principles of conduct. Being unable to make satisfactory adjustments to certain phases of their environment—family, school, or friends—they become negative to all values associated with those groups; they tend, therefore, to develop a morality which represents the reverse of the one expected of them. A cynical attitude is usually developed, which, although sometimes penetrating and critical, seldom results in a constructive personal code of conduct.

CONCLUSIONS AND IMPLICATIONS

1. The moral beliefs of adolescents in Prairie City are strongly conditioned by their families, the community mores, religion, and peer influence. These influences include many stereotyped concepts about good conduct and, when successful, lead to a rigid and inflexible code of behavior. The influence of the school affects primarily the sense of responsibility and honesty; it is less effective as far as loyalty, moral courage, and friendliness are concerned.

2. Moral beliefs are formed by accumulating reactions to immediate situations, not by a conscious formulation of a generalized code of conduct. This reflects the fact that the teaching of what is right and wrong is done with reference to isolated, concrete acts of behavior; relatively little effort is made to help young people generalize from these situations or to help them develop a coherent moral philosophy. The development of a personal and rational code, when it does take place, grows out of the accidents of personal make-up and patterns of adjustment. Under these circumstances, maladjustment rather than adjustment tends to be the stimulating force toward reflection, criticism, and personal orientation.

3. The ability to apply moral beliefs to an increasing range of conflicting life situations is quite undeveloped at the age of sixteen. These subjects see the more obvious lines of action but seem at a loss whenever a subtle weighing of values is called for. They find conflicts hard to face; they tend to solve conflicts by using slogans rather than by using concepts of the relative significance of values.

4. Most of these young people seem to be eager to respond to moral values. Even those who rebel against their environment seem to cherish an inward ideal of desirable conduct. It seems, therefore, that rebellion and bad conduct are usually rooted in causes other than rejection of moral values themselves. It need hardly be said that the development of character, as is true of any socializing process, takes place in an emotional context and in relation to other personalities. The byplay of feelings and emotions has a profound influence on the nature of moral beliefs and their efficacy in influencing conduct. Good emotional adjustment is, therefore, an important prerequisite for desirable character development in adolescence.

5. There is too little flexibility in Prairie City in the means by which individuals are permitted to achieve a code of behavior. Good conduct is imposed both by the family and by the community in the form of a rigid code. Personal differences in attempting to restyle social demands to suit personal drives are discouraged and punished by the school, by the family, and by the peer culture.

People with a high degree of moral and personal sensitivity are especially at a disadvantage. Since their reactions to the environment tend to be more complex than the average, they usually have more difficulty in making adjustments. As a result they are often unsuccessful in living up to social expectations. Since they are judged by the end result of their behavior, rather than by their efforts to cope with their difficulties, social approval is often withdrawn, and these individuals are left to deal with their problems unaided.

9

The Relation of Values to Character

Chapter 9 reports a study of moral values as expressed in essays written by Prairie City adolescents. The study is of primary interest as an experiment in methodology.

The relationship between values, as expressed in essays, and character reputation is found to be positive but low. In suggesting factors which may influence this relationship, the closing sections of the chapter bear upon the problem of the nature of character formation.

A person with high values has good character. This statement seems at first to make such obvious good sense that one is inclined to accept it as needing no scientific verification. If we should define a person's values by what he does rather than by what he says, high values and superior character become, in fact, synonymous.

If, however, values are defined as objects or states of affairs which are desired by an individual, then we can be sure that a person's behavior will fall short of his values. It was on the basis of this latter definition that values were studied in relation to character reputation. It was assumed that an individual's verbal statements are true reports on his values. Subjects were asked to write essays on topics which would indirectly elicit information on values. Essays on the topic "The Person I Would Like to Be Like" were analyzed with this objective in mind.

The situation was planned so that the subjects would feel free to express themselves without fear of affecting their status in school or in the community.[1] The instructions were:

Describe in a page or less the person you would most like to be like when you grow up. This may be a real person or an imaginary person. He or she may be a combination of several people. Tell something about this person's age, character, appearance, occupation, and recreations. If he is a real person, say so. You need not give his real name if you do not want to.

[1] For a more detailed description of the "test" situation, see Chapter 24.

97

In order to deal quantitatively with the data, a "scale of values" was designed and applied to the essays. The scale assigned numerical weights to verbal statements, from low to high, along a continuum from the selfish and materialistic to the altruistic and spiritual. Three judges, working independently, ranked the essays in order of merit on this scale, and an average or composite rank was assigned to each essay. This rank was used to compare values with other factors, such as reputation, school achievement, IQ, and social-class position.

The scale itself, the methods of rating and ranking, of checking objectivity and consistency of judges' rankings, and of checking reliability of students' responses are all discussed in Chapter 24, "Methods of Studying Values."

The following papers, written by three boys and three girls, have been selected to illustrate high, medium, and low values, as judged by the authors.

High

A. This person is between 30 and 40 years old, is kind and tries to help everyone he can. He will always stop what he is doing and tell you about anything you want to know concerning him or his work. He is good looking and not very many people have a grudge against or disagree with his way. This person is a livestock farmer in the corn belt area who gets along good with his neighbors and is known very well for that. He helps his neighbors secure good animals and helps finance them also at times. He invites them over to see his livestock and shows his neighbor how to pick out a good one. He helps young boys in 4-H or F.F.A. get a start and keeps them going. He belongs to farm organizations and helps them many times. For recreation he likes most any outdoor sport.

B. The person whom I hold in my mind as my ideal woman is a combination of several people. I picture her as being in between 25 and 30 years. She has a very pleasing personality, is patient, kind, understanding, has a good sense of humor, very easy to get along with, and very trustworthy. This person is very interested in church work. She also has many other interests, such as music, sports, young people's organizations, etc. This woman is very well groomed. Through her life the world should be made a better place in which to live. She shall serve humanity.

Medium

C. When I am an adult I want to be an understanding person, both with children and other adults. I do not want to be fat nor thin in appearance. My hair would not be short nor glued to my head. I want to be a good dresser. I want to be lovable with all and courteous but not so courteous that I would make others unpleasant. As for my occupation if I had to work then I would like to sew and make clothing for people. I would like to spend my recreation time traveling, reading, seeing a movie occasionally, ice skating, and seeing well-known performances out of town. As for my character, I want to be a jolly and good-natured person, but not the type of person who makes a fool of herself.

D. There is a man I would like to be like and that is my boss because of his witty humor, a good business man and also that he treats all people alike rich or poor. He has very good judgment and when there is a job to do he does it and doesn't waste any time doing it. He also has the ability to get along with people no matter who they are.

Low

E. First of all I'll say my ideal, Robert Taylor. I don't know what I'd do first if I could become his twin brother right now. The main things I like about my ideal are his looks, occupation and his beautiful female surroundings. When I go to a picture played by Robert, I sit and envy him most of the time and don't get much meaning from the picture. The age, I am not sure of how old Robert Taylor is, but I'm sure he is over twenty-three, the age I would like to be this instant. In that case that would have to be Mr. Taylor's age also if we were to be twin brothers. When I am old enough I am going to try every means possible to improve my looks. I am going to wear a Taylor mustache, train my hair to be nice as to my liking. I have light hair, brown eyes. According to this it would be quite easy to make my hair darker.

F. The person I would like to be like is real. She has everything. She is the same age as I am, seventeen. Her character is practically perfect, she is always neat, and clean. She wears her clothes well, and she has plenty of them. Her occupation, at the time being is just an ordinary Senior like me. I would love to be able to bowl like her, that's about all the recreation she does that I don't feel like I can do.

RELATION TO REPUTATION AND OTHER FACTORS

The first question which arises is whether individuals with high rank on the scale of values have good character reputations. The relationship between value rankings and reputation, computed by statistical methods, was found to be positive but not high.[2]

Rank on the scale of values was also compared to intelligence (as measured by the Stanford-Binet IQ) and to school achievement. In both cases the relationships were positive but low, the relationship being slightly higher between values and school achievement than between values and IQ.[3]

[2] The rank order correlation coefficient was 0.40, which corresponds to the product-moment coefficient of 0.42. When corrected for attenuation, the correlation becomes 0.61. See Chapter 24 for discussion of these points.

[3] The rank order correlation coefficient for essay scores and Stanford-Binet IQ was 0.33; for essay scores and school achievement, the latter expressed by averaged school grades, the coefficient was 0.39. When corrected for attenuation, these coefficients become 0.48 and 0.66 respectively. See Table 45, Chapter 24.

A fourth factor considered in this analysis was social-class position. The relationship between values and class position, while positive again, was low—the lowest of the four relationships.[4]

These relationships tell us that there is a tendency for sixteen-year-olds with high values scores on the essay to have good character reputations, to do well in school, to be of good intelligence, and to come from families high in the social scale. But there will be many exceptions to these generalizations. It will not be at all unusual to find lower-class boys and girls with high scores on the essay. It will be unusual, but not surprising, to find boys and girls with below-average reputations and high scores on the essay.

Comparisons by Quartile Standings

A clearer picture of the degree of relationship existing between values scores and other factors is given by analyzing the distribu-

TABLE 16   ANALYSIS OF VALUES SCORES AND OTHER SCORES BY QUARTILE STANDINGS

Values N, 78	Reputation N, 74 *				Binet IQ N, 75				School Achievement N, 71				Social Class N, 78	
	Quartile				Quartile				Quartile				High (U, UM, LM)	Low (UL, LL)
	I	II	III	IV	I	II	III	IV	I	II	III	IV		
Q I N, 19	8	3	4	3	7	4	4	3	7	6	3	1	9	10
Q II N, 20	5	7	4	3	8	4	4	3	6	5	6	2	10	10
Q III N, 20	3	8	3	4	3	6	5	4	4	4	4	6	13	7
Q IV N, 19	2	0	9	8	2	2	4	10	1	3	5	8	13	6

* There were a few subjects for whom scores were not available.

tions of subjects according to quartile standings. This analysis is given in Table 16.

[4] Tetrachoric *r* was computed between social class and values, using upper, upper-middle, and lower-middle classes as indicating above-average rank and upper-lower and lower-lower classes as indicating below-average rank; the upper 50 per cent were used as high rank on the essays and the lower 50 per cent as low rank. The correlation was found to be 0.27.

The table is to be read as follows: Of the nineteen subjects who were in the highest quartile on values (Q IV), eight were in the highest quartile on character reputation, nine were in the second highest quartile on reputation, and two in the lowest quartile. Similarly, of the nineteen, ten were in the highest quartile on IQ, eight in the highest quartile on school achievement, and thirteen had relatively high social position.

From this table one generalization emerges immediately. Those subjects who are in the upper quartile on values tend to be high on all the other measures in the table.

In contrast, subjects in the lowest quartile on values are to be found in all quartile positions on the other measures, except for school achievement where most of this group is definitely low.

Individual exceptions to the general rule can be selected from this table and studied. For example, there are two individuals in the upper quartile on values who are in the lowest quartile on reputation. These two subjects belong to the lower social classes. One is Polish, which, in Prairie City, tends to lower his reputation automatically. The parents of the other subject have been engaged in a disreputable occupation and thus may have lowered the reputations of their children.

Another striking exception to the generalization is the presence of three persons in the upper quartile on reputation but the lowest quartile on values. These three subjects are very ambitious persons. It is probable that their ambition leads them to conform to the values of the school situation, although their personal values may be decidedly selfish and materialistic.

Still another factor that operates to reduce the relation between values and reputation is the friendliness element in the reputation score. Several persons, although ranking high on values, were rated unusually low on reputation for friendliness. Their friendliness ratings were of considerable importance in bringing their average reputation scores down to the first or second quartile. On the other hand, all three individuals in Q II for values and Q IV for reputation are in the highest quartile in friendliness. Probably the subject who emphasizes friendliness in his essay does not thereby add much to his values score, whereas a friendly disposition tends to raise his reputation score.

This kind of analysis can be continued with other sections of the table. Most of the apparent exceptions to the generalization that high values correlate positively with good character, high achievement, etc., are easily explained when one turns to the individual case material. These exceptions are due, of course, to other factors which affect values or reputation or achievement—factors which have not been expressly considered in this analysis.

One conclusion to be drawn from this study is that adolescent boys and girls with high values tend to have good character reputations but that those with low values are not so definitely marked by low reputations.

Another conclusion has to do with the quality of the values expressed by the subjects of the study. Their scores on the scale of values were found to be low. Although there is as yet no definitive study of the validity of the methods here described, the tentative judgment of the authors is that the quality of values expressed by these adolescent boys and girls falls short of what the community desires.

10

Personal-Social Adjustment and

Character Reputation

This chapter studies the relationship between character reputation and personal-social adjustment, the latter being measured by a standardized questionnaire. Adolescents of high and low reputation are compared, and a description is given of the adjustment tendencies of subjects of low reputation.

The material applies most directly to theories of character formation and to the relation of character to other aspects of personality.

The boy or girl who enjoys a good reputation in the community is often described as "better adjusted," both to himself and to society, than the boy or girl of unfavorable reputation. This may mean several things: the well-adjusted individual behaves in accordance with the expectations of responsible people; his goals and aspirations are likely to be socially approved, and the means and techniques he employs to secure them are not likely to lead him into unexpected trouble; he is not likely to feel disliked, avoided, or ridiculed and hence not likely to feel inferior or worried over becoming a social misfit or outcast. All these are types of "adjustment," and they are part of what we understand by "good character" and "good reputation."

But, if adjustment can mean many things, a person well adjusted in one direction may be badly adjusted in another. Even a boy or girl of good repute often feels himself poorly adjusted in some ways. Hence, we must always ask what particular directions or kinds of adjustment tend to correspond to reputational differences.

THE HYPOTHESIS

The guiding hypothesis in attempting to answer this question, as well as the general procedure for testing it, and the conclusions reached are described briefly in this chapter. Further details as to methods and findings will be found in Chapter 25. The hypothesis may be stated as follows:

The behavior of an individual in morally significant situations and his consequent reputation are partly determined by certain characteristics of personal and social adjustment, including, among others:

1. Certain temperamental and conative qualities evoked by social situations (dominance, reclusiveness, independence, etc.).

2. Favorable or antagonistic sets toward particular objects and situations, which influence his conduct toward these or similar situations.

3. The degree of confidence he possesses in his psychological competence for good social adjustments, as evidenced by his possession of social skills, acquaintance with and respect for social codes and standards, and his degree of adjustment to family, school, and community.

4. The kind of person he believes (or wishes to believe) himself to be and the intensity of his drive to defend and maintain that conception.

Of these four possible "personality" determinants of conduct and reputation—temperament, attitudes, adjustive efficiency, self-concept and self-feeling—evidence has been obtained only on the third and on certain aspects of the fourth. The first (temperamental traits) and second (particular attitudes) cannot be directly tested by the technique here employed; hence no conclusions are drawn as to their mode of operation. They seem, however, to help account for many details of the findings, and their operation is apparent in several of the studies described in other chapters, particularly in the individual case histories.

THE INSTRUMENT

How to get reliable information about people's emotional, intellectual, and behavioral adjustments is not an easy problem to solve. Several methods are in use—interviews, continued observations, performance-test situations, ratings by self or associates, questionnaires, and other devices—each with its own merits and defects. In the belief that an "adjustment inventory" or questionnaire would yield a maximum of relevant information, the "California Test of Personality, Secondary Series, Form A" was selected.[1]

This instrument consists of 180 questions about the subject's thoughts, feelings, habits, opinions, and experiences, each question

[1] By E. W. Tiegs, W. W. Clark, and L. P. Thorpe. Los Angeles: California Test Bureau, 1943. Permission of the publishers to reproduce parts of the test is hereby acknowledged.

to be answered "yes" or "no." Half the questions refer to facts about the individual's own mental and emotional attitudes, and half to the effectiveness of his adjustments in various social relationships, including family, school, and community. The questions are grouped into twelve subtests of fifteen items each, designated as follows:

Part 1. Self-adjustment
    1A Self-reliance
    1B Sense of personal worth
    1C Sense of personal freedom
    1D Feeling of belonging
    1E Freedom from withdrawing tendencies
    1F Freedom from nervous symptoms

Part 2. Social adjustment
    2A Social standards
    2B Social skills
    2C Freedom from anti-social tendencies
    2D Family relations
    2E School relations
    2F Community relations

For some items of the questionnaire the favorable answer (indicating good adjustment) was "yes"; for others, it was "no." The score (subtest or total) is the number of favorable replies.

It may be asked whether one can take at face value subjects' replies to questions about their personal and social attitudes. Certain criticisms have been leveled against questionnaires of the type used here. It is argued that a person cannot always be depended on to tell the truth about himself, especially an embarrassing or humiliating truth; that often he is unable to appraise himself accurately even if he wishes to; and that questions are often so ambiguous or general that a one-word answer cannot be wholly truthful.

Granting the importance of these objections, responses to such questionnaires can be accepted as giving a fair picture of the subject's feelings and opinions about himself, or at least what he is willing to have people think those feelings and opinions are. For the purposes of this study, how factual and exact his statements are is of less importance than how the subject conceives of himself and his adjustments. His replies are taken to mean no more than this.

RELATIONS BETWEEN REPUTATION AND ADJUSTMENT

The first general question which arises is, how close a relationship exists between the adjustment scores of sixteen-year-olds on this instrument and their reputation ratings? Analysis of the two sets of data showed that, although the relations are positive, they are low—so low that they warn against identifying good reputation with good adjustment.[2]

This finding confirms the suggestion made earlier that one must go beyond the total scores to inquire what particular *kinds* and *directions* of adjustment are related to reputational differences.

DIFFERENCES BETWEEN HIGH- AND LOW-RATING INDIVIDUALS

To study the particular kinds and directions of adjustment suggested by the hypothesis, a comparison was made of the average scores on the personal-social inventory for two contrasting groups, subjects with high reputation ratings and subjects with low reputation ratings.

For each of the five character traits the "high-rating" group is defined as those sixteen-year-olds who received reputation ratings of 22 (D-scores) or higher;[3] and the "low-rating" group, those rated 18 or lower. The "intermediate" or "average-rating" group, scoring 19, 20, or 21, comprising approximately one-third of the whole group, were omitted from this comparison.

Composition of the high-rating group varied from trait to trait, although twenty persons rated 22 or higher on all five traits and thus were found in all five high groups. There was more variation in the low-rating groups, although twelve people tested rated 18 or lower on four of the five traits. At the time the questionnaires were administered, a larger proportion of the low-rated than of the high-rated persons were out of school and not available for testing.

[2] Coefficients of correlation between ratings on each of the five traits and self-adjustment scores range from 0.20 to 0.39; for each of the five traits and social adjustment, from 0.02 to 0.29. See Table 46, Chapter 25.

Comparable data on ten-year-olds in Prairie City showed much higher relationships between reputation and personal-social adjustment. See Chapter 25 for a detailed discussion of these age differences and their bearing upon the nature of the instrument.

[3] See Chapter 19 for explanation of D-scores.

Since the contrasted groups were of unequal size it was necessary to employ group averages in comparing their scores.

Scores on Self-Adjustment and Social Adjustment

Table 17 shows the average scores made by the high ratees and low ratees on the two main divisions of the inventory, "self-adjustment" and "social adjustment." High- and low-rating groups are shown separately for each character trait.

TABLE 17   PERSONALITY ADJUSTMENT SCORES FOR SUBJECTS OF HIGH AND LOW CHARACTER REPUTATION

Rated on	Number		Self-Adjustment			Social Adjustment		
	High	Low	High Ratees	Low Ratees	Differ- ence	High Ratees	Low Ratees	Differ- ence
Honesty	40	20	70.8	63.3	7.5	74.9	65.0	9.9
Moral courage	40	25	67.3	63.4	3.9	71.5	68.2	3.3
Friendliness	33	15	70.9	59.4	11.5	72.5	65.5	7.0
Loyalty	46	19	70.2	56.8	13.4	73.6	65.7	7.9
Responsibility	46	21	69.6	63.0	6.6	74.4	65.2	9.2

Taking all five traits together, the high ratees averaged 8.5 more favorable responses (about 14 per cent) on the ninety self-adjustment questions and 7.5 (about 11 per cent) on the ninety social-adjustment questions.[4]

If the trait moral courage is omitted, the differences become somewhat greater, the percentages becoming 16 and 13, respectively. Differences between high- and low-rating groups on moral courage are not so clearly reflected as in the other four traits, possibly because this trait sometimes means a kind of social defiance or non-conformity, i.e., non-adjustment.

Scores on the Twelve Subtests

More significant differences emerge from a study of the twelve subtests in the inventory. Table 18 shows the differences between high- and low-rating groups on subtest scores. Again, high- and low-rating groups are shown separately for each of the five character traits.

[4] See Chapter 25 for a discussion of the significance of these differences.

From Table 18 we see that "1C Sense of personal freedom" and "2F Community relations" show only a little difference between the two rated groups, and "1A Self-reliance" and "2E School relations" do not show much more. But subjects who rated above average on the four reputation traits, honesty, friendliness, loyalty, and responsibility, show more freedom from nervous symptoms (averaging 2.25 points higher in a total of 15 points), stronger sense

TABLE 18   DIFFERENCES BETWEEN SUBJECTS OF HIGH AND LOW CHARACTER REPUTATION ON PERSONALITY SUBTEST SCORES

Subtest	H *	MC	F	L	R
1A Self-reliance	0.7 †	1.4	1.8	0.8	0.8
1B Sense of personal worth	2.0	1.0	3.2	1.7	1.7
1C Sense of personal freedom	0.3	−0.5	0.4	0.1	0.6
1D Feeling of belonging	1.2	0.6	2.5	1.6	1.2
1E Freedom from withdrawing tendencies	2.0	0.8	1.8	1.3	0.6
1F Freedom from nervous symptoms	1.8	1.4	2.6	2.6	2.0
2A Social standards	2.1	0.6	2.0	1.2	0.9
2B Social skills	1.4	0.4	1.8	1.7	1.1
2C Freedom from anti-social tendencies	2.4	1.0	2.3	1.9	2.0
2D Family relations	1.8	1.0	3.0	1.4	1.1
2E School relations	1.0	0.3	1.1	1.0	1.3
2F Community relations	1.3	0.2	0.4	0.7	0.8

* H, MC, F, L, R refer to the traits honesty, moral courage, friendliness, loyalty, and responsibility.

† High ratees minus low ratees.

of personal worth (2.15 points), greater freedom from anti-social tendencies (2.15), better family relationship (1.82), stronger feeling of belonging (1.62), higher social standards (1.55), better social skills (1.50), and more freedom from withdrawing tendencies (1.42). In terms of percentage differences based on the average scores earned, the high-reputation people scored, as a rule, from 13 per cent to 28 per cent higher on these eight general adjustment traits than did persons of low reputation.[5]

Moral courage gives a rather different kind of adjustment picture than do the other traits. Ratings on this trait, whether made

[5] See Chapter 25 for a discussion of the significance of these differences.

by age mates or by adults, appear to be based on different considerations than ratings on honesty, friendliness, loyalty, and responsibility; this difference is reflected in the subtest scores. (What people interpret as moral courage appears at times to be that conduct which defies social conventions. One might raise the question whether that which goes by the name of moral courage is not sometimes as much a case of "I don't give a hang what people say about me" as it is a case of defending one's moral principles.) On the "sense of freedom" questions, the high ratees on moral courage actually make a somewhat poorer adjustment score than do the low ratees, who perhaps feel less constraint upon their conduct. On six more traits the average score difference is less than one point, too small to be significant; on three more, sense of personal worth, freedom from anti-social tendencies, and family relations, it is just one point. On self-reliance, and freedom from nervous symptoms, as one might anticipate, the high ratees on moral courage scored higher (1.4 points) than the low ratees.

One reason why differences between high- and low-rating groups on the twelve subtests are not greater is that the high and low groups are not very sharply contrasted. The high group includes several pupils of D-score 22, loosely "high average"; and the low group, several 18 D-scores, or "low average." A study of score differences was made with the contrast sharpened by taking as a "very high" group those who rated 23 or higher, and as a "very low" group those who rated 17 or lower. Although this diminished the number of individuals to be compared, it increased the differences by more than one-third in fifty-one of the sixty comparisons. Of the remaining nine comparisons, two were left unchanged, and seven were decreased. These score differences may be taken, therefore, as indication of some real relationship between kinds or directions of adjustment and reputation.

Differences on Individual Test Items

The twelve subscores cannot be interpreted as being exact measures of the trait names attached to them. In many of the subtests, items of questionable appropriateness are included, although equally appropriate items are placed under other categories.

A more definite picture of the kind of responses which distinguish ratee groups can be obtained by an item analysis. Individual responses to each of the 150 items were counted, and for each item the frequencies of unfavorable ("maladjusted") replies made by the two groups were compared. This analysis was made for each of the five reputation traits separately.

The differentiating value of each item can be stated in terms of its "percentage difference," i.e., the percentage of the low-rating group responding unfavorably minus the percentage of the high-rating group responding unfavorably. This method, employed in the list below, is admittedly crude; a percentage difference of 35 might mean that 85 per cent and 50 per cent, respectively, of the two groups gave unfavorable replies; or it might mean 35 per cent of one and 0 per cent of the other. For readers desiring more complete information, Table 48 in Chapter 25 gives the low- and high-group percentages for each significant item for each of the five traits.

Drawing representative items from the longer list shown in Chapter 25, we can sketch a composite picture of the sixteen-year-old who has a less-than-favorable reputation on one or more traits. These items have been reworded to express the "unadjusted" response; otherwise the meaning is left unchanged.

In the brackets following each item is given by initial the trait which it serves most clearly to contrast and the percentage difference for that trait. Thus, an item annotated "H34, R22, F21" means that 34 per cent *more* of the low-honesty group failed this item (i.e., failed to give a favorable reply) than of the high-honesty group; although on responsibility and friendliness the differences were 22 per cent and 21 per cent. No percentage differences below 15 are included.

The following general statements can be made:

1. Low-rating pupils are more prone to feel that they are not liked or respected by their associates; and to feel inferior in status.

I am not usually considered brave or courageous [F34].

My folks do not seem to think that I am going to amount to something [F31, R31, L28, MC24, H19].

My friends do not seem to think I have likable traits [F24, L17, R15].

I do not feel that people recognize my social standing as they should [MC29, H24, L20, F18].

I am considered a failure in many of the things I do [H22, R22].

I do not feel that I am an important part of my school [F43, L21].

My folks appear to doubt whether I will be successful [F38, H22, R15].

2. Many low ratees are deficient in the social skills which promote harmonious social relationships.

It is not easy for me to introduce or be introduced to people [F20].
It is hard for me to admit it when I am in the wrong [H32, MC25, F25, L23, R19].
I do not often assist at planning parties [H37, R20, L18].
I usually feel uneasy when I am around people I do not know [R27].
It is hard for me to lead in enlivening a dull party [F31, MC15].
It is difficult for me to compliment people when they do something well [L22, R22, F15].
I frequently find it necessary to interrupt a conversation [R21, L18].
I find that many people are easily offended by me [L26, F21, R20].

3. They have not learned or wished to accept and carry out social responsibilities.

I dislike to take responsibility for the welfare or safety of children or old persons [H22, R19].
I do not like to take care of my own or some neighbor's pets [H21, L19].
I feel that I am not good at handling money [H23, R20, L18, MC17].
My folks do not give me a reasonable amount of spending money [H34, R22, F21].
I do not like to go to school affairs with members of the opposite sex [F25].
The police officers are not of such a character that I should like to help them [H32, L29, R28, MC25, F21].

4. Boys and girls of low character reputation are conscious of their personal as well as their social deficiencies.

It is hard for me to continue with my work when it becomes difficult [F21, R15].
I do not give much thought to my future work or career [F35, L25, R16].
I do not do things that are good for me if I do not like them [F46, MC36, R28, H25].
I usually get discouraged when other people disagree with me [MC23, L19, R18, H17].

5. They feel unhappy, discontented, frustrated, left out of the group.

I feel that people often treat me rather badly [F20].
My friends and acquaintances seem to have a better time at home than I do [F21].
I am not often invited to mixed social parties [F23].
My responsibilities and problems are often such that I cannot help but get discouraged [L27, H22].
I am scolded for many little things that do not amount to much [F25, L22, R21].

I usually like to be somewhere else than at home [H33, R33, MC21, L17, F16].

I am not usually given credit for the good judgment that I show [F22].

I sometimes feel like leaving home for good [F27].

If it were right, I would stay away from school as often as possible [R36, L33, H32, F24, MC15].

6. Their unsatisfactory adjustment often expresses itself in neurotic symptoms.

I have many problems that cause me a great deal of worry [R31, L25].

I have the habit of biting my fingernails often [L30, F26, R24, H22, MC19].

I sometimes have nightmares [L31, H25, F22, MC17].

I find that I am tired a great deal of the time [F37, H17, R16].

7. Feeling these conditions intolerable, the low ratees have recourse to self-assertive, defiant, or even anti-social conduct.

It is right to create a scene when parents refuse to let people of high-school age go to the movies [F28, H19].

High-school students do not need to follow their parents' instructions if their friends advise them differently [F21, L19, R16].

It is all right to disobey teachers if their requests appear to be unfair [H33, R18].

Certain people are so unreasonable that I can't help but hate them [R47, F34, H20, MC17].

A person does not need to be courteous to disagreeable people [H24, R23].

I am often forced to show some temper in order to get what is coming to me [R30, H26, L16].

People are often so stubborn that I have to call them bad names [MC23, H16].

I often have to quarrel or fight to get my rights [H48, R40, MC23, L20].

Little "kids" often get in my way so I have to push or frighten them [L24, R16].

Many of my classmates are so unkind or unfriendly that I avoid them [L25, R18].

I know people who are so annoying I would like to molest them [L23, R22, H20].

This analysis gives, in rough outline, a picture of the self-adjustment and social-adjustment tendencies of the sixteen-year-old rated low on reputation. His low ratings on honesty, moral courage, friendliness, loyalty, and responsibility may be either a cause or an effect of his blundering and misguided attempts to improve an intolerable status. Probably they are both. He may be caught in a vicious circle from which he can escape only by changing his habits—habits which he feels under the circumstances he has no choice but to continue. Yet the use of such techniques does not alleviate, but perpetuates and complicates, his maladjustments.

PART 3

Character and Personality Types

11

Studies of Individuals

Although the group studies which have preceded this chapter have pointed out a number of factors which influence character, they do not further our understanding of the development of character in individual boys and girls nor of the ways in which character operates in the living, growing personality.

To understand the dynamics of character development, the authors undertook to study individuals by means of case studies. This part of the research was planned with a further objective in mind—that of drawing generalizations from the study of individual subjects which would apply to other boys and girls. Very often the study of individuals is limited to a series of case studies, each one giving more insight into character and personality but leaving the research worker and the reader with no other generalization than that all persons are different. This type of research is unsatisfactory to the person who wishes to predict behavior, or wishes to plan a program of character education with some degree of assurance that it will be pertinent to the needs of large groups of boys and girls. The study of individuals must, therefore, be combined with some procedure for generalization of the findings and for their application to future situations.

With these objectives in mind, an initial group of nineteen boys and girls was selected for intensive study. The nineteen, comprising one-fifth of the number on whom there were enough data to attempt case analyses, were chosen because they presented a wide variety of characteristics. Some were high on all measures of character reputation; some were low on the same measures. Some made contradictory showings on certain tests. One boy and one girl of low social status but of high character reputation were included. The most popular person in the age group was included.

Seven of the authors, organized into a Clinical Conference Group, prepared case studies of the selected subjects, organizing the data according to the following pattern:

 a. *Character reputation.*
 b. *Social contexts.*   Family social position; relationships in the family; social interaction with age mates; relation to the school, church, and job; ethnic group; etc.
 c. *Personal characteristics.*   Appearance; intelligence; moral beliefs; interests; emotional make-up; self-adjustment; attitudes toward other people; attitudes toward authority; attitudes toward work; etc.

CHARACTER AND PERSONALITY

In the course of discussing these case studies it soon became clear that moral character could be understood only in relation to the over-all personality of the individual. Good character means one thing in one type of personality and something quite different in another type; character is formed differently in different personalities. For example, two girls who will be described in the following chapters, Minerva and Sally, have very nearly identical character reputations, yet they are entirely different in personality. Minerva is a sober, conscientious, rather rigid person, while Sally is gay, outgoing, pliant, and kindly. Both are popular. Both are leaders. Both are thought to have very good character. But it is clear that a quite different set of factors has operated in each case to produce good character and that the two girls will behave differently in situations which test character.

Thus moral character can be studied only in relation to the total personality of which it forms a part. As a result, the case studies became personality studies rather than character studies in the narrower sense. The total organization of a person's values, attitudes, impulses, abilities, and habits became an essential part of the character study.

THE DELINEATION OF PERSONALITY TYPES

By the time nineteen case studies had been made, it was clear that the group was composed of several subgroups whose members were similar to each other. There were five differentiated groups or types which were named as follows:

> The Self-Directive Person
> The Adaptive Person
> The Submissive Person
> The Defiant Person
> The Unadjusted Person

These groupings were empirically, not theoretically, arrived at. The Clinical Conference Group, after analyzing and reanalyzing the data, observed similarities among certain subjects of their study; they grouped similar subjects together, and they described the common characteristics of each subgroup. They then drew up, for each subgroup or type, a profile of personality and character factors which characterized each member of that type, but no others, and which, at the same time, included those factors which are generally conceded to be most important in describing an individual.[1] These profiles are shown in Table 19.

[1] This method of delineating personality groups or types, which may be called the conference method, is, of course, only one of several possible methods. As compared with techniques of syndrome analysis, factor analysis, and inverse factor analysis, it is open to the criticism that it is the most subjective of the methods. It seemed, however, best adapted to an exploratory study such as this and to the types of data available to the Clinical Conference Group. Further claim can be made for the conference method in that it makes use of the clinical intuitions of trained and qualified students of personality, who have observed the subject as a living, functioning individual and who have thereby gained valid impressions that cannot be obtained from the mathematical analysis and synthesis of data.

TABLE 19 PERSONALITY PROFILES OF ADOLESCENTS

Area	Instruments or Methods	Personality Type				
		Self-Directive	Adaptive	Submissive	Defiant	Unadjusted
Social personality	Observation, Sociometric tests, Interest Inventory, Essays	Ambitious, Conscientious, Orderly, Persistent, Introspective	Outgoing, Confident, Positive, favorable reactions to environment	Timid, Does not initiate action, Stubborn, Avoids conflict	Openly hostile, Self-defensive, Blames society for failure	Discontented, Complaining, Not openly hostile
Character reputation	Reputation instruments	High, Higher on H and R than on F	High, Higher on F than on H and R	Average to high, Higher on H and R than on F	Very low, Higher on MC than on other traits	Low to average
Moral beliefs and principles	Student beliefs, Life problems, Essays	Variable, High uncertainty	High, Little uncertainty, Adopts current standards	High, Some uncertainty	Low	Low to average
Family environment	FR Questionnaire, Interviews and reports on family, Interest Inventory, Mooney Problem Check List	Strict family training, Some conflict with family	Permissive family training, No conflict with family	Severe family training, No conflict with family	Family training inconsistent, provides no basis for constructive character formation, Conflict with family, Early neglect	Variable family training, Conflict with family

		Leader	Very popular	Follower	Unpopular / Hostile to school activities / Quarrelsome	Unpopular / Hostile or indifferent to school activities
Social adjustment with age mates	Sociometric tests / Interviews / Observation	Active in school affairs / Awkward in social skills	Active in school affairs / Social skills well developed / Popular with opposite sex	Nonentity / Awkward in social skills	Hostile to school activities / Quarrelsome	Hostile or indifferent to school activities
Intellectual ability	Intelligence tests	Average to high	Average to high	Low to average / Seldom high	Low to high	Low to high
School achievement	Academic grades	High, or higher than IQ would imply	Fair to high	Fair / Seldom high	Low, or lower than IQ would imply	Low, or lower than IQ would imply
Personal adjustment	Interviews / Personality Inventory / Interest Inventory / Thematic Apperception / Rorschach / Mooney Problem Check List	Self-doubt / Self-critical / Some anxiety, but well controlled / Concern about moral problems / Average aggressiveness / Moves away from people / Lack of warmth in human relations / Gains security through achievement	High on all adjustment measures / Self-assured / No signs of anxiety / Unaggressive / Moves toward people	Self-doubt / Self-critical / Submissive to authority / Unaggressive	Hostile to authority / Aggressive impulses / Inadequately socialized / Moves against people	Aggressive impulses / Feelings of insecurity

THE TYPE ANALYSIS APPLIED TO THE TOTAL GROUP

The type analysis was then applied to the total group of sixteen-year-olds, or to as many of them as were represented by a substantial amount of data. Each subject was compared with the characteristics of the five types, to find out who fitted a given type. A master score sheet was drawn up for each individual to show the data from a variety of instruments. From this sheet could be read at a glance whether the person was in the first, second, third, or top quartile of the group on any of a dozen tests or rating procedures.[2]

With the aid of the master score sheet a profile was made of each individual's characteristics. Since the profiles characteristic of the five personality types had already been determined, it was a matter of finding out whether the profile of an individual was a fair match for any of the type profiles.

The distribution of subjects among the five groups is shown in Table 20. Since there was not enough information to permit classification of fifty persons, about a third of the group, the distribution is based upon ninety-four cases.

Twenty-nine individuals, or 31 per cent of the group, could not be placed in any of the five types and are therefore put into a "mixed" category.

[2] The Master Score Sheet contained scores by quartiles for the following instruments or procedures:

Social status
Character reputation (average of the five traits)
Character reputation (average of honesty and responsibility)
Character reputation (friendliness)
Intelligence (Stanford-Binet)
Intelligence (Wechsler-Bellevue Performance Scale)
School achievement (average of last year's grades)
Student Beliefs (a test of moral values)
Life Problems (a test of ability to apply general moral principles to specific situations of conduct)
Mooney Problem Check List
Family-Relations Questionnaire (a test of emotional relations in the family)
Personal adjustment (the California Test of Personal Adjustment)
Moral values (a rating of the moral values shown in an essay "The Person I Would Like to Be Like")

TABLE 20   DISTRIBUTION OF SUBJECTS BY PERSONALITY TYPES

	Number			Percentage
	Boys	Girls	Total	
Self-Directive Person	8	12	20	21
Adaptive Person	2	8	10	11
Submissive Person	6	10	16	17
Unadjusted Person	8	7	15	16
Defiant Person	3	1	4	4
Mixed	13	16	29	31

THE CONCEPT OF PERSONALITY "TYPES"

A typology such as the one described here is likely to meet with certain objections. Certainly there is a great deal of literature, both pro and con, concerning the concept of "type" and its usefulness in the social sciences. In general, it may be said that sociologists tend to favor the use of the concept as a scientific tool, although psychologists (with some notable exceptions) disparage it.

Some of the disagreement might be avoided if users of the term were clearer as to the meanings they intend it to have. Winch has recently helped to clarify the meanings of the concept by distinguishing between heuristic (ideal) and empirical types. He says:

. . . An empirical typology is derived primarily from data rather than from theory; it functions to summarize observations rather than to enhance vision or to illustrate the existence of essences; it describes modal rather than extreme characteristics; and stands logically between observation and the reformulation of theory.[3]

As has already been pointed out, the typology used in these studies is empirical and is therefore free from certain of the objections usually levelled at more theoretical typologies.

Not only is this typology warranted from a study of the data, but it is also defensible on other grounds as well. Although all the literature in defense of typologies cannot be marshalled here,

[3] R. F. Winch, "Heuristic and Empirical Typologies: A Job for Factor Analysis," *American Sociological Review*, 12, pp. 68–75, February 1947.

two recent studies are of particular interest. One is the study undertaken at Harvard University by Sanford and others.[4] Using methods quite different from those used in these studies, Sanford isolated and described a number of personality types, four of which correspond closely to four of the types described here. The Self-Directive Person is the Structured Personality of the Harvard study; the Adaptive is the Social Being; the Submissive is the Timid Child; and the Defiant is the same as the Defiant in the Harvard study.

Karen Horney, in a volume published subsequent to the Prairie City research,[5] describes three personality types.

Dr. Horney suggests that every child, when very young, experiences to a greater or lesser degree the feeling of being isolated and helpless in a potentially hostile world. Made anxious by these disturbing conditions, the child gropes for ways of coping with such a world and gradually develops one of three basic strategies, or ways of life: the child can move *toward* people, *against* them, or *from* them.

These give rise to personality types which have a resemblance to those found in the present studies. The child who moves away from people develops a "detached personality" or becomes the Self-Directive Person. The child who moves against people becomes an "aggressive personality" or the Defiant Person. Horney's "compliant personality," or the child who moves toward people, has some of the characteristics of the Adaptive Person and some of those of the Submissive Person. The authors suggest that the "compliant personality" may be divided into these two subdivisions.

The Unadjusted Person of the Prairie City studies is not a separate personality type, as is pointed out elsewhere, but is a member of one of the other types who finds himself in a frustrating situation and who is seeking, unsuccessfully, a more congenial environment.

Thus the personality types empirically arrived at in these studies are similar to types found in other studies where different methods and concepts have been used.

[4] R. N. Sanford and others, "Physique, Personality, and Scholarship," Monographs of the Society for Research in Child Development, 8, No. 34, Washington, D. C.: National Research Council, 1943.

[5] Karen Horney, *Our Inner Conflicts*. New York: Norton, 1945.

If a typology is used cautiously, without attempting to force every individual into one or another type (31 per cent of Prairie City subjects could not be classified) and without minimizing the differences between individuals who fall into the same category, then the type analysis is a useful one. It serves a practical purpose in enabling the investigator to generalize from his data and to make recommendations regarding educational programs aimed at serving groups of persons rather than individuals.

In the next five chapters illustrative case studies of the five personality types are presented. These case studies are disguised so as to avoid causing embarrassment to the individuals concerned, but there has been no basic alteration of essential items.

12

The Self-Directive Person

The Self-Directive Person is conscientious, orderly, and persistent. He sets high standards for himself and is seldom satisfied with his performance. He is ambitious, strong-willed, and self-sufficient, yet characterized by self-criticism and self-doubt.

CURT

"The best thing that could happen to me is to become important in the college or university I hope to go to," writes Curt at the age of sixteen.

He is an ordinary-looking boy, in that period of rapid physical growth preceding maturity. His most striking feature is the intense gaze which he levels at the world from his deep-set brown eyes.

Curt's character reputation is very high. In moral courage, loyalty, and honesty his reputation scores put him very close to the top of the group. In friendliness and responsibility he is slightly lower, though still well above average. His own comments show that he wants responsibility but is not sure that he can handle it. He regards this as one of his greatest problems in life.

When asked to say what he believes on a variety of moral issues, Curt proves to be extremely uncertain. This uncertainty and a tendency to hold back from making decisions or committing himself to a course of action are characteristic of the boy. He has not thought his way through to clear-cut moral principles, but he continues to try to do so. Consequently, he cannot decide on a moral issue quickly. He restrains himself from following his impulses in such matters and thinks situations through carefully. A description of this moral uncertainty is given by Curt himself when he says:

"I never can decide what to do or where to go. When the time comes and I have to do it, I always make a decision, and it works out all right. Ever since I can remember I've had that trouble when I had a choice to make."

This self-critical, soul-searching attitude proves to be characteristic of all the Self-Directive subjects. They are puzzled by the many moral problems that confront them, and they are uncertain and somewhat worried.

Curt is one of several children in an upper-middle-class family. His father is a professional man and is said by leading citizens to be "one of the finest men we have in town." His mother comes from a "good family." According to their minister, "They do everything to give their children the proper advantages." Both father and mother are leaders in community affairs. The father is known as an independent thinker and sometimes makes people angry by his outspoken comments. The family training has been rather strict, and Curt has learned to obey his parents and to depend on them. At seventeen he is just beginning to show signs of being irked by family control.

Curt has matured socially rather slowly. He is still very uneasy in the presence of girls, as is evidenced by his report that he has difficulty in talking to girls and that he does not go out with girls much. For several years up to the age of sixteen, Curt was an ardent Boy Scout, and he spent his leisure time with three friends of his own age, hunting, fishing, and practicing photography. When he realized that he was being left out of the developing social life of his class, Curt did the characteristic thing. He thought the situation over soberly, and then decided to learn to dance and to make himself take part in social activities. These things he did, with surprising success. He developed a very acceptable set of social skills and became one of the leaders of his class by the time of his senior year in high school. He took part in class plays, was a class officer, and an athlete.

On tests of intelligence and academic achievement Curt does extraordinarily well. His school grades place him in the top quartile of his class. He likes science and mathematics and plans to become an engineer. This seems to be an appropriate choice for a boy with his abilities, interests, and background.

Curt impresses the observer as having a "strong" personality but not an easy or smooth one. His manner of dealing with people is too direct and humorless for them to like him very much, though they are bound to respect him. He holds himself under control at all times and cannot, as he puts it, "cut loose." For example, he once said: "I can't spend money like the other fellows do. Some of them can take ten dollars and blow it just like that. Gee, ten dollars lasts me three weeks."

When asked what abilities he would like which he does not now have, he said: "I need the ability to make up my mind."

On psychological tests which aim to probe the emotions and to get at the basic forces of the personality, Curt shows a good deal of unrest and anxiety. He is holding his impulses in check and is somewhat bewildered and alarmed at his adolescent emotions. This is not unhealthy in a boy like Curt, though it causes him considerable discomfort.

Beneath his rather conventional behavior and attitudes Curt carries a burning ambition to amount to something in the world. We have already noted his desire to "become important in the college or university I hope to go to." In an essay on "The Person I Would Like to Be Like" he said: "I would like to be financially all right with authority over a group of people."

In the Interest Inventory, he scored above all others in his class in his liking for leadership activities. At the same time, he was very high in his dislike of submitting to the authority of others.

But his characteristic uncertainty and self-doubt crop out again when, on the Mooney Problem Check List, he underlines as his greatest problem "lacking leadership ability."

DAVID

"The best thing that could happen to me is to somehow obtain much money and talent which would enable me to very well carry out the profession I have in mind." So wrote David as a junior in high school. "The worst thing," he went on, "is to utterly fail to accomplish the profession I have in mind or some worth-while profession—fail in life."

David is a slender, blond boy. People who see him get the impression that he is still in the early stages of adolescence, both in physical growth and social maturity. He dresses poorly, though neatly.

His character reputation is very high, both with adults and with his age mates. He was rated at the very top of his group on moral courage and responsibility. There was only one trait, friendliness, on which he was rated below the highest quartile.

David's own verbal responses to questions and situations involving moral beliefs are rather uncertain, especially in the areas of responsibility, loyalty, and friendliness. His moral principles seem to be clearly defined in the areas of honesty and moral courage but not in the other areas. Like other Self-Directive Persons, he has not yet organized in his own mind the area of moral behavior, but he is working hard to do so. He has very strong religious beliefs and conforms without question to the rigid moral code of his church.

David comes from a lower-class, "poor but respectable" family. His older brothers and sisters have not gone to college, though they were good students and very successful in high school. His parents had only grammar-school educations. The father works in a factory and has had a difficult time supporting his family, though he is an industrious, hard-working man. The family are active, loyal members of the Lutheran Church. They have family devotions every day. An upper-class man speaks of the family as "good stuff." David has been brought up strictly but also with a good deal of affection. He has been encouraged by his family and by several professional men in the town to plan to go to college and enter a profession.

Because of the poverty of his family and also because of his belonging to the Norwegian Lutheran group, which frowns upon such activities as dancing and movies, David has not been acti socially. He does not go with girls and is uneasy in their company.

In spite of these things he is still one of the outstanding persons in his class, has held class offices, and is admired by his age mates. On a guess-who test, David was given first rank by his classmates on the item "likes school," second on the item "plays fair," and third on the items "clean" and "nice manners." An older girl said: "For intelligence and manners I think little David probably rates higher than anyone else down there at the high school."

In his school work David is near the top of his class. His intelligence is superior but not as high as that of Curt. He is a hard worker in school and is thought by some people to be almost too conscientious about his studies.

In all the tests which he took, he tried to follow directions with an exactness which was almost painful to watch. His attitude toward teachers and other adults is one of obedience and respect. On the interest inventory he was second highest among the boys in liking activities which involve submitting to the authority of others. This is in contrast to Curt, who has a great dislike for submission to authority.[1]

One characteristic of David's personality, then, is that of conformity to what certain people stand for—these being the middle-class professional people who represent everything that David wants in life. On projective tests of personality we find David displays a need for *succorance*—for help from good and powerful people—in meeting the problems that beset him.

On tests exploring his feelings about himself and his estimate of his own personality, he ranks low. He has much self-doubt and feels uneasy and inadequate in social situations. On a check list of personal problems, David checked more problems than most of the other boys.

David's predominant desire is to make something of himself. On a test of moral ideals he listed as good things to do: to "get the most out of school," "work hard for what you get," and "do what you are told," while a bad thing to do was to "waste your life."

His first reaction in meeting a situation is to ask: "How will it affect me?" Whatever he does appears to be done because of its value to him and him alone. For example, he says he is ashamed, "when I displease people or do or say something quickly, without thinking, that makes people have a bad impression of me." He says he is angry "when people make it hard for me, somehow, in what I may be doing."

To move up from the lower-class position in which he was born to the middle-class position to which he aspires, he has learned the necessary skills and attitudes. He is a hard worker, has good manners, and takes care to maintain a good reputation. Furthermore, he has no strong personal attachments to people, and he will always be able to subordinate friendship and emotional relation-

[1] Although we shall not attempt an explanation here of the dynamics of personality formation, it is perhaps pertinent to point out a difference between Curt and David in their early family relationships. There is considerable evidence in Curt's case of repressed hostility towards the father, which may underlie his resistance to authority.

ships to his desire to get ahead in the world. He is the type of person who may be expected to leave the small city where he grew up and search for success in a larger community.

MINERVA

"Minerva is the most townish country girl I have ever known. She is definitely a leader. Everyone likes her. She is popular, and she could be even more so if she were not held back by her folks." This comment was made by an older girl. Minerva is a short, blue-eyed, pleasant-looking girl, dressed neatly but inconspicuously.

Her character reputation is very high—she is in the upper tenth on all five character traits.

Her verbal responses to questions of moral judgment show some uncertainty. Like Curt and David, she refuses to agree with some of the moral clichés on the Student Beliefs Test, and she is somewhat confused in applying moral principles to concrete situations.

Minerva is one of several children of a leading farm family. Her father is known as a good farmer and is active both in politics and church work. He had an eighth-grade education. Her mother had some college training and is a leader among farm women. Both parents are continually at work on one community project or another. The older children have been sent through college, and Minerva will be sent to college also. The parents believe in education. When an older sister was married as soon as she graduated from college someone told Minerva's mother that it was useless to have given her a college education. "Such a silly thing to say," she commented, "I rode the tractor in the field so that they could be in school, because I know that an education helps you all of your life."

The father and mother have given Minerva a strict Lutheran training, against which she has begun to rebel. Recently, since she has become interested in social activities, there has been a good deal of conflict over her choice of friends. On one questionnaire, Minerva was asked to write the names of the boys and girls who were her friends and the names of the boys and girls with whom her parents wanted her to be friends. In the first list, she wrote the names of a dozen of the most popular boys and girls in school. In the second list she wrote the names of six outstanding Norwegian

Lutheran boys and girls, all very well known, who were known especially for faithful adherence to the moral beliefs of the church concerning dancing, card playing, and movies. Finally, when she was asked to give the name of the one person she would like most to have as a friend, she named a very popular boy, known as rather "fast" with girls.

On several other instruments Minerva showed some resentment against her parents. She answered "yes" to the question "Are there things about one or both of your folks that annoy you?" and also to the question "Are you troubled because your folks differ from you regarding the things you like?" On the Family-Relations Questionnaire she responded to the question, "Do your parents seem old fashioned in their ideas about how young people should act?" by saying that this happened "frequently." She singles out her grandmother for special praise because she has a more lenient attitude toward young people. She says: "I wish to be like my grandmother because she is the most broadminded person I know and really knows how to get along with young people."

To the question "Do you sometimes feel like leaving home for good?" Minerva responded by first marking "yes," then erasing and marking "no."

In school Minerva is quite popular and active in extracurricular affairs. She is the best known and most active of the rural students. Her school achievement is quite good, and she ranks between Curt and David on an intelligence test.

She was the top student in the rural elementary school which she attended before going to Prairie City High School.

Minerva has the same combination of ambition and self-doubt that we have seen in Curt and David. Her drive for achievement is reflected in her conscious attempts to be "urban" and not "rural" in her attitudes and behavior, and to win recognition. For example, as the "best thing that could happen," she thinks of being chosen in a state-wide contest to enter a nation-wide contest. On the Interest Inventory she indicates a strong liking for leadership activities. At the same time, on the Personality Inventory she shows that she is easily hurt and often feels neglected by others. She ranks low, in the third quartile, on "personal adjustment" as measured by this inventory.

A good deal of Minerva's doubts and worries center about her social relations, especially with boys. She says that she dislikes "thinking about sex" and "going 'steady' with someone." She declined to respond "yes" or "no" to the question "Do the young men like you?"

The activity of a severe conscience is indicated by the fact that she double-checked the problem "Can't forget some mistakes I have made" on the Problem Check List.

Minerva seems to take her problems seriously. She double-checked ten problems on this list, an unusually high number; among them the items "confused on some moral questions," and "doubt the wisdom of my vocational choice." She is undecided about vocational choice; at present, she is interested in social work and teaching.

SUMMARY

The Self-Directive Person enjoys a very good reputation, especially for responsibility and honesty. He is known as a conscientious person, who can be counted on to do what he says he will do. He is orderly and persistent in his work. He is known as a leader in school and in the organizations to which he belongs. He accepts leadership as a responsibility, though he does not always enjoy it. He is very self-critical, sets high standards for himself, sometimes doubts that he can achieve his goals, but drives ahead until he accomplishes what he has set out to do. He is strong willed and may be somewhat stubborn. He is said to have a "strong" personality. He is usually a good student.

The moral values of the Self-Directive Person are somewhat uncertain and even inconsistent at the age of sixteen. Although his actual behavior is nearly always proper, as is evidenced by his good reputation, his ideas about what is right and what is wrong reflect uncertainty and self-criticism. Morality presents a problem to him. His fantasies often deal with moral conflict, involving individuals with strong characters. On a scale of personal adjustment this person is seldom as high as the upper quartile.

The Self-Directed Person is self-sufficient and does not go out of his way to seek companionship. During the middle years of adolescence he is likely to be socially backward. He does not begin keeping company with the opposite sex as early as the average person, and probably his sexual impulses are more strongly inhibited than is the case in other personality types. He does not rely upon sexual attractiveness for acceptance and popularity.

A variation of this type is found in certain upper-middle-class youths who are "independents." They appear to be more sophisticated and almost a little weary of the life of ambition, thrift, and severe morality. They are "mavericks" who belong and yet do not belong. They may have artistic or literary interests. To adults they are more interesting and attractive than the orthodox members of the type because they seem to understand themselves better and to have more "depth" in their personalities. At the same time, they are often moody, self-critical, and uncertain of themselves.

Another variation is the boy or girl of below-average intellectual ability. Such boys and girls rarely develop personalities of this type, probably because at an early age they learn the limitations of their abilities and lack the experience of success upon which ambition feeds. There are a few persons, however, who seem to fit this type even though they were in the third or fourth quartile in intellectual ability. They are very hard workers, usually one or two quartiles higher in school achievement than in intelligence. They are good citizens and are liked by their classmates, by their teachers, and by adults.

The Self-Directive Person is introspective, and he has a strong and rather severe conscience. This results in a good deal of anxiety, in the form of fear that he will do something wrong or that he has done something wrong. This anxiety is constructively handled in most cases. It leads this type of person to better performance and serves, so to speak, to keep him on his toes.

Compared with the other groups, the Self-Directive Person places a strong emphasis upon self-achievement—achievement *per se* appears to be his goal in life. This person has probably had less than the usual amount of emotional warmth in his relations with his parents and with other adults. They have taught him that he can attain security only through performance. He learns not to expect to be appreciated for himself but for what he can accomplish.

The Self-Directive Person has a well-developed sense of self, or ego, which seeks gratification through personal attainment. It is as if he gains a sense of self-worth only by demonstrating to himself and to others his ability to achieve. This enables him to be self-assertive, ambitious, and to turn things to his own advantage.

There is a tendency for upper-middle-class youth to be Self-Directive Persons, as is shown in Table 21.

Of ten upper-middle-class boys and girls, six were in the Self-Directive category. This might have been predicted, for the characteristic upper-middle-class child-rearing procedures seem most likely to produce ambitious, responsible, conscientious individuals with a strong drive for self-achievement. This kind of training in the home, coupled with favorable family economic and

TABLE 21 PERSONALITY TYPE IN RELATION TO SOCIAL CLASS

Social Class	Personality Type											
	Self-Directive		Adaptive		Submissive		Unadjusted		Defiant		Not Classified	
	M.	F.	M.	F.	M.	F.	M.	F.	M.	F.	M.	F.
U, UM	3	3	2	1	0	0	0	0	0	0	1	0
LM	2	5	0	4	4	4	1	1	1	0	8	9
UL	3	4	0	2	2	3	7	5	1	1	3	6
LL	0	0	0	1	0	3	0	1	0	0	1	1
Totals	8	12	2	8	6	10	8	7	2	1	13	16

social position, should produce a maximum number of Self-Directive Persons.

The Self-Directive Persons who come from lower social classes differ from those in the upper-middle class much as David differs from Curt. They are more conventional in their behavior and more subservient to powerful people in the school and community who can help them get ahead.

The Self-Directive Person develops good character as part of this total pattern. Conformity to the values of the community results in a favorable reputation—itself a worth-while goal—and at the same time smooths the way for other types of achievement.

13

The Adaptive Person

The Adaptive Person is sociable, friendly, vivacious, and outgoing in manner. He has what is often called good "social intelligence." Usually he is good looking and has great physical vitality. Though he enjoys leadership, he does not strive hard for it. He fits readily into almost any social situation and seems to conform naturally to the expectations of the people with whom he is associated.

MAISIE

Maisie is a very good-looking girl. She is physically mature and has a feminine beauty that is attractive both to boys and girls. Her vivacious, friendly personality made her one of the most popular persons in school.

Maisie's character reputation was uniformly high. On all five traits she was rated well toward the top of the group, and on friendliness she was given a score slightly higher than on the other traits. Her own responses to the Student Beliefs Test indicate that she accepted the prevailing moral standards in a discriminating way. Only in the area of moral courage did she fall below the top quartile. In this area it seemed that she was reluctant to let a blunt outspokenness interfere with social amenities or with friendly relations with other people.

Her beliefs about behavior reflect her practical common sense, her sensitivity to what is socially acceptable, and her strongly developed feeling for friendly social relationships. In a moral ideology test she stated as good things to do, "It's always a good thing to help a fellow in need. He would approve and so would all who found out about it. . . . Develop yourself along at least one line like music or athletics. That helps yourself. You come in contact with other people. . . . Be a good sport; that makes more friends. Helps yourself and people with whom you come in contact. . . . Help your folks. . . . Liking other people . . . making other people like you. In other words develop personality. Influences those with whom you come in contact."

In this same test, under bad things to do, Maisie listed things which would bring social disapproval. "Give up after first try is bad. Hinders yourself and those with whom you are working. . . . Engage in brawls and stealing. Ruins reputation. . . . Being a show-off, egotistical. People disapprove. . . . Visiting places that have bad reputations, habit forming and ruins own reputation. . . . Selfishness is bad. Sometimes hurts those with whom you come in contact. Nobody with common sense likes selfish people."

Maisie is next to the youngest in a large Irish family which has been in Prairie City for two or three generations but has "never amounted to very much." The reputation of the family has improved somewhat in recent years, but people have not forgotten past history. "That family used to be one of the toughest families in the community. They were always getting into trouble. The old man wasn't worth a damn, and his wife didn't have a very good reputation either." . . . "The family used to have a bad reputation . . . but the children have rather pulled the family up in late years." . . . "The mother and father don't amount to a great deal, but they've certainly done a swell job on their kids."

The family is regarded as definitely lower class. "You can't mix classes. . . . Now you take Maisie. She doesn't belong in that high-school crowd she runs with. She comes from one of the poor Irish families that has a bad name in the community." . . . "Maisie travels with the group who run the junior class—but they're not allowed to go to her house." Furthermore, "The family aren't regarded very highly by the other Irish here. For one thing, they haven't kept up their religion."

Maisie's home is an interesting one. There is nothing unusual about the house itself. It is clean and neat, and its only modern features are electric lights, an electric refrigerator, and a radio. It is small and crowded—too small and too crowded for the number of people that come and go, or come and stay, as the years go by. But the life within the home is rich and warm, and Maisie's mother deserves much of the credit. It is "Mom" who really "runs the home," and Pa, good natured and easygoing, doesn't seem to mind taking second place. Mom's rule over her family is by no means harsh; she dominates by the strength of a personality that is unusually warmhearted and understanding. She is the kind of person who wants her children and her grandchildren about her—and they come, because they are glad to be with her. It is quite the usual thing for one of the married daughters to bring her children and move in with Mom for a while.

In this friendly, easy atmosphere the members of the family have developed strong feelings of affection and loyalty. Whatever the community may think and say about the family and however the family may feel about the low regard in which they are held by their neighbors, the children have found a satisfying feeling of security in their home.

Maisie reflects this security. On the Family Relations Questionnaire she gave a picture of a satisfying home situation with a secure, cooperative, pleasant relationship between herself and her parents.

Maisie's father and mother had very little formal education themselves, but they are proud of the progress their children have made. A son and a daughter older than Maisie went to high school, were good students, and were well liked by their fellows. The boy in particular was outstanding, continued his education beyond high school, and has been very successful in a business he set up in another community. He is known as "the Irish kid who really made good and is going places." His success has helped the reputation of his family and no doubt made the way easier for Maisie.

Maisie's popularity in high school was evidently not affected by her low social status. The Guess-Who Test showed her as one of the most popular girls in her age group, liked and accepted by boys and girls from the middle and upper classes. On this test she received 153 mentions from classmates, six times as many as most of the girls received, and all but six of the mentions were favorable. She was never mentioned unfavorably by any of the boys and girls from the upper class, and she was mentioned more often by them than by persons from any other social class. In her own response to this test, Maisie mentioned people from her own status group and from the lower-middle class unfavorably and people from the upper class favorably. From this test it appears that Maisie was well accepted by the upper-class group, that she was striving, perhaps unconsciously, to improve her own social position with them, and that she therefore rejected young people in her own social class.

Maisie is a highly intelligent girl. She ranked in the upper fourth of her class in intelligence, as well as in school achievement, and teachers and peers alike respect her scholastic ability. Her intelligence makes it possible for her to do good academic work and still have time left over for participating in many activities. She belonged to a number of clubs, she sang in the chorus, she worked on committees for school functions, and went to school dances and parties. She was one of the leaders in the school; the other leaders, boys and girls from the middle and upper classes, were her best friends.

Adults in the community liked Maisie and recognized that she had a strong position in her peer group, but they were skeptical of her future place. "I don't know about Maisie. I think maybe she'll revert to type. All her friends will go away to college, and she won't fit in with them any more." . . . "She'll probably get a jolt when she finishes high school and finds out that she can't continue to run with that group that she's in." "Maisie is fooling herself. She hasn't got the stuff that it takes to stay there. Her family background is all wrong. Upper-class people run around with her now because she has some talent and a lot of personality, but later on they won't recognize her."

On all tests of personality adjustment, Maisie ranked very high. She had few doubts about herself. Her conscience never seemed to bother her. She liked to be with people and to do what other people did. On an interest inventory she was the only one in her class to indicate a liking for every school activity on the list. She absorbed the group pattern of behavior without any strain or difficulty; she was unaggressive, not critical of others, and had no unusual desires or convictions.

The story of Maisie will be continued beyond her junior year in high school, because of the important changes that took place in her personality.

Had Maisie been reared in a middle-class home she would have gone on to college, with her parents' approval and support, and she probably would have repeated there the social and academic success of her high-school career. But, because she came from a lower-class family, the situation was more complicated.

She received a number of scholarship offers; and one adult in the community set up a cash scholarship award expressly for her.

She could go on to the college which had been selected by most of her friends and be assured of getting along financially. But to do so involved a departure from the standards held by her family and her social class, and a break with her mother and the things her mother understood and valued. Consequently, the adults who knew Maisie and liked her watched with interest as her high-school career drew to a close and she faced the inevitable choice between her family, with the security and support they gave her, and a journey into a world where she would have to leave the family behind.

As the end of her senior year approached, it became obvious that Maisie had given up her earlier intention of going to college. She refused to discuss the matter with teachers and other adults who wanted to help her. At the same time, her interest in school work waned, and she went through her last semester in high school with a moody, almost sullen, manner that puzzled and hurt her friends.

About this time she stopped going with the upper-middle-class boy who had been her "steady" for more than a year. There was no special talk about the break. It just seemed to "happen," as far as the friends of the couple could tell. She did not go out socially very much for several months. She seemed to retire to her home and to spend more time with her mother.

When school was over Maisie took a clerical position in town and worked at it steadily. She was seldom seen at dances or parties, although she occasionally came to school games, alone. All of her best high-school friends went off to college.

During the Christmas holidays when they returned to their homes, they got together for two or three parties and told each other what good times they were having and what they were doing at their various colleges. Maisie came to the first of these parties, and to everyone's surprise she was mean and rude. She did not come to their next party.

One of her adult friends, when questioned about her a few months after this, said: "She's gone back across the tracks and so far as I know has little or no connection with the people who were her friends."

It seems to us that Maisie's behavior at the end of her high-school course was to be expected of an Adaptive Person faced with a conflict between the values symbolized by her home and the values symbolized by the school. Had she been a Self-Directive Person, she would have decided to go on to college, in spite of the breaking of home ties. But Maisie was the product of a warm, permissive home environment, deeply attached to her mother. This gave her the pleasant, friendly and outgoing personality which assured her of social success in any group of people, but it failed to give her the drive and ambition for achievement which alone could have enabled her to leave her lower-class home and make her way into a middle-class world.

With her intelligence, vitality, good health, beauty, and friendly disposition, success had come easy to her in high school. She was able to adapt to a middle-class social environment without much effort and without giving up her family and all the latter stood for. But further progress along the path she followed in high school would take her more and more away from her home, not only physically but spiritually. For the first time, she faced a problem difficult to solve and which involved effort and determination. Being an Adaptive, rather than a Self-Directive personality, she chose what seemed to us to be the easier solution. She continued to be the creature, and not the master, of circumstances.

SALLY

Sally is a slight, pretty girl, very graceful, quick, and lively. She makes a definite impression on any observer because of her unusual animation. She has a craving for being sociable and is always seen with a group of people.

Sally's character reputation is very similar to that of Maisie. She is almost at the top on all of the five character traits and highest of all on friendliness.

Her responses to the Student Beliefs Test place her in the highest quartile on friendliness, loyalty, and moral courage and about average on honesty and responsibility. In contrast to the Self-Directive Person, she is uncertain about very few items. On the Life Problems Test, she shows herself to be highly consistent in applying moral principles. On the problems which involved a conflict between honesty and friendship she chose friendship.

Sally comes from a lower-middle-class family of German background; the family is considered respectable and financially stable. "They're good people. They have had some financial difficulty, but they're all right now." . . . "Sally's parents haven't had much education, but they're good intelligent people. Her mother comes from a bright family." . . . "They have a small business, but they do pretty well with it."

Sally's father has owned a small grocery store in Prairie City for years, and he and his wife have run the store without extra help most of the time. When Sally was a child she spent much of the time in the store with her parents. Her popularity seems to have begun back in those early years when she played in her father's store and in the other business houses along Main Street. "She was always the pet of Main Street. Everyone along there has known her and liked her since she was a small child."

Sally's parents are not active in either civic or social affairs, but they are not unfriendly or disinterested, and they are proud of their children's popularity in the community. Sally is the youngest child; there are two boys, both considerably older than she, who were prominent in high school and in college. "They're not socially inclined, but it's a friendly family."

Sally's home life has been very irregular in many ways. Since her mother has usually helped out in the store, she has not had time to prepare meals for her family and to supervise closely the routine living habits of her children. Sometimes Sally eats in a restaurant; sometimes she gets a hot meal from the restaurant and eats it at home alone or with one of her parents; sometimes she just "has a pickup lunch from the store." She spends very little time in her home, which is a rather small apartment and has apparently never been expected to take responsibility for household duties. "Sally has never had to help around the house as most Prairie City girls do, and perhaps that explains her social ability. She always has time to do things."

Sally's home environment, like Maisie's, is a permissive one. She is free to go out with boys, to go to movies, to dances, and to parties. Her parents approve her friendly relations with others and do not place restrictions on her activities. She says: "I never was punished, and so I never was afraid of my parents like some of the kids are." In contrast with Maisie, however, Sally has not developed a particularly close relationship with her parents. This may be because she has not shared many experiences with her father and mother, even in the daily routine of living. Whatever the reason, as she grows older Sally shows herself to be increasingly independent of her parents. Affection for her family remains, but their authority is gradually weakening.

Sally's religious affiliation is with a church which places few restrictions on the social activities of its members. Shortly before she was ready to enter high school, she made her own choice of the church to which she wanted to belong. She chose one which is regarded as the "upper-class church," has a liberal point of view, and is not critical of the social diversions she and her friends enjoy. Her parents approve her choice, but they rarely attend church themselves. "Sally's mother is very infrequent in her attendance, but Sally is active in the young people's organizations."

At school Sally takes part in everything. She and her friends are the leaders in practically all school activities. They make up "the" crowd, the one which is the most desirable in the eyes of most of the high-school girls.

Sally's popularity, as indicated by the Guess-Who Test, is even greater than Maisie's. She is mentioned over two hundred times by other high-school students and only one mention is unfavorable. About one-third of the mentions come from boys, and the people who mention her are from every social class. They say she is the kind of person their parents would want them to associate with, that she is good looking and well dressed, that she is a leader, participates in many activities, and always has a good time.

In her own response to this test, Sally mentions upper-class students proportionately much more often than any other on items relating to etiquette, clothing, and popularity. On items which have to do with friendship and personal associations, she mentions her own social class more than any other. "Best friends" are from the lower-middle class; but when she names boys and girls her parents would want her to go around with she names not only this same group of friends but also people from the upper class. This may indicate that her parents have exerted some pressure on her to advance in the social scale.

She has an excellent school record, which is in keeping with her high intelligence. Though she has no outstanding talents, she can do everything in school uniformly well. When asked whether she had any unusual ability, she said: "I like to meet people and be with them."

In many ways, Sally shows herself to be a socially mature person, sincerely interested in people and concerned with their welfare.

For example, in the Moral Ideology Test she lists, under good things, "Entering into games at parties cheerfully even though you detest them. . . . Being sincerely nice to everyone. . . . Trying to defend another person who is unable to defend himself. . . . Encouraging people who are discouraged." As bad things she lists "Holding grudges. . . . Snobbishness. . . . Talking about people behind their backs and betraying confidences. . . . Complete selfishness."

In her fantasies Sally shows her insight into and her consideration for the feelings of others. In her stories the characters are intensely human, full of imperfections, and faced with all kinds of problems. The problem of the boy-girl relationship appears frequently and is solved sometimes with adult help and sometimes by going against adult advice. She seems to be moving toward increased self-reliance and toward a mature understanding of the complexity of human behavior.

Sally is not concerned over many problems. In the Problem Check List she marked fewer than the average number of problems, and those she mentioned were of minor importance. She is a little worried about problems of finance because she feels her parents are sacrificing too much for her. As she came nearer to the time for college entrance, she showed increasing concern in these areas. "I know it cost my folks a lot to send my brothers to college, but it was more important for the boys to have an education. My folks want me to go though." She expects to earn part of her expenses. "We figured that if I could earn enough to pay my tuition, my mother could buy my clothes, and I could go."

Sally talks rather vaguely about a career after she finishes college, but her main ambition is to make a successful marriage. She doesn't feel that she has any special talents or abilities beyond that of making friends, and she is not seriously concerned. In writing about "The Person I Would Like to Be Like," she concludes: "My greatest ambition is to be a woman. It probably sounds silly because, in one sense of the word, physically, I'll have to be, but I don't mean just physically. There are so many things you have to be and do, it seems to me, before you really are a woman."

In summary, Sally is a well-adjusted person, somewhat mature for her age, congenial, self-confident, and unusually secure in her social relations.

Like Maisie she has a strong desire for social approval and friendly contacts, and, like her, she has personal qualities which make it easy to win approval and make friends. In addition, she has what Maisie lacks—a family that has a fairly good social standing and is able and willing to help her maintain her strong social position.

SUMMARY

Some persons—the Adaptive type—acquire a code for conduct by effortless absorption from the social environment. In so doing, a person may learn what is right and what is wrong without necessarily developing a clear-cut rationale of character values, without being deeply contemplative about what is right and what is wrong, and without working through any particular conflicts. These people are successful conformists and have good character reputations by virtue of adjusting to people around them and adopting an appropriate conduct as a by-product of that adjustment. The main characteristic of this personality type is the almost unconscious adoption of good patterns of conduct. Good character develops easily and naturally.

This means of achieving acceptable character is not, however, open to all persons, as we have seen in our discussion of the Self-Directive Person and as we shall see again in our discussion of other personality types which follows. This easy adjustment to the demands of society is predicated on the possession of certain personal characteristics and certain favorable conditions in the environment. Although all the factors listed below are not necessary to the development of the Adaptive personality, they tend in this direction. They are aids which give the individual an "edge," so to speak, in adjusting to the group. The individual who has attributes which appeal to the group more easily wins group approval and, in turn, finds it easier to identify with the group.

One of these factors is an above-average intelligence. For sixteen-year-olds, the school plays a large role in social acceptance. School achievement is an important factor, and at least average intelligence is needed to maintain an acceptable school record. This is particularly important for individuals who do not belong to the dominant social class. A lower-class girl or boy must have a good school record in order to earn the respect, or at least the good will, of the teachers.

Intelligence is a less-important factor for individuals from higher social groups. For them, school achievement is less necessary for social acceptance. Coming from well-established homes, they can count on a certain degree of acceptance, regardless of their personal attainments.

Good looks, appearance, health, and energy are important, though not essential, qualities. Good looks are helpful in social gatherings and in being attractive to the opposite sex. This, in turn, creates opportunities for abundant social experiences which otherwise would be absent. Energy and health are important, because, lacking them, an individual could not carry on adequate school work and a wide program of social activities. Whenever school activities are cut down, chances for popularity and acceptance are also diminished. Part of the picture, particularly for girls, is the presence of a marked degree of sex appeal. This is a potent factor in social standing in high-school groups and is particularly important for girls from lower social classes. Being liked by boys fosters popularity with girls. This in turn helps keep up social relations, makes adjustment to the dominant social values easier, and thus tends toward the development of favorable character reputation.

An outgoing, amenable personality, a friendly disposition, and a lack of aggressiveness are essential to the Adaptive Person. Such people seldom have unusual desires, convictions, or interests. They can be absorbed into group patterns of behavior without any strain or difficulty because they are able to suppress easily any unique features they may possess. In an adolescent group the Adaptive Person does not have very strict moral criteria. Ability to take situations as they come and to live up to group expectations as they come are prerequisites of the successful social conformer.

An important factor in the development of personality is, of course, the nature of the family relationships. The Adaptive Person must have had an affectionate, permissive family environment. Discipline must have been easy, and the child must have been given a complete feeling of security and affection in the early years. The moral views of the parents are broad and tolerant so that they do not set restrictions on their child's social participation.

The Adaptive Person has a highly developed ego or sense of the relation of himself to his environment. His sense of self enables him to size up the reality of various situations and to respond to them readily and effectively in ways which bring a maximum of pleasure and success. His ego develops in the direction of identification with the group, in contrast to the ego of the Self-Directive Person, which seeks gratification through personal attainment and personal recognition.

The Adaptive Person contrasts with the Self-Directive Person also in severity of conscience. The severe conscience of the latter makes him cautious and self-critical, whereas the permissive conscience of the Adaptive Person allows him to act with great self-assurance.

The Adaptive Person seems unusually mature in his social contacts during adolescence. He gets along well and easily with both sexes and has a greater fund of experience in human relations than most others of his age.

This personality type is more characteristic of girls than of boys in our sixteen-year-old group. More needs to be known about personality characteristics at other ages before this finding can be explained; but part of the explanation may lie in the fact that the feminine sex role in our culture calls for behavior a great deal like that of the Adaptive Person. As a consequence, perhaps, the family and social groups beyond the family train and reward girls for being Adaptive Persons.

As shown in Table 21 in the preceding chapter the Adaptive Persons come from all social classes. Possibly the lower classes will have relatively fewer of this type in a social environment dominated by the middle classes, because a number of potential Adaptive Persons from the lower classes will suffer from social discrimination and thus will move into the Unadjusted group.

14

The Submissive Person

The Submissive Person is one who will not initiate action. He waits for others to take the lead. He never shows signs of overt aggression and rarely of covert aggression. He lives by authority.

ANNE

Anne is not well known either to her age mates, her teachers, or to other adults in the community. Those people who know her agree that she has a good character. She is rated among the top 25 per cent of the sixteen-year-olds on honesty, above the average on moral courage and loyalty, and average on responsibility. Only on friendliness does she rank below average—and, on this trait, informants agree in placing her well toward the bottom of her group. She is thought of as being socially withdrawn— "never has a good time"—but as being "hard working," "virtuous," "good."

Anne has rather high moral values, but they are not self-formulated, nor are they backed by strong personal convictions. The moral beliefs which influence Anne's behavior seem to come from her mother and father. In a test of moral ideology she was asked to list "good" and "bad" things to do and to indicate who would approve the good and disapprove the bad. In every instance she mentioned her mother and father as the people who would approve or criticize. As good things to do, she listed: "Try to be helpful, try to be friends with everybody, go to school dances, play different games, be a good sport." Under the bad things to do she said: "Don't go around with tough kids, don't have a bad reputation, don't go with boys till of age, don't be lazy, don't stay out late at night."

Anne is one of the older children in a large lower-class family that has a reputation for low intelligence, economic instability, and a careless and casual pattern of living. At present both the father and the mother are employed, but in the past it has been the mother who has been employed most consistently. The father is known to relief offices as "a long-time case. He gets a lot of help and has received it through every agency." Of the family it is said: "They're always on relief and spending their money on permanent waves for the girls."

In spite of being regarded as shiftless and economically incompetent, the family has escaped being branded immoral and nonrespectable. "It is a big family. They beg for all they can get. They are very poor, but there has never been anything bad said about them." There was a single instance of a petty theft committed by one of the children, and the feeling in the community was that the publicity given to the theft was unwarranted and unfair.

The home situation is poor from the standpoint of both physical equipment and adult supervision. Their present home, like others previously, is shabbily furnished, overcrowded and cluttered, and lacking in facilities for comfort and convenience. Anne accepts responsibility for much of the care of the home and is given credit by outsiders for keeping the home clean and in fair order. She finds this a difficult task, however, and resents the lack of cooperation from her family. She thinks of herself as being a highly responsible person in the sense of being prompt, neat, and orderly. "I try to be always neat. When I come home from school, I have to clean up the house. My mother isn't there and seems like I'm always picking things up off the floor and the table. I clean up so many times! I tell my mother and the kids at home, but they still don't seem to pay any attention. Sometimes it gets me so mad, but I don't say anything."

The children, particularly the younger ones, have an uncared-for appearance, are dirty and untidy, and are both physically and mentally retarded. The parents are in the home very little, and the children spend much of their time on the streets or at the movies.

Anne's family is not much interested in education. Her father and mother had no formal education beyond the eighth grade, and they have not encouraged their children to remain in school any longer than necessary. Her mother is rather proud of Anne's achievement in going through high school; on the other hand, she is said to have advised Anne last year to quit school and take full-time employment.

In many respects, Anne stands out in marked contrast to her family. Although she retains an allegiance to them and seems also to be quite dependent upon her mother, she has departed from the family behavior pattern and is conforming as closely as she can to middle-class standards. Conformity has meant, for her, remaining in school to the completion of high school, keeping up a very neat and attractive personal appearance, having a good moral reputation, and adhering quietly and unobtrusively to standards of personal conduct that are beyond criticism. In any mention of her family, she is singled out as one who has worked hard to make something of herself and who has been fairly successful in spite of family handicaps.

She is eager to get a job so that she can earn enough money to buy good clothes and have an attractive place in which to live. "I'd like to have a room that I could go home to and don't have to worry about it being all messed up. So I'd like to get a room somewhere that I could have for myself and keep it neat."

At the same time, she is not ambitious about the kind of job she is to have but wants to work in reasonably pleasant surroundings and prefers lower paid office work to a factory job. "One of my friends is a file clerk. I want to get a job like that, or typing. I don't want to get a job like out there where they are making powder and stuff like that. You make more money doing that, but I'd rather make less and work somewhere else."

Anne thinks of herself as being a very shy person. She said: "At school when I don't answer questions they probably think I am awfully dumb. I know the answer, only I am always afraid it is wrong, so I don't speak out." Her teachers agree that she is handicapped by her timidity; it is difficult for her to recite or to take part in class discussions. She has a strong feeling of inferiority, is ill at ease in most social situations, and avoids situations involving social contacts with people above her in social status.

She takes very little part in school activities and rarely attends school functions. Her feeling of being excluded and her desire to be accepted come out in response to a question as to what changes she would make in her school situation, if changes were possible.

"I'd select a school where the kids mingle together and associate with everybody instead of just certain ones."

By her behavior, Anne has not achieved popularity among her peers, nor has she gained social acceptance beyond her own status group. But she has won respect, particularly the respect of adults. At the same time, the fact that she is mentioned so seldom on the rating instruments, by either peers or adults, indicates that she has been a very inconspicuous member of the school community.

On the tests that were administered, Anne measured low average in verbal intelligence, low in reading ability, and high in performance tests of ability. Her school achievement, which rests heavily on verbal intelligence and reading ability, is low, but she puts forth considerable effort and does as well as she can.

She accepts responsibility, but she does not show initiative except in occasional activities with her very limited group of friends. She works well under direction, but she proceeds cautiously, protecting herself from making any mistakes that might come from misunderstanding instructions or from using her own judgment.

She has no desire to be a leader or to be in any way aggressive. On the Interest Inventory, she was one of the very few people who expressed absolutely no interest in activities that require leadership, and she showed practically no interest in activities that call for some show of aggression.

In her fantasies Anne reveals her dependence upon adult authority. In the Thematic Apperception Test she showed little imagination and did not get beyond a general description of the situation presented in the pictures. In almost every instance, she made some reference to adult authority, usually expressed through a mother figure.

She continues to be a self-effacing person, conscious of her personal limitations and those of her social class and resigned to mediocrity. She has some worries about her appearance, her social incompetence, and her self-consciousness, but she takes her difficulties for granted and blames no one for them. Occasionally she feels some vague discontent and resentment, but, in general, she finds adequate satisfactions in the approval her quiet and submissive behavior brings to her.

In all likelihood, Anne's behavior had its genesis in the experiences of her early years. Severe home training, with approval for unquestioning obedience, may have been an early causative factor. A little later, when she entered school, she must have found that teachers approved her because she was quiet and obedient as well as neat and clean. It is important that she had no special intelligence or abilities to use in making a place for herself, and she must have relied heavily on conformity and submissiveness for acceptance. She has developed honesty, loyalty, and responsibility as integral parts of the pattern. These types of behavior have won commendation from the persons in authority, are therefore successful behaviors, and tend to be repeated. In time, they have resulted in a "good" character reputation.

MARTHA

Martha has a uniformly high character reputation. She is rated by both age mates and adults among the top few sixteen-year-olds on responsibility and honesty. On moral courage and loyalty, she stands somewhat lower but still within the highest 25 per cent of the group. On friendliness, she is rated somewhat above average.

She is not a conspicuous member of her peer group, however, and receives relatively few mentions from peers on the guess-who tests. Within her own small circle of friends, she is well accepted and apparently feels quite secure. Her social relationships, both in school and out, are limited to this small group—all of whom belong to the same ethnic-religious group as Martha.

Her reputation among adults indicates that she has qualities which adults rather than peers are likely to notice and value. She is spoken of as "A perfect girl—kind, courteous, social, and a Christian." "Unusually courteous and thoughtful." "A perfect lady and always kind."

Martha has conservative moral beliefs that she has taken on from the adults with whom she has associated most intimately. She believes that people should be honest, conscientious, responsible; that they should take part in "good, wholesome" activities, and read "good" literature; and that they should avoid gambling, dancing, smoking, drinking, card playing, and lawbreaking. Her behavior is in conformity with these beliefs. At the same time, she has some self-doubt, and in conflict situations—as on the Life Problems Test—she is sometimes confused and inconsistent. The issues in many areas, particularly loyalty and moral courage, are not clear to her.

Martha has grown up in an atmosphere of strict morality. Her home and family background, quite unlike Anne's, is eminently respectable. Her father has a small but apparently stable income; and by the exercise of thrift and good management the family, classified as lower-middle class, is able to live comfortably on this income. The only criticism of the family stems from their unswerving allegiance to the strict social and moral code approved by the ethnic-religious group to which they belong, the Norwegian Lutherans. Such criticism comes occasionally from people outside the group who feel that this code is unnecessarily strict and confining.

Martha's father and mother have good cultural and educational backgrounds. They are deeply interested in the welfare of their family but are not striving for social mobility. Within the family there is strong parental control directed toward maintaining the behavior pattern approved by their religious group. Their minister says: "Their home training is the strictest of anyone's in the church." There is much shared activity and a strong family solidarity.

Martha is an unaggressive and rather inconspicuous member of her class in school, but her position is quite different from Anne's. In both intelligence and school achievement she ranks in the top quarter of her group. She participates with considerable success in some school activities but limits her participation to areas in which there is no conflict with the standards of her church group. For example, she has some talent as a violinist and takes part in school music activities, but she does not enter into school social activities. At school parties there is likely to be dancing or card playing and these are types of entertainment which she does not approve. She does not question the standards or the authority of her religious group, nor does she defend them against opposition. She simply withdraws from conflict situations and remains submissive to the authority she has always accepted.

Martha is docile and rather timid, and she avoids situations that call for aggressive behavior and the exercise of leadership qualities, even within her own clique group where she is highly regarded. She is active in the church but she is not often an officer, even there. She is not an aggressive girl or a leader, but she is a good worker."

She seems to be a fairly well-adjusted person. On a problem check list she checked vague and stereotyped problems—her complexion, how to save and spend money, how to study effectively, and the like. When she was asked in an interview what difficulties she had at school, at home, at work, she said: "The most important difficulty I have at all three of these places is that of not wasting my time. At school especially do I seem to lack the ability to, or to know how to, concentrate on what I am doing."

Martha is not aware of many problems in her life, probably because she lacks a critical and analytical attitude toward herself and toward others. Her adjustment is on an immature and superficial level. It is the result of withdrawing from conflicts, rather than having faced them and worked them out to her own satisfaction.

In her fantasies Martha gives further indication of stereotyped thought, dependence upon adults, and acceptance of a rigid code of behavior. Her stories in the Thematic Apperception Test have a definitely moralistic tone. Selfish people see the error of their ways and reform; family responsibility for providing good moral training is stressed; success and good fortune are on the side of the angels.

Martha plans to be a nurse, and in making this vocational choice she seems to be motivated by an ideal rather than by a strong personal desire. Her choice is highly approved by her family and her ethnic-religious group, and both the training for the work and later employment can be carefully supervised.

There is ample evidence to indicate that Martha's behavior has been guided throughout her life by well-defined standards which were laid down for her and which she has accepted without question. Given the strict moral standards of her group, her good character has developed as a direct consequence of her submissiveness.

In a sense, the submissive quality of Martha's personality is even more striking than Anne's. Anne, though ostensibly more shy and more withdrawn than Martha, reached beyond her immediate family to find a pattern of values to which to conform—in this case, the middle-class morality dominant in the community. Martha, on the other hand, seems never to have deviated from the family code accepted docilely in early childhood.

LESTER

A third example of the Submissive personality is that of Lester. In contrast to Anne and Martha, his reputation for character is somewhat below average, although not markedly so. He is in the third quartile of subjects on honesty, responsibility, and moral courage. On friendliness and loyalty, he is average. There is and has been nothing outstanding in his behavior to lower or to raise his reputation, and his scores are based on a relatively small number of ratings by adults and age mates, indicating that he is an inconspicuous member of the group. His highest ratings come from his employer, in whose grocery store he has worked week ends and summers for two years.

In his moral beliefs and values, Lester shows himself ready to observe behavior standards that are appropriate for one who wants to be a respected, well-liked member of the community, a follower but not a leader. He will accept responsibility, word hard, avoid "bad" companions, and be obedient to authority. In a test of moral ideology he lists as good things to do: "help at home, work and give your folks some board, be obedient, buy defense bonds and stamps, don't be always borrowing money." Under "bad" things, he says: "Don't be disobedient to anybody, don't run around at nights too much, don't go with boys and girls you know that are bad, don't do things you're not supposed to do at work."

Lester is a rather colorless boy, both in appearance and in personality. He is of average height, very slender, neither handsome nor unattractive. There is nothing about his behavior, either negative or positive, that serves to differentiate him to the casual observer.

Like Anne, he is from a lower-class family, although his family stands a little higher in the social scale than does Anne's. His father has had steady employment in a factory, and although his income is small the family is independent and strives to maintain a fairly good home. Lester's mother says: "It was sort of slow at times during the depression, but he (the father) always had work. I guess we're lucky compared to some people. We own our own home so that helps."

Comments about the family show them to be "common folks"— "They are poor but respectable." "The father is hard working and honest. The mother is, too. They try to improve their home."

Lester seems to have had considerable affection from his family but not a great deal of guidance and direction. He has a feeling of dependence upon his parents and a feeling of obligation to them. Of his relationships with his family he says: "I get along with my family swell. I try to be good to them all the time. Dad and Mother have quite a responsibility. I try to make it pleasant for them, as much as I can. I think Mother and Dad have a pretty good opinion of me. They like me, I know. When I was smaller— well, it seems like since I've been in high school I've got to appreciate my folks more."

Like Anne and Martha, he is an insignificant member of the school group, more likely to be forgotten than to be looked down upon. But in contrast to the two girls, Lester is a rather outgoing person who makes a definite effort to enter into activities and who obviously desires to be friendly. His lack of success in this respect is probably because his peers find him uninteresting.

Lester ranks in the third quartile in intelligence and in the fourth in school achievement. He is not seriously concerned about his poor school achievement; scholastic attainments are not very important to him.

Lester ranked well above the average in mechanical aptitude tests, although he has not made much use of mechanical abilities. When his scores on performance and aptitude tests were interpreted for him, he seemed surprised and pleased.

He indicated, on the Problem Check List, a wide variety of problems that bothered him. Almost none were home or family problems. He indicated that he is worried about his health and his appearance; about school; about his personality; about his limited participation in sports; about his awkwardness in meeting people; his dependence on other people; his relations with the opposite sex; his future education and vocation. He is also worried about family financial difficulties. In an interview, he said: "I don't believe I recite enough in one of my classes. I've been disappointed with girls. One particular one. I don't know—I guess I just figured I could go in and pick out a girl and that would be all there was to it, but it didn't work that way. . . . I was disappointed with myself in sports. I figured I should have done a lot better, but I guess I just wasn't qualified. . . . Then I'm disappointed in school this year. Things just don't pan out like you want them to. . . . I'd like to improve my personality and that. . . . I'd like to improve my physical, well, condition, I guess you'd call it. I'd like to be taller and heavier."

He desires the approval of adults who are courageous, decisive, successful; but he has little confidence that he is or can be any of these things himself. He speaks admiringly but not resentfully of more successful people. "I'd like to have ability like some other kids do. Everything they go into just comes natural to them. They just seem able to do everything. If I do anything I sort of have to work up to it."

Lester says that he would like to be the manager of a grocery store. In choosing this vocational goal he seems to have given thought to his interests and abilities and to have made a rather realistic choice.

In summary, Lester is shy, passive, and submissive to authority. He is basically dependent upon his parents, immature, and undifferentiated as a personality. He feels somewhat frustrated by circumstances of family finance and is not sure of his abilities. However, he accepts his limitations realistically. He makes a reasonably good, although inconspicuous, member of a community.

SUMMARY

The Submissive Person is one whose attitude toward his surroundings is one of passive acceptance. He lacks self-confidence and gains security by conforming to standards imposed by more aggressive personalities. For the most part he derives his satisfactions from the approval he gets for doing what is expected of him.

He has little or no desire to be a leader. He feels more secure in following the lead of others than in initiating action himself. Consequently, he avoids situations that would involve him in leadership activities.

The Submissive Person wants to avoid conflict and stays away from situations where conflicts are likely to arise. If he does find himself in such a situation, his immediate tendency is to withdraw. Martha, for example, in conforming to the strict standards of her religious group, remains aloof from school social activities and thus avoids conflicts.

In peer groups the Submissive Person is frequently a nonentity, ignored rather than actively approved or disapproved. He may have a lower reputation for friendliness than for other traits, not because he wants to be unfriendly but because of his inconspicuous behavior or because of his tendency to withdraw. As mentioned earlier, Anne protects herself from possible rebuffs by remaining aloof, thereby giving the impression of unfriendliness.

The reputation of the Submissive Person ranges from good to excellent. Some groups place high value on obedience and un-questioning acceptance of authority; and the person who conforms to those standards will have a good reputation with the members of the group. One such group, and there are obviously many others, is the adult school personnel. Teachers approve the Submissive Person because he is docile and uncritical and causes no disturbance. He rarely shows initiative, but, in doing what is expected of him, he acquires some reputation for being a responsible person.

The Submissive Person is not submissive to everybody he meets. He has standards and a strong sense of duty. Often his conscience is extremely severe. Therefore, he may exhibit a moral stubborn-ness that appears surprising in one whose behavior is usually meek and mild. No doubt Martha would show an extremely stubborn adherence to her standards if she was put into a group with differ-ent moral practices. The Submissive Person has accepted a given pattern of external authority and has made it part of himself so completely that he cannot exercise independent judgment. But neither does he shift from one moral authority to another, as the Adaptive Person is able to do, for he lacks the freedom of action that accompanies a well-developed sense of self.

Although the conscience or superego is well developed and quite severe in the Submissive Person, the ego or sense of self is relatively undeveloped. This type of person has very little creativity or sense of freedom. He must cling to an early accepted set of stand-ards, without which he would be insecure and helpless. Lacking any strong sense of identity, his behavior pattern is one of appease-ment; he makes his way by submitting to his particular authority.

The development of the Submissive Personality is fostered both by personal characteristics and environmental factors. Personal characteristics which make it difficult for an individual to compete successfully with others may operate to make him unaggressive and submissive. A person who feels inferior because of mediocre intelligence, lack of physical attractiveness, or lack of physical energy may find it easier to admit his inferiority and stop striving for leadership or even independence.

From the standpoint of environment, anything which encourages the feeling that standards are imposed from without and anything which discourages belief in individual ability or the individual's right to pass judgment on those standards may well foster the development of the Submissive personality.

More specifically, the following environmental factors, operating singly or in conjunction with others, seem to be significant in the development of the Submissive Person:

1. A home dominated by authoritarian parents; parents who are "never wrong"; or parents who deny their children opportunity to question the wisdom of parental judgment. A home in which there is a lack of emotional backing and warm attachments to offset the influence of rather harsh and sometimes puzzling parental requirements.

2. A strong social or ethnic group that sets up standards of behavior and invokes the authority of tradition to uphold them.

3. Frequent association with strong aggressive personalities whom it is difficult and usually unpleasant to oppose.

4. A school environment that is authoritarian in nature and that contains characteristics similar to those of the authoritarian home.

Would the Submissive Person, if reared in a bad moral environment, develop a bad moral character? Since this type of person is unaggressive, he probably could not show aggressive types of delinquency, such as fighting, deliberate cruelty, or predatory stealing. However, he could be a liar, irresponsible, and a moral coward, if those whom he recognized as his authorities taught him to be so.

The data suggest that Submissive Persons tend to come from the lower-middle and upper-lower classes (see Table 21, Chapter 12). If this is true, the explanation would seem to be that a number of children from these classes are reared very strictly, given little opportunity in the home for development of independent judgment and responsibility, and then encouraged by the social environment of the school and peer group to follow the submissive pattern they learned in the home. However, the fact that these two social classes produced as many Self-Directive Persons as Submissive Persons should warn against the converse of the proposition stated above. The lower-middle and upper-lower classes have no greater tendency to produce Submissive than Self-Directive Persons.

15

The Defiant Person

The Defiant Person is openly hostile to society. He shows his hostility by doing poor school work, refusing to conform to social expectations, and sometimes by attacks upon property which land him in jail. Because he has been neglected or mistreated by society he bears a never-ending grudge which prevents him from making any constructive adjustment to his age mates, to his family, to school, or to a job. He is definitely a maladjusted individual.[1]

None of the sixteen-year-old subjects was so definitely maladjusted that he was a good example of this type, but Smoky was closest to it, and his case illustrates at least certain characteristics of the Defiant Person.

SMOKY

"The way I am now, nobody's going to hurt me any. If they want to treat me O.K., all right; if not, all right. It's not going to bother me any. I don't show no consideration for other people—

[1] Needless to say, the Defiant Person illustrates only one kind of personality maladjustment. Each of the other personality types described in this section may include individuals whose behavior patterns are so deviant in one way or another that they no longer fall within the range of the "normal."

However, maladjustment characterizes all members of the Defiant-Person type, as we have defined it. It is a characteristic of the type itself and not merely of a few extreme individuals within the type.

It is for this reason that none of our Prairie City subjects proved good examples of this type. The true Defiant Person is probably not represented within the average high-school population; by the age of sixteen, he is likely to have found his way into a corrective or penal institution. On the other hand, a discussion of the Defiant Person is included here to help the teacher differentiate between the "problem" adolescent, so often found in our high schools, and the more deep-seated maladjustment of the Defiant personality.

not as much as I should, I guess—but if they want to be nice to me, I'll be nice to them. Otherwise, what difference does it make?"

And that is Smoky. He feels he has been "kicked around," and he knows he has been hurt; but, if he can help it, he won't be hurt again.

Unfortunately, he cannot help it. He has even less faith in himself than he has in others. He continues to be dependent and unhappy, while he struggles for independence chiefly by taking a negative and defiant attitude toward society.

Smoky is dark eyed, with black curly hair. He has very good, delicate features. When the young woman field worker first saw him, she wrote: "He impressed me as nice looking, someone who would like to be friendly and to accept friendliness but who has long been wary of people." He was very careless about his appearance and became more so during his last two years in high school. On the occasion of her last interview with him the interviewer wrote:

As I have seen Smoky this year, his appearance has been successively less attractive. The last time he was quite unkempt and dirty. His hands were very dirty. He was wearing a pair of dirty overalls, and he left his cap on throughout the interview. He did not give the impression of wanting to be disrespectful and inconsiderate. He seemed rather to be preoccupied and unhappy, unaware of the fact that he might not be doing the considerate thing.

Smoky is rated by adults and by his age mates in the lowest quartile on moral character. In fact, he is nearly lowest in his group on responsibility and honesty.

At the same time, he is rated about average on moral courage. This relatively high rating on moral courage is to be expected for Defiant Persons, since they are known to be openly critical of teachers and other authorities and since the ability to defy authority is often taken as evidence of moral courage.

On the Student Beliefs Test, Smoky was in the lowest quartile in all areas. Again, on the Life Problems Test, he accepts almost none of the usual statements of moral principles. The conclusion from these tests is that Smoky has none of the accepted standards of conduct.

Shortly after Smoky entered elementary school his parents separated, and since that time he has lived with his mother in the otherwise childless home of her married brother. This family is a lower-middle-class family, which is respected in the community and which takes a minor part in community activities.

Smoky's father was a traveling man. He made a fairly good salary, and Smoky, the only child, had plenty of nice clothes and toys during his early childhood. But his parents quarreled a good deal during the brief periods when the father was at home. Their separation was unpleasant for Smoky. Ten years afterward he was asked to answer a questionnaire which contained, among other items, the following: "Describe briefly some conditions or situations in which you had a lot of unpleasantness or disappointment." He said, in answer to this: "About the only one I can remember is when my folks separated." Later in discussing this reply, Smoky said he could remember very well everything that happened. He said: "It wasn't much fun" and shook his head.

On the questionnaire about family relations, Smoky said that he had no recreation with his family and that he did not eat regularly with them. He said that his family very often nagged at him and were suspicious of him.

This "family" to which Smoky referred consists of his mother, uncle, and aunt. Some people say: "His aunt and uncle spoiled him." Others say: "They always expected too much of him. They've thought he ought to act like a grownup ever since he was a kid." Smoky himself says: "There's three people yelling at me at home, and that's too much."

On another questionnaire, Smoky said that he felt his parents were not interested in him and that he often wanted to leave home for good. On a questionnaire about his interests, he was lowest among the boys of his group on liking activities with his family.

On a check list of personal problems, Smoky checked fewer problems than any other boy, perhaps indicating that he was unwilling to face some of his difficulties. He checked only 10 of a list of 330 problems. Six of the ten fell into the area of "family relations." They were:

> Parents separated or divorced (double checked)
> Father
> Mother
> Talking back to my parents
> Parents not trusting me
> No one to tell my troubles to

Though several adults, including two or three of his teachers, sensed that Smoky was more to be pitied than blamed, there was only one person who gave a really favorable report on him. This was his employer, a gasoline-station proprietor for whom he had worked after school and on Saturdays for nearly a year. This man said that Smoky was "absolutely dependable and reliable."

Smoky's poor reputation has developed gradually since his early adolescence. As a little boy, he was thought by his teachers to be "cute," and he was quite popular with other children. He belonged to the same Sunday-school class as Curt and joined the Boy Scouts at the same time.

But Smoky gradually drifted away from his peer group. He stayed only two years in the Scouts. He lost his friends and spent a good deal of time by himself. When he was fourteen he got in trouble with the school authorities because he would go to the elementary-school playground at night and tie knots in the swing ropes so that the children could not get them down. By the time he was sixteen he could usually be seen in the evening sitting alone on the steps of stores on the main business street, idly watching the passers-by.

In talking with the field worker, Smoky once commented on his unsatisfactory relations with other boys during his early adolescence. He said:

Well, when I was younger, when I was growing up, I used to run around with a bunch of kids, and their folks are respectable and pretty well-to-do and everything, and then I stopped going around with them and began to go around with another bunch of kids that didn't amount to much. My mother can't understand it. She always wants to know why I don't go around with those good kids any more.

Then he said he didn't know himself what had been responsible for the change—that it just happened, he didn't know why.

By the time he was a junior in high school, Smoky had a reputation for being anti-social and unfriendly. On the Guess-Who Test, he was tied with another boy for being mentioned most often as having bad manners, and he was in fifth place on the item, "dislikes school." He himself named fifty boys on this questionnaire, thirty of them unfavorably and twenty favorably. This was unusual, since most students named more people favorably than unfavorably.

To show Smoky's antagonism to his peer group and to the school, several items from the Student Beliefs Test have been selected with Smoky's responses contrasted with those of Curt, who was described in Chapter 12.

	Curt	Smoky
1. If your home room or class decides to do something which they know you do not care to support, you have the right to refuse to help them.	D[1]	A
2. Everyone should belong to several friendship groups, "gangs," or clubs.	A	D
3. Students who do not attend the school games, plays, and parties are poor citizens.	A	D
4. A busy person has the right to refuse to do a job which will benefit a club to which he belongs but which will not benefit himself.	D	A
5. Students who are not willing to do the minor and somewhat-boring tasks to help the school and teachers are not really good citizens of the school.	A	D
6. A club should not expect you to do tasks which you are not willing to do.	U	A
7. One should not stick with an organization, no matter how worth while, whose members often do not come to meetings and where in general there seems to be little enthusiasm for the organization.	D	A

[1] Code: A, agree; D, disagree; U, uncertain.

Smoky's academic record in high school is very poor and places him in the lowest fourth of his group. It is probably because of this record that his peers regard him as "not very smart," when actually he is above average in intelligence. In tests of mechanical aptitude he is superior. His grade-school teachers thought of him as a bright boy. "He did good work while he was in grade school and seemed to get along all right." His high-school teachers recognize that he has more ability than he makes use of, but their attitude toward him has been colored by the fact that he has been a behavior problem and a source of irritation.

The psychological tests which go more deeply into the structure of the personality show that Smoky is in a state of severe emotional conflict. He manifests a degree of anxiety well beyond the normal range, which reduces his ability to use his intellect. In his stories on the Thematic Apperception Test he frequently includes a sympathetic and affectionate mother-figure. One story about a lonely scientist ends with this statement, ". . . they talked to him and he went back to work, and he did the experiment successfully and it turned out all right, and all he needed was a little companionship."

Smoky is an unhappy boy who feels that the world, the quite "respectable" portion of it in which he is expected to live, has given him a raw deal. He proposes to get even by being contemptuous of the standards of that society and by refusing to conform to them. He failed to find in his family the kind of affection and security that he needed, and he is not a strong enough person to face the world and make an adequate adjustment without that security. He lacks faith in himself, and he lets self-pity get in the way of a realistic understanding of himself and his problems. He is weak willed rather than "bad" and needs outside support if he is to develop faith in himself and if he is to use constructively the good intelligence that he has.

Smoky is not a typical Defiant Person for several reasons: he is not aggressively anti-social; he seems to be making a satisfactory adjustment to his job; he has periods of blaming himself rather than society, and of wishing for sympathy. On the other hand, his insecurity, his anxiety, his hostilities to school, family, and age mates are indices of deep-seated maladjustment which is not likely to be remedied merely by changes in the environment.

SUMMARY

There was no one in the sixteen-year-old group who was so anti-social that the authors felt he would end up in prison. There are a few such people who as early as the age of sixteen are incorrigibly aggressive and hostile toward society; but Prairie City did not provide such a person.

More often the Defiant Person at sixteen is verbally hostile to the school, the church, the community, and the peer group but takes out his aggression by being irresponsible, defiant, and blaming society for his own failure. His future course will in many cases lead him to more open defiance and aggression.

In general, the Defiant Person is one who has had early and continued experiences of neglect and frustration. Society, represented at first by his family and then by the school and the peer group, has not satisfied his needs; and he, in turn, has failed to incorporate the ideals and values of society. Thus he grows up without knowing the satisfaction of being rewarded for socially acceptable behavior or of making sacrifices for the welfare of others.

He is unable to cooperate with others in group activities and becomes aggressively selfish and self-centered. He is quarrelsome and bitter. He blames other people or external factors for his shortcomings. If he is intelligent, as Smoky is, he refuses to use his ability to do the things which are expected of him at school.

The moral character of the Defiant Person is sure to be bad in every kind of social environment, for he has never learned to make the personal sacrifices that moral behavior demands. He will be dishonest when it appears to be to his advantage; he will be irresponsible, disloyal, and a moral coward. He will be unkind and unfriendly. It is a hopeful sign for Smoky that he is still able to be responsible and honest on his job and in his relations with his employer and a few other adults. This shows that Smoky is not completely unable to meet social expectations.

The Defiant Person is so definitely maladjusted that a mere improvement in his social environment will not help him much. In this respect he differs from the Unadjusted Person, to be described in the following chapter. The Defiant Person needs the help of a psychiatrist, who can treat him as a sick person and who can help him repair his inner resources for dealing with the world.

Smoky appears to us to be on the borderline between the Unadjusted and the Defiant Person. He needs not only an improvement in his environment but also personal help from a therapist to enable him to respond adequately to an improved environment.

To avoid possible misunderstanding it should be pointed out that the Defiant Person is not the same as the social reformer who rebels against some of the social conventions in order to find a higher and better kind of social behavior. The Defiant Person is anti-social in the true sense of the term. He is unable to cooperate with other people in the pursuit of any social end. Therefore his moral behavior is sure to be bad when judged by the standards of any group in which he finds himself.

16

The Unadjusted Person

The Unadjusted Person is discontented, insecure, frustrated; usually he is having difficulties with his family; in school his work is not up to the level of his ability. However, he is not openly hostile to society or definitely maladjusted as is the Defiant Person. He is actively but as yet unsuccessfully seeking to establish a satisfactory relationship with his environment.

DARLENE

"I don't like school, I just simply don't like it."

"Did you like school better when you were in the grades?" asked the field worker.

"Yes, I liked it then and I liked it when I was a freshman in high school, but I just don't like it at all now.

"Another thing, my folks won't let me go out nights. They say I can go out one night a week, and I have to be in by ten o'clock. Well, if I go to a show or go skating with some of the girls, I like to go down to the candy kitchen afterwards and talk to the kids and drink cokes. But you can't do that and be home by ten. And then I like to go riding in cars and my folks won't let me do that, either."

"How about Sunday school, Darlene, and young people's meetings at the church. Do you like to go there?" asked the field worker.

"No, I dropped out of Sunday school last year. There was a bunch of snobs in there. They just quit talking to me and quit paying attention to me. They had better clothes than me. So I just quit going there."

This was Darlene's situation when she was sixteen. She was at odds with school, home, and church. Only with a small clique of friends, who shared her social difficulties, did she feel that she was liked and accepted.

Darlene's character reputation is low. She is in the lowest quartile on all the traits, and adults as well as peers give her low ratings. The impression one obtains from studying her reputation data is that people agree in putting her well down the scale except in specific instances where they happen to know something good about her.

In her moral beliefs Darlene seems to be at loose ends, with no fixed standards. She gives no indication of feeling loyal or responsible to school standards; and she shows no feeling of allegiance to her peers. She does not apply moral principles consistently to concrete situations.

Darlene is a tall, big-boned girl. She is not pretty, rarely smiles, and has a rather sullen expression, as though she anticipated unfriendly reactions from others.

Her parents are respectable lower-class people. Neither of them went beyond eighth grade. They go to church and have the reputation of trying to cooperate with the school in matters affecting their children. Darlene's father and mother have kept a strict eye on her, and until recently she showed no sign of rebelling against them. When she comes home at night she always goes to her mother's room and tells her about the evening.

Darlene's social participations were quite normal until recently. She belonged to the Girl Scouts, attended Sunday school faithfully, and liked to skate and do the other things that girls enjoy in their early teens. But since her freshman year in high school she has dropped out of the social life of the school and church. She has associated with a small group of girls who, like herself, are not well adjusted to the life of the school. The leaders of this group are actively hostile to the school; they skip school when they can do so and go with boys who are not in school. Darlene is a peripheral member of this group. Her parents do not approve of them, and she, herself, is critical of them at times.

Information about her social adjustment in the school was secured by a field worker, who talked with her about her reactions to the interest inventory, on which she had indicated an unusually high number of dislikes for school activities.

"Are you in any clubs in school, Darlene?" he asked.

"No, I don't belong to any. I was in a club my freshman year but not since then."

"Would you like to belong to some?"

"Well, I would really like to be in dramatics."

"Well, why don't you join?"

"It's too late now. Besides, my folks wouldn't let me out at night. You see, they practice plays at night."

"Do you get along all right with the other girls?"

"Well, with my crowd I'm perfectly happy. We have a lot of good times. But some of these other girls in my classes, they just don't treat me right. They look down on us girls. They think they're somebody. They think they're better than we are. They have a lot of money and they look down on us."

Since the family has very little money, Darlene has done housework to earn what she needs for books and other school necessities, but she does not like this kind of work.

As a junior in high school, she shows much discontent. On an interest inventory which inquired about her likes and dislikes for school subjects, she marked only the "dislike" column. On another inventory she was the lowest in her group in "likes" for school activities and for leadership activities.

Darlene has good intellectual ability. She ranks above average in verbal intelligence and in the highest quarter of her class on a performance test of intelligence. Her school work has been average, indicating that she is not making the most of her abilities in her studies but also that she is not rejecting school entirely.

In her choice of a vocational goal she has vacillated considerably, although she did try to enter nurses' training. She wanted to drop out of school at the end of her third year and enter a nurses' training school, but her father refused to give his permission. She has at other times wanted to be a beauty operator and an office worker.

Darlene is negativistic, insecure, and unhappy. She feels that people are constantly criticizing her. On an essay describing the person she would like to be like, she writes: "This person would not consider the younger generation as being bad. I think it is awful the way people talk about other people when they really know nothing about them. This person would not be a gossip." She is concerned over her own lack of physical attractiveness, but she does very little about her appearance.

Beneath the surface Darlene seems to be a passive person, emotionally dependent on others, with rather weak impulses. She easily becomes anxious, and cannot be actively hostile toward people. She withdraws from situations if they seem to require independence or aggressiveness. Her only strength lies in a sense of duty, which keeps her doing the things she believes are right even though she gets no reward for them.

If this girl were better looking, had more physical vigor, had some talent, or if her family had better social position, she probably would have made a reasonably good adjustment to her social environment, and she would have a much better character reputation. But, as things were in her junior year, there seemed to be little chance for her situation to improve.

In her final year in high school, however, the picture changed radically. During the summer between her junior and senior years, Darlene got a full-time clerical job in an office and handled the work quite well. She continued with this job on a part-time basis as her work assignment in the cooperative work-study program which she entered when she went back to high school in the fall.

On the day she came for a conference with the field worker, she was attractively dressed and her hair had recently been shampooed and set. She appeared more serene and at ease than ever before. The field worker asked her a number of questions, including, "How does what other people think of you differ from the way you think of yourself?" Darlene's reply was: "Some people think I am given too much freedom as to where I can go and what I can do with the money I earn. I don't go to the church that my parents belong to. Some people think that is wrong. I think we have freedom of religion and I am taking advantage of it. I choose my own doctor, dentist, clothes and places to go because I am old enough to know what I want, and I don't do anything wrong. My money I earn is my own and I spend it as I see fit."

To another question "Describe any important or unimportant difficulties you have at school, at home, at work," she replied: "I don't have any difficulties at school except that I just don't like it. The only difficulty I have at home is that I cannot stay out as late as the other girls; otherwise we get along wonderfully well."

To the question "Describe briefly some conditions or situations in which you had a lot of fun and enjoyed yourself," she said: "I always seem to have fun when I go skating or to a movie. I enjoy church on Sunday. I never cared for it much before. I am cheerful more than otherwise. When the girls I go around with and I are together, we can always find something to laugh about."

The key to the changes in Darlene's personality seems to have been the getting of a job as part of her school program. This was an office job, carrying with it much higher social status than the housework she had done previously. Since the job was counted as part of the school program, she now felt better disposed toward the school.

The money she earned allowed her to have her own choice of a doctor, dentist, and clothes. The ability to stand on her own feet in these matters was a symbol to her that she was no longer a child, and she could be more independent in her dealings with her parents. This independence paid dividends in her change of churches. She left her former church, where she had been snubbed by a group of middle-class girls, and in spite of criticism from her relatives, she went to a church with a larger lower-class membership, where she found people more friendly to her. Thus the environment changed for Darlene, and she was able to make a better adjustment. She still disliked some aspects of her environment, including school, but she resented them less because her adjustment had become better in other areas.

The case of Darlene illustrates the fact that the Unadjusted Person does not characterize a basic personality type in the same sense as the other four categories. It includes individuals who, for one reason or another, are having difficulties with their environments and who have not yet developed clear-cut and differentiating patterns of adjustment. With changed environments, many persons move from this category into one of the others previously described.

NICK

"If I were 21, I sure as hell wouldn't be spending much time in Prairie City," wrote Nick when he was sixteen.

Nick does not usually express his hostility so emphatically. Certainly he is hostile towards life in Prairie City, but, unlike Smoky, he is not a belligerent, deliberately conspicuous non-conformist. He says, in effect:

> I am not impressed by what most of you people here in Prairie City seem to think is important. I'll conform to some of your standards because I believe in them myself; I'll conform to some of them because it takes effort to fight against them and it isn't worth the effort. I'll ignore the rest of them, and it doesn't matter to me how you feel about it or whether you even notice it.

Nick's reputation for honesty and responsibility places him in the lowest quartile of the group. On the other three traits he is rated somewhat higher, and on friendship he is rated slightly above average. Adults tend to rate him lower than do his age mates.

In his response to the Student Beliefs and Life Problems tests Nick is either uncertain or negative toward the generally accepted moral values. He is especially low in respect to responsibility, where he seems to feel that a high-school student need not assume any responsibility except for himself and his own interests. As regards honesty, he is willing to be dishonest if some personal advantage results.

Nick is the second of three boys in an upper-lower-class family. His father has a good income, but he makes his money in a business that is not considered respectable—he runs a tavern. He knows the "best" people in town, but he is not socially acceptable to them, nor does he, for that matter, show any desire to be accepted. He is regarded as a strong-willed, independent individual who is not concerned about public opinion.

It is difficult to judge accurately Nick's relationship to his family. There is some indication that he feels rather ill at ease and restless at home, and there is no indication of close emotional attachments or strong feelings of loyalty to his family. Yet he seems to have considerable freedom about the use of his time outside school hours and apparently is not under strict parental discipline. He says he is "nervous, but I guess that's more physical than mental." He tries to account for this in part by his irregular eating and sleeping and then adds: "Another reason is being oversensitive, I suppose." He seems to be indicating here a home situation that is upsetting to him but that could be tolerated if he were not "on edge" and oversensitive.

Nick's parents have a limited educational background, but they have been insistent that their children finish high school and are apparently willing to finance college training. It is the father rather than the mother who has opposed Nick's desire to leave school. "I was all set to quit school this spring but my dad talked me out of it—talked me down rather," Nick said with a grin. He said, too, on another occasion, that if he wanted to go to college the matter of finances would not be a problem.

Nick is well above average in intelligence and ranks in the top fourth of his group. However, he refuses to apply himself at school, and in achievement he is in the lowest fourth of his class. He appears to be critical of what the school has to offer, but his usual attitude is one of indifference and boredom rather than one of open rebellion. On one occasion he said: "I suppose I am capable of better school work, but daily assignments seem to me to be too unimportant or trivial to be worth the task of preparing them. I guess I'm just lazy."

He is not overconfident of his ability, nor is he completely satisfied with his indifferent attitude toward school achievement. When his intelligence-test score was interpreted to him he seemed genuinely surprised to find that it was so high, and he commented: "I guess if I'm as smart as that I ought to know enough to settle down and accomplish more. . . . Sometimes I get down and concentrate for about a week, but I slide right back again. Except to get through and get a diploma, school just doesn't seem important."

In spite of his negative attitude toward routine school assignments, Nick has obviously spent considerable time, there and elsewhere, in reading. He has an excellent vocabulary and expresses himself unusually well both orally and in writing.

In an essay on "The Person I Would Like to Be Like," he says:

The Person I would like to be like is mostly imaginary. He is a man who knows how to make plenty of money and how and when to spend it. He also knows how to get along with any type or class of people he should come in contact with. He is personable, neat, and well-mannered, having a great general knowledge of books, travel, music, and other arts. He drinks and smokes with moderation, is not overly religious, and is not afraid to voice his opinions if it becomes necessary. He will not be married until he is about thirty, having a substantial business, and a bank account that would be sufficient to ease the responsibility of supporting a wife and children. He is active in all social events, and a member of many clubs and fraternal organizations.

And on an essay, "Where Do I Get My Ideals?" he says:

The person from whom I get my ideals is imaginary. His ideas and ideals come a great deal from books. He learns a lot about life in this manner. He reads mostly books on life such as most of Sinclair Lewis' are. However, the greater and more impressive ideals come from his social activity and the type of people he associates with. His moral standards are high or low according to the collective moral standard of his social group. Other sources of ideals are his business or occupation, and athletics. Athletics give him a solid foundation for high ideals and ideas. They form in him a feeling of self-respect, and a feeling of respect for good sportsmanship.

Another area in which Nick performs well is art. He likes to draw and paint, but he gets no particular recognition of this ability, for he works alone most of the time and gets no help from the school.

Nick's participation in school activities is limited chiefly to athletics. He is considered a good football player and belongs to the "P" Club, an organization of boys who have won the school "letter." Occasionally, but not often, he goes to school dances.

Observing him, one gets the feeling that here is a boy who could be very popular with his peers if he would accept overtures or make them himself. He is tall, well built, and attractive in appearance; he is courteous and well mannered; he has considerable poise; and he has a keen sense of humor. A popular girl in his class says of him: "He's a rather strange boy—'devil may care.' He notices things but says little. He is well liked." In general he is regarded as a "nice kid," "smart," "good in music and sports," but "stand-offish."

Nick impressed the field workers as being more grown up in his understanding of human relationships than any of the other boys in his group. Yet he is childish and irresponsible in much of his behavior. He is absent from school as much as possible, although when present he is not a trouble maker. "When it comes to absence and tardy behavior, Nick is probably the greatest offender we have in the high school. Otherwise he's not a behavior problem," says the principal. He recognizes his immaturity in these respects, and it gives him some concern. He says he wants to "get some place where I'd have to work. I just don't do it without someone pushing me into it and making me do it."

Psychological tests disclose a very severe emotional conflict in this boy. He has strongly aggressive impulses, combined with deep-seated inferiority feelings that rob him of the drive to make good. Nick has some understanding of his difficulty. He spoke to the field worker of his lack of self-confidence and his inability to settle down and concentrate on the things he knew he should be doing. Then he said: "I guess maybe it's more a sickness than a fault."

Nick seems to be unadjusted all along the line—in school, among his age mates, in the community. What Nick wants more than anything else is to escape from Prairie City and to try to make his mark in the world outside. In Prairie City his family's reputation holds him back, and his peculiar artistic and literary interests gain him little reward or companionship.

Probably such a move would be good for Nick. In a new setting, with a congenial, challenging atmosphere, he might become a happier and more effective person. Given a more favorable environment, his present personality conflicts would not be serious enough to destroy his creativity.

ALDEN

Alden is a small fellow, thin and nondescript. Some of his teachers say that he looks like a squirrel—alert, suspicious, and restless.

His reputation varies from average in moral courage to very low in honesty. Teachers were the only adults who rated him, and they placed him considerably lower than did his peers.

On Student Beliefs his scores are about average. His responses on the test of ability to apply moral principles to actual situations are confused and inconsistent.

Alden's family is lower-middle class. His father has a minor supervisory position in a factory. Although the family is not very popular in the community, they are respected, and they appear to form a closely knit group. Alden enjoys being with his family, taking vacation trips with them, and seems to feel under no pressure from his parents.

His participation in school activities has been limited to the band, which he dropped after two years. He is not widely known in school and has no close friends. He was a Boy Scout for two years and attended Sunday school while he was in the seventh, eighth, and ninth grades. Since his sophomore year in high school Alden has belonged to no organizations. Yet he is not a solitary sort of person. He is often in mischief, and some of the teachers dislike him. One of the men teachers said: "He can't settle down. All the time he is popping off. One of these days I'm going to pop him one."

Alden's intelligence is quite limited. He is in the lowest quartile of his group, and his school work is also in the lowest fourth. Since most persons with as low intelligence as his (IQ 96) have considerable difficulty with abstract high-school subjects, it is not surprising that Alden reported difficulty at school with algebra and Latin.

His ambitions are limited. In his essay on the subject, "The Person I Would Like to Be Like," he wrote:

When I get to be an adult, I would like to be exactly like a man who comes into the store where I work. He has a new car, and a fine wife. For his recreation he goes and bowls, he also likes shows very much, and he and his pals go up to the Eagles and play cards and drink beer. He is very friendly. If you meet him walking down the street he will say "How do you do" even if he has never seen you before. He is always willing to do anything he can for other people. If he is driving around town, and he sees you going home, he will ask you if you want a ride home.

The personality tests indicate that Alden has an unstable, childish personality. He is impulsive, anxious, and becomes confused when he meets a conflict. His behavior is unpredictable. Sometimes he is anxious and troubled, and other times he is boastful and impudent.

Alden has made a poor adjustment to school, probably because his academic ability is limited. Although he tries to keep up with the social life of the school and has his parents' approval and support in this, he lacks the intellectual ability to play an important part in the more serious school activities, and he does not have the physique for athletics.

Alden's adjustment improved when his school work was associated with a job. Between his junior and senior years he took a summer job as clerk in a chain store and made a success of it. During his senior year he kept this job on a part-time basis—as his assignment in the cooperative work-study program. Although his afternoon work took him even more out of the social life of the school, it gave him a valuable sense of self-confidence. In an interview with the field worker he listed his work as one of the most enjoyable aspects of his life. He said: "I learned a lot on that job. I can go anywhere now and get a job as a grocery clerk."

Alden is still an immature boy, still boastful and insecure, but his job has given him something real to depend upon, some assurance that he can be a man. With added maturity he will probably make a reasonably good adjustment to life.

SUMMARY

The three Unadjusted Persons described here are basically different in personality. Alden's situation seems due principally to his relatively low intelligence and social immaturity. Darlene seems to suffer mainly from her family's low social position and her own lack of physical beauty. Nick's is a more complex case, in which a rather deep emotional conflict combines with his family's poor social position and his unappreciated literary and artistic abilities to make him dissatisfied and unhappy.

In these and other individuals of this category, the person becomes discontented and insecure and often shows hostility to school, family, and community.

His character reputation will be low, for two reasons: First, it is difficult for him to accept and live up to the standards of a social situation which does not reward him; second, his habitual discontent and negativism will make people react unfavorably towards him, even though there is nothing morally wrong with his behavior.

The Unadjusted Person is not a definite personality type as are the other four. Rather, he tends to be a potential Self-Directive, Adaptive, or Submissive Person who is barred by adverse circumstances from achieving a reasonably good adjustment in one of these roles. Since the problem for this person lies in his relation to his social environment, changing the environment often helps to solve the problem. In this study, where lack of adjustment to the school seems to be a major source of difficulty to persons of this type, changing from the school situation to the job situation, or changing the school situation so as to include a job, resulted in much better adjustment.

The Unadjusted Person came overwhelmingly, twelve out of a total of fifteen, from the upper-lower class (see Table 21, Chapter 12). The explanation of this is probably that the adolescent social environment of Prairie City discriminates against children of this class on social and economic grounds. They lack adjustment to the peer group because it is geared to middle-class values and expectations.

PART 4

Suggestions for Character Education

17

Conclusions and Implications

All the group and individual studies have been concerned with variations of two basic questions:

1. To what extent is character development influenced by the social environment of the individual?

2. To what extent is character development influenced by the individual's personal make-up?

FINDINGS FROM GROUP STUDIES

In the group studies which constitute Part II of this book, character reputation was studied in relation to each of a series of factors—factors in the social environment and factors within the personal

TABLE 22   CORRELATIONS BETWEEN CHARACTER REPUTATION AND VARIOUS FACTORS

Character Reputation Scores Related to:	Correlation Coefficient
Social-class position	0.52
School achievement (school grades)	0.74
Intelligence (Stanford-Binet IQ)	0.49
Values and ideals (essays)	0.42
Self-adjustment (California Inventory)	0.32
Social adjustment (California Inventory)	0.16
Moral beliefs (attitude scale)	0.34
Religious activity (rating)	Low

make-up of individuals.   The principal relationships between character reputation and these various factors are summarized in Table 22, where the relationships are expressed in terms of correlation coefficients.

It will be seen from Table 22 that, with the exception of school achievement, all the relationships are low. In other words, although social-class position, intelligence, values and ideals, and so on, are each related to character reputation, the degree of relationship is so low as to be of little predictive value; that is, one cannot predict an individual's character reputation from knowing his social-class position, from knowing his IQ, or from knowing where he stands on a test of social adjustment.

The low relationships obtained may be due, in part, to the fact that the methods used in some of the group studies were not always successful in attaining their purpose. For example, there is reason to doubt that the "social-adjustment" score of the California Personality Inventory is a good measure of social adjustment for sixteen-year-olds. It measures the individual's feeling of status in the family, school, and community; but the adolescent may be so uncertain about himself as to underrate his status with his social group and thus to score lower on the test than he does in the judgment of other people. Again, certain individuals with good character are so torn with self-doubt that they make low scores on tests of moral beliefs.

But such considerations of methodology are probably secondary in importance. The primary explanation for the low correlations is undoubtedly the fact that character, social environment, and personality are related in complex ways and not in simple one-to-one relationships which can be expressed by coefficients of correlation. In fact, the results shown in Table 22 might well have been anticipated.

Even where the relationship between two single variables is shown to be high, as is the case with school achievement and character reputation, the correlation coefficient fails to tell the whole story. As was described in Chapter 5, school achievement, as expressed in terms of school grades, is a complex measure. It reflects not only the student's academic abilities but also his attitudes toward school, his acceptance of school values and standards, and his desire to make the most of what school offers him. It becomes a measure of the degree to which the adolescent is well adjusted to the school environment, and since the school stresses middle-class values it becomes a measure of the degree to which he is conforming to middle-class standards of conduct.

It appears, then, that the adolescent who has a good relationship to the social environment, as constituted by the high school, is the one who enjoys good character reputation. The majority of young people in Prairie City try to live up to the standards and expectations of the school. For this, they are rewarded by the approval of most of their age mates, their teachers, and most of the adults of the community. Their behavior in the school environment tends to be honest, responsible, morally courageous, loyal, and friendly, because they are rewarded for this behavior.

In Chapter 5 it was pointed out that those boys and girls with low reputations came largely from certain lower-class homes which have not supported the values of the school. Where the home is at odds with the school, the child's behavior and reputation are usually unsatisfactory. This is true of two groups considered in Chapter 4, the out-of-school group and the unadjusted group in school. The actions of members of these groups will in general be irresponsible, unfriendly, disloyal, and even dishonest in relation to the school's values.

This finding of the high relationship between good adjustment in the school and good character reputation poses two questions: (1) Is good adjustment the cause of the individual's good character? or (2) Is good character the cause of the individual's good adjustment?

Probably the best answer to these questions is "both." Certainly any change in the school which improves the adjustment of certain students will help those students to become more responsible, loyal, honest, and so on; just as certainly any change which occurs in certain students to make them more responsible, loyal, and honest will improve their adjustment to the school.

All the evidence from both group studies and the studies of individuals points to the strategic importance of the school in the lives of the adolescents of Prairie City. The school, for certain individuals at least, makes up for shortcomings in other areas of the social environment.

On the other hand, the school, as presently organized in communities like Prairie City, is in many respects inadequate as an agency for character formation. Although this point is discussed in more detail in Chapter 18, it should be pointed out here that the school, in its stress upon academic achievement, is unable to reward all kinds of youth for loyal, responsible, and honest behavior. Many boys and girls, no matter how much they try to live up to the expectations of the school, will be rebuffed and discouraged. The school must itself be changed if it is to serve more effectively in the formation of good character. It must make room for the deviant student. It must be more tolerant of boys and girls with unusual or non-academic abilities and interests.

These conclusions concerning the relation of character to good adjustment in the school and other social situations support the hypothesis that good social adjustment contributes to good character. Any young person who experiences success and security in home, school, church, and other groups is influenced strongly to adopt the prevailing code of morality and to govern his actions accordingly.

FINDINGS FROM STUDIES OF INDIVIDUALS

The studies of individuals, reported in Part 3 of this book, yield, on the whole, more insight into the complex relationships between character, personality, and social environment than do the group studies.

Perhaps the most significant conclusion of the individual studies is that moral character, personality, and social environment are related in systematic ways and that moral character cannot usefully be studied apart from the total personality.

Individuals of different personality types may have very similar character reputations. Minerva, Sally, and Martha, described in Chapters 12, 13, and 14, all have the same high reputations for honesty and responsibility, though they are quite different in personality. Similarly, Nick, Smoky, and Alden all have low reputations for honesty and responsibility, yet they fall into quite different personality categories.

The Relation of Character to Personality Type

Good character (or bad character) may have a very different meaning in the lives of two individuals, when seen in the total configuration of their personalities. Character develops differently in boys and girls of different personality types; it is influenced by a different set of causative factors and by a different set of learning experiences.

One finds, for example, that certain personality types are much more concerned about moral beliefs and principles than are other personality types.

Adaptive Persons take on the beliefs and principles of their social environment readily, without much question and without much inner commitment. They seem to have no moral struggles.

On the other hand, Self-Directive Persons are reflective and critical concerning morality. Although their moral behavior may be very similar to that of the Adaptive group, they are characterized by self-doubt and turmoil over the moral choices they must make. They are engaged in the painful process of working out moral principles for themselves.

Submissive Persons, too, are very self-critical concerning their moral behavior, but their doubt springs from a very different source. Unlike Self-Directive Persons, they are worried, not by the problem of whether or not they are living up to their own principles and whether or not those principles are the correct ones to follow, but by whether or not they are living up to the expectations of persons who are in authority over them. For Submissive Persons, the question is not "Is this really the *right* thing to do?" but rather "Is this really the thing to do to keep me out of trouble?"

The Unadjusted Persons are confused over moral beliefs and principles. Caught in an environment which fails to reward them sufficiently for good behavior, or which poses moral choices which cause them severe conflicts, they are unable to see a clear and consistent relation between a set of moral beliefs and principles and the feelings of personal satisfaction and social approval which they are striving for.

The Defiant Persons have rejected the generally approved moral beliefs and principles. They have not experienced satisfaction and social approval for good behavior to a degree sufficient to learn the beliefs and principles which lie behind good behavior. They are ruled by selfishness and aggressive impulses.

In general, the character differences between the various personality types may be attributed to differences in the nature and severity of the moral conscience, together with differences in the development of the sense of self, or ego. The Self-Directive Person has a strong and severe conscience, combined with a well-developed sense of self. His sense of self consists of a cold and objective understanding of the relations between himself and other people and of a drive for achievement and independence in those relationships.

The Adaptive Person has a more permissive conscience and thus is ruled more by social approval and disapproval than by inner feelings of right and wrong. At the same time, the Adaptive Person has a well-developed sense of self—which means a clear understanding of how he stands in relation to his social environment—combined with a desire to make a good impression by getting along with others.

The Submissive Person has a strong and severe conscience combined with a weak sense of self. The weak sense of self means a loose grasp on reality, combined with a tendency to retire from the struggle to impress others.

The Defiant Person has a very weak conscience and a poorly developed sense of self. This type of person lacks both inner and outer control over his impulses and thus is selfish, dishonest, disloyal, and irresponsible, as the impulse strikes him.

The Unadjusted Person is one of the first three types caught in a frustrating environment.

Character and Personality Type in Relation to the Social Environment

Further progress can be made in the attempt to evaluate the character potentialities of the various personality types by asking how the character of a given type is related to the social environment.

In the stable social environment of Prairie City, where middle-class ideals are the accepted pattern, there is not much difference in the moral behavior of the Self-Directive, the Adaptive, and the Submissive Persons. In general, they behave honestly, responsibly, and loyally. The Defiant Person and the Unadjusted Person, according to Prairie City standards, are less honest, responsible, and loyal.

It might be anticipated that the first three personality types should all have rather similar character reputations, if they go to high school and are thus subjected to the middle-class pressures of the high-school environment. Their reputations and their characters should be acceptable, for they are reasonably well adjusted to the environment in which they live. Certainly it is to be expected that a large majority of people will show good moral behavior if they live in an environment that rewards conformity.

The group who are not subjected consistently and continuously to a middle-class environment should show greater diversity of moral behavior and reputation. This is true of those who do not attend high school. Also, the lower-class group who stay in high school should show more diversity of moral character and reputation because they are subject to a lower-class environment outside school. This was found to be the case, as was shown in Chapter 5. Moreover, a large proportion of the Unadjusted Persons are in the lower classes. This may be because many lower-class children learn habits and values from their lower-class family and neighborhood environments which are different from and often antagonistic to the habits and values found in the middle-class school environment. The persons caught in this situation will show evidences of lack of social adjustment and consequently will fall into the Unadjusted group.

To repeat, then, it is to be expected that, as long as boys and girls remain in the environment of Prairie City, the Self-Directive, Adaptive, and Submissive types will have high character reputations; the Unadjusted and Defiant types will have low character reputations. But what if these boys and girls are placed in a different social environment? What will be the effect upon moral character?

It appears that the Self-Directive and the Submissive Persons, by the time they reach early adult age, are likely to maintain their moral behavior in spite of changes in their social environment. They can do this because they possess a strong conscience and because they are consciously committed to a set of moral principles. If they move from a morally wholesome environment into a morally bad environment, they will follow their principles, even though this makes them unpopular in their new situation. The Self-Directive Person has an advantage over the Submissive Person, however, in that he can apply his moral principles more freely to new situations and he can reorder his principles on a rational basis. The Submissive Person may be unable to apply his moral values wisely to new situations because he has adopted them blindly from authority and does not really understand them.

The Adaptive Person will change his moral behavior if the expectations of his social environment change. The reason for this is that he is primarily dependent upon social approval and disapproval for his moral conduct. His major moral principle is conformity to the mores of his environment.

The Defiant Person will persist in bad moral behavior in spite of changes in environment. Because he is basically maladjusted to social life, he cannot be responsible, loyal, or honest in his relations with any social group.[1] For persons of this type, the basic difficulty lies in their own personalities and can be cleared up only by a thorough change of personality. Or, to put it in another way, the Defiant Person has started so early and has lived so long in a bad environment that his personality has been injured by it, and he will not be helped much in late adolescence unless changes in the environment are accompanied by mental-hygiene measures applied to his own personality. (A Defiant Person who grows up in a morally bad area of a city does not thereby develop *good* character, in "defiance" of the mores of his environment. A Defiant Person would have a bad moral character in any environment because he is basically a maladjusted person.)

The moral behavior of the Unadjusted Person is determined largely by his lack of adjustment to the social environment. Consequently his behavior will change if his environment changes in any important respect. The Unadjusted Persons in these studies had poor reputations and often bad moral habits when judged by the standards of the dominant middle-class environment. If, however, one should study a group in a "delinquency area" of a large city, the Unadjusted Persons in that group might have moral habits which would be judged fairly good by middle-class standards. They might be too honest for thievery and too friendly and kindly for fighting.

WHAT IS "GOOD" CHARACTER?

The case studies give several examples of persons who have good character reputations but whose characters leave much to be desired. Anne, a Submissive Person, for example, is voted high on most desirable characteristics, but she has achieved this reputation by accepting unquestioningly the authority of parents, teachers, and peers. She tries to be what other people expect her to be, without fully understanding what those expectations are or why they exist. She has no conscious moral principles. Is Anne's type of "goodness" desirable in our society?

[1] This statement applies only to the "ideal" Defiant Person, of whom no case was found in the Prairie City High School.

Would it be better if she were more self-directive, more aware of and more analytical of the values which seem to direct her life and conduct?

Curt, a Self-Directive Person, has a high character reputation, but he is uncertain about moral values; every decision involves a good deal of worry and anxiety. He is developing character, but at considerable cost to his personality. Is Curt's type of "goodness" the type we should try to develop in our young people?

Perhaps one thing to look for in appraising the "goodness" of character is its stability. Not all people who at the moment enjoy a good reputation can be expected to retain it. For example, the Adaptive Persons whose main source of conduct is an unconscious absorption of values from their social environment may or may not continue to behave in the same way, depending upon the nature of the group with which they associate. To the extent that the individual lacks control over what he accepts or rejects in his environment, the socially imitative character is an unstable one and is therefore less desirable than one which is grounded in more stable factors, such as personal clarity about and conscious choice of values.

A similar criticism may be made of the character of a Submissive Person. His conduct depends largely on the kind of authority that has sway over him. If the authority is consistent and exercised in a constructive direction, the result is good. Should there be conflict between various authorities, such as the home and the school, uncertainty, conflict, and confusion are likely to be the end results.

For the Adaptive Person and the Submissive Person environmental influences must be constructive, consistent, and stable to produce a continuing good character. These, however, are conditions that can rarely be counted upon. For this reason, although these sources are quite acceptable for initiating perception of moral values and development of good conduct, one would like to see these influences succeeded by a measure of personal conviction. Even if authority remains the chief source of moral judgments, one would like this acceptance to occur because the person has considered these standards and found them good. Similarly, although a degree of submissiveness to social standards and conformity to group expectations may be part and parcel of moral behavior in any community, submissiveness which produces personal uncertainty and insecurity is in the long run an undesirable way of achieving moral character.

In other words, good character—the kind of character which is desirable in our society—develops when the external and automatically accepted influences are transformed gradually into inner, conscious, and personally directed criteria of behavior.

Another consideration in appraising "goodness" of character may be the quality of the motivation leading to acceptable conduct. As was pointed out earlier, good character reputation can be developed as a means of realizing certain ambitions. Thus, David was conscientious and responsible because he was trying to improve his social status. He was striving for acceptance into the middle-class group and was therefore accepting middle-class standards of conduct.

Such an ambition is a valid one and is likely to continue to exert pressure toward socially acceptable conduct. One can, however, conceive of ambitions which, although productive of acceptable conduct at the moment, are neither constructive nor conducive to stability of good character. Ambition for power or for money can easily become indiscriminating as to the means by which it is achieved. There is also a question whether a certain ambition represents an individualistic, selfish achievement or a socially oriented one. Some ambitions are capable of remaining permanently a constructive source for character building, whereas the constructive influence of others may be only temporary. Some lead to socially acceptable personality, while others are destructive of humane and sociable characteristics.

The case studies show that people of different personality types have different character structures, even though they may have rather similar character reputations. In all probability they have arrived at their present characters by different routes and through different learning experiences.

If the student of character formation were interested only in character at the level of conformity to social conventions, he might have no preference among the various personal characteristics which accompany good moral reputation. All people are different, he might reason, and it takes all kinds of people to make a world. It is enough if they learn how to behave morally in the conventional sense.

But one who is interested in character at the higher level—that of conscience and the adherence to moral principles—must be concerned with the personal characteristics which favor the development of character on this level.

First among these characteristics is an intelligent understanding of moral principles and the ability to apply them to problems of daily conduct. Second, and more important, is the conviction that moral principles are worth sacrifice—even the sacrifice of social acceptance and popularity.

Only with these characteristics will a person possess a stable character; and only then can he behave with true morality in the ever-changing situations of modern life. This person will be able to discriminate among values and to deviate from the moral status quo of the community, when such deviation is necessary to the realization of higher moral principles. This person alone can become a moral leader.

To this person society must look for progress in morals. He has the ability to conceive a moral principle, to accept it as right, and to defend it when the moral judgments of the community seem to violate it.

How such persons can be discovered, and, above all, how such persons can be produced in greater numbers is the major problem for research in character formation.

18

Objectives for Prairie City

Prairie City has the advantage of being an integrated community, with lines of communication well established from any social group to any other. There are no boundaries, such as those found in large cosmopolitan cities, which prevent the communication of moral approval and disapproval from one section of the community to another. Consequently, Prairie City can have a single, coordinated program of character development. Such a program would operate through several agencies—principally the home, the school, youth-serving organizations, the church, and certain organizations representing the community as a whole. Through these agencies the community should devote itself to four principal tasks.

1. *Extend the emotional experiences which are basic to developing moral values.* Many well-meaning parents do not understand the importance in character development of the child's emotional experiences. They mistakenly suppose that, if the child is punished regularly for what is wrong and is told to do what is right, this regime alone will build satisfactory character.

But every child in the process of growing up must curb many of his impulses and must yield much of what seems desirable to him. In return for giving up these things, the family must offer the rewards of love and the satisfaction of other impulses. If these rewards are not given, the child is left to build his character upon the negative and inadequate foundation of punishment and self-denial. Only if the child feels loved and basically secure will he readily take on the moral values of his family.

If the family gives adequate affection, together with consistent discipline, the child develops a conscience, which is at first the internalization of the punishing and rewarding voice of the parents; and he develops rudimentary moral principles which grow out of

190

he regularities of his early moral training. The family thus lays
he foundation for good character development. If the family
ails, the other institutions which deal with the child face a tre-
nendous, usually impossible, handicap.

Consequently, there should be a program of parent education in
Prairie City, to increase people's knowledge of this part of their
ob as parents. Responsibility for such a program in a community
ike Prairie City must probably rest upon the school, though the
churches might well play a part.

The school should also act directly to extend the emotional experiences upon which moral values are built. The school offers
boys and girls opportunities for living together on a relatively wide
cale. Children of all social classes, from all kinds of families, with
ll kinds of values are together in school. These children form
trong emotional attachments to each other and to some of their
eachers. Children respond to these teachers and to other children
by taking on their moral values.

The teacher who gives her children emotional security is the one
who has the most influence on their characters. She gives them
vidence of her liking for them. She views their shortcomings with
understanding, even though she lets it be known that she disapproves. Teachers should be selected for their personal attitudes
oward children. Only those teachers who really like children can
ave a positive influence upon them.

Emotional relationships among children also provide a basis for
earning moral values. The more popular children are imitated
by others. Consequently the school should try to discover the
hildren with the finest moral qualities and to help them develop
nto leaders. Some of the instruments used in these studies might
e useful in discovering the children with the best moral qualities.
Check lists, the Guess-Who Test, essays on moral values, and ob-
ervation by the teachers would all serve this purpose.

The youth-serving organizations—the Boy and Girl Scouts, the
Campfire Girls, the 4-H Clubs, the YMCA and YWCA—should
elect and train the leaders of youth knowing that children and
oung people will form strong emotional attachments to these
eaders and will tend to take on their moral values. These or-
anizations need better support from the community, and they
eed to be brought into the lives of more boys and girls, par-
icularly those of lower-class families.

The churches should apply similar considerations in their choic
of leaders for work in the Sunday church school and the youn
people's organizations. They should select their ablest and mos
attractive young men and women and give them all the trainin
that is possible through training institutes and through the per
sonal attention of the clergy. It is clear that most of the churche
fall far short of what they might do in the character formation c
their youth. The church leaders know this and complain abou
the poor attendance and lack of interest, especially on the part c
teen-age youth. To a very considerable extent, the difficulty ma
lie in the absence of young men and women in the churches wh
are willing to give time to boys and girls.

2. *Develop a social environment which rewards good moral behavio
in all kinds of boys and girls.* The social environment which pro
motes good character is one that systematically rewards good mora
behavior. Prairie City people should work to create a series c
social situations in the home, school, youth group, church, an
community, all of which consistently reward good moral behavio
in boys and girls of all kinds of ability and all social back
grounds.

The family should teach the child that reward or approval fol
lows right actions, and punishment or disapproval follows wron
actions. The family should make clear, consistent demands fc
conformity to certain moral rules.

The school is potentially an excellent situation for learning mora
behavior because the child spends so much of his time there an
because he feels so keenly the pain of social disapproval from hi
age mates and his teachers. If a child achieves a good relation t
the social environment in the school, if he gets enough reward an
not too much punishment, he is likely to adopt the moral standard
presented to him there.

For the school this should mean extending and making mor
careful use of extracurricular activities. Through these activitie
children can be given more opportunity to take responsibilities, t
exercise judgment, and to take the consequences of their mistake
Opportunities should be provided for self-government in matter
important to children. Boys and girls should be given the ex
perience of making rules of their own, of obeying them and bein
rewarded with social approval, or of breaking them and being pur
ished by social disapproval. It should be kept in mind that, fc

most children above the primary grades, approval from the peer group is more important than approval from teachers.

With a widely varied program, the school could offer something worth while to every boy or girl, bright or dull, upper, middle, or lower class. There should be opportunities for everybody to do something satisfying—something that is within the reach of his abilities and interests. This is especially necessary for the deviate individuals, who, because of their particular experiences or their particular personalities, do not quite meet the usual school expectations. The young artist, the intellectual genius, and the lower-class child are often deprived of ways of meeting the expectations of the social environment, when actually they may have unusual capacities for morally constructive behavior.

At the elementary-school level a greater variety of facilities is needed—better facilities for work in shop, in art, and in home arts. Only in music is Prairie City already reasonably well equipped to reward the child who has unusual ability. The high-school program, too, needs broadening, in directions which will be specified later in this chapter.

The youth-serving organizations of Prairie City, although rich in potentialities, are altogether too limited in their appeal. They reach relatively few lower-class boys and girls. One possibility worth trying is to discover some existing cliques of boys or girls who are not now in the Scouts or other organizations of this type and to build new troops or groups about these cliques. Another suggestion is to secure as leaders young men and women from the lower class who have made a good adjustment to the community but have kept their lower-class status. Maizie, for example, would make an excellent leader for a group of Girl Scouts, and she might welcome this chance to be active in community life.

The churches, through their Sunday schools and young people's organizations, should provide a companion social environment to that of the school. This is especially important for those churches which believe that their members should live up to a moral code different from that of the community in general. They can teach this moral code to their young people only if they create a social situation that rewards it.

For the young people who have dropped out of school, the church should assume a special responsibility, since it provides almost their only opportunity to associate with a group of their age mates. The church should offer them opportunities for leadership and in every way possible seek to encourage these boys and girls, knowing that many of them are uncertain of themselves because they have not done well in school.

Through the service clubs, the women's clubs, and other all-community agencies a community program to improve the social environment should be developed. A committee to promote wholesome recreation should be made up of men and women from a dozen or more organizations. For example, a community recreation committee might be created to supervise the skating rink and swimming pool at the municipal park; to meet monthly with the theatre managers to discuss the quality of the movies being shown; to get on friendly terms with and advise the proprietors of pool halls, bowling alleys, skating rinks, and dance halls; and to call the attention of the District Attorney, when necessary, to violations of the law.

The employers of Prairie City should recognize a responsibility to provide a certain quota of jobs for young people of high-school age and to think of these jobs as part of the community's program of character building. They should work closely with a high-school faculty member who is in charge of the school's cooperative work-study program. Their aim should be to create situations outside school in which young people can get satisfaction from practicing the qualities of responsibility, honesty, industry, and ambition.

3. *Encourage the intellectualization of values and moral experiences.* The third task is to provide for the intellectualization of values and moral experiences. Thinking about moral experience leads to the formation of moral principles. Applying moral principles intelligently to the varied situations of modern life requires practice under guidance—guidance such as an educational institution is best fitted to give. The school has the greatest opportunity to supplement moral habits with moral thinking.

For the school to realize its opportunity in this connection, two major improvements must be made. First, the school must bring a greater part of its own organizational life under the control of the moral decisions reached by the students. Second, the school must train children systematically to study moral problems and to apply moral principles to a wide variety of situations.

Even though students may take a great deal of time in thinking and talking through the moral issues of their group life—time that is saved when the school authorities make the rules and require unreflecting obedience to them—the school should consider this time well invested in the making of character. The school can add to the value-building experience of the pupil in three ways, all of which are now used too meagerly:

First, the school can create situations which open up new moral values or extend the application of already accepted ones. Students who think of loyalty in terms of support of the football team may be taught to enhance the school's good name through working for harmonious relations between the racial groups in the school. Those who have learned to be responsible for academic tasks may be induced to feel equally responsible for equality of opportunity for everyone in the school.

Second, the school can open up more opportunities for self-expression and self-examination. Book reviews could change from the formality of dates of birth and marriages and accounts of plots to occasions for appraising moral values and examination of one's own values. There should be more chance to talk and write about things involving conduct, motivation, and personal feelings about values.

Third, the school could use the reading of fiction and biography and the study of history and social studies to extend moral perceptions and to lift concepts of good and bad behavior above the level of the obvious and the immediate. Literature and history, of course, are filled with moral issues of all kinds, and the solutions of those issues are so varied as to protect students against a kind of moral provincialism which they might otherwise develop—a provincialism which approves only a certain set of moral practices and which penalizes individuals who have unusual moral sensibilities. In these ways the conscience of the student could be clarified and sensitized.

The school's counseling program offers many opportunities for aiding students to develop moral principles. The counselor deals with a student at crucial points in his moral life. If the counselor will take the time to work the situation through with the student on a rational, reflective basis, his influence will extend much further than the immediate occasion of the conference.

The youth-serving organizations have their moral codes which youngsters are often asked to memorize and which are discussed in meetings. The group leaders should work to give these discussions concrete meaning for boys and girls. For example, they might take the principle of loyalty in "A Scout is loyal" and help boys and girls to apply it in one situation after another, showing it in conflict with other values, such as honesty or friendship. They would thus help their youngsters to work out a scale of values to be applied to new situations.

The churches should also take every opportunity to teach moral principles in terms of their applications to everyday situations. They should try to make their sermons and their lessons more concrete and less abstract.

4. *Provide continuity and consistency of morally educative experience.* Greater continuity and consistency of experience is needed. Psychologically, there is a certain sequence of steps from the simplest moral experience to the more complex intellectualization of experience. For example, persons who have not had sufficient experience with basic value building situations cannot profit from intellectualizing about them. The school should provide these steps in the sequence most conducive to effective learning. Moral teaching must not take place "upside down," such as talking about principles, before boys and girls understand the concrete situations on which the principles are based; meting out punishment when the individual is not yet able to realize the consequences of his acts; or requiring obedience to rules before the reasons for those rules are understood.

A PROGRAM FOR PRAIRIE CITY HIGH SCHOOL

Of all the areas of social environment, the school is the most important in the character formation of the adolescent. Even though the School Board and the high-school faculty may not talk about character education or plan for it explicitly, almost every decision they make has implications for character formation. Therefore it would be well to examine in greater detail what the high school might do as its share of a community-wide program of character education.

Character Education for the Total High-School Population
The four objectives of character development stated earlier in this chapter can all be achieved to some degree for all students in the high school. The first of these objectives, the extension of emotional experiences which are basic to the development of moral

values, is illustrated by the following story told by a businessman in Prairie City.

> You know, when I look back on it, I come to the conclusion that one man probably did more to shape my life than anyone else. The fact of the matter is, I think there's one man in every man's life that molds him for better or worse.
>
> Now when I was in high school I was just a playboy, I guess you'd call it, for the first two or three years. I just fooled around. I never had any ambition. Then we got a new principal. He taught mathematics. Well, you know, that fellow always had some respect for me, and, I'll tell you, I really had respect for him. If I wanted to leave the room to go somewhere, I'd always ask him, and he'd say: "Go ahead, and come back when you've finished."
>
> Well, one day I was feeling sick. I'd been sick the night before. I was sitting there in math class when suddenly I knew I had to get out of that room. I didn't have time to raise my hand or say anything to him, I just beat it straight to the door and got out just in time. Well, when I came back, he looked at me, and I didn't say anything. Then I went up at the end of the hour and I said to him: "Mr. Harris, I'm sorry that I had to leave without your permission, but it was necessary."
>
> He said: "Dick, I'll tell you. You may do anything without my permission, as long as it is necessary and you think it honorable. Now, always in life if you have to do a thing, if it's necessary and you consider it honorable, do it, and don't worry about the consequences."
>
> Well, you know, that hit me, and ever since then I've always thought of that. That's been kind of the guiding principle of my life.

Every teacher in the high school has the opportunity to serve boys and girls in this way, but it goes without saying that not every teacher has the moral stature to stand as an example and a guide to students.

Not the teachers alone but also the leaders among the students set patterns in moral behavior which are imitated by other students. During the high-school years there is an almost slavish adherence to the fashions in dress, speech, and behavior of the adolescent peer culture. It is a mystery, sometimes, who sets the fashions; but the patterns of moral behavior will usually be found to stem from small groups of the older and more mature students.

The teachers will find their own personal influence multiplied manyfold if they can establish their influence over a few students in key positions.

The second task of the high school is to create a program broad enough and democratic enough so that literally everyone of high-school age can find something that satisfies him and at the same time is recognized as a worth-while part of the school's program. The school should widen its scope of activities, both in curricular and extracurricular offerings.

The cooperative work-study course is one of the best aspects of the Prairie City high-school program for character development. It helps to put many students in a better relation to the school, with a resultant improvement in their characters. Other vocational courses should be offered, and the facilities of the school for work in shop, domestic arts, and fine arts should be improved. The case of Nick, described in Chapter 16, seems to be one of a very able boy who lacks motivation for strictly academic studies, yet whose abilities could be released by more interesting courses in literature, arts, music, and social studies.

In addition to adding to the curriculum, general education courses could be made more effective to the degree that they are made more relevant to students' interests and are given more meaning in terms of concrete applications to students' lives.

Extra curricular activities offer countless possibilities for the development of good character. An example is given in the following statement written by a teacher:

Democratic living, or good citizenship, or whatever you want to call it, is not just talking about how children ought to behave. In the newspaper group it is taking turns; it is sticking to a job because the group is depending on you; it is showing someone else how to use a stylus; it is putting the scissors back in the drawer where the next group can find them; it is picking up a pin from the floor (even if "I didn't put it there"); it is moving the typewriter carriage over when erasing; it is calling up a pal to say, "Please take over for me; I have a cold and Mother won't let me come to school;" it is distributing copies of the paper without causing a commotion; it is using the paper-cutter for its legitimate purposes, not "just for the heck of it"; it is trying to put into the paper the names of boys and girls who are seldom mentioned; it is putting the papers in the teachers' mailboxes without disturbing the office staff; it is turning out the light and locking the door if the typewriting room is to be left empty.[1]

Beyond establishing a broad and varied program, the school must search systematically for those individuals who need special help, either because they are not well adjusted to the school program or because they give evidence of unsatisfactory moral conduct. No matter how broad and rich the school program will be,

[1] Nellie L. Merrick, "The Class Newspaper as a Learning Experience," *School Review* 53, pp. 218–226, 1945.

there will inevitably be some misfits and some moral deviates. To help these people the school should have a well-planned guidance program with a specially trained person in charge.

Once having identified the small group who need special attention, the next step is to plan a program for each one. In one case it may be a matter of encouraging a positive relationship between the student and one of the teachers. This teacher may provide the understanding and the conduct examples which are lacking in the home and neighborhood life of the student. In another case it may be a matter of working with the minister in one of the churches. Another case may involve finding a job for the student under an especially intelligent and sympathetic employer. Still another case may require helping the student to make one or two good friends in the school.

The third task of the high school is to encourage the intellectualization of moral experience. The courses in English, history, and social studies should be taught with this as one of their purposes. In literature, for example, many of the books usually read in a desultory way by high-school students can be brought to life and their moral meaning made clear by good teaching. Such books as *The Scarlet Letter*, *Macbeth*, *Arrowsmith*, and *Crime and Punishment* can be dull stuff, or they can be turned into profound moral experience, depending on the way they are taught.

In history there should be special attention to the great ethical characters, the prophets and martyrs of our culture, and to the great ethical movements. It should be made clear by the teacher that these persons often had to go against popular approval and popular morality in order to be true to their own moral principles. In social studies the moral issues involved in social problems should be pointed out. The problems of peace, international organization, capital and labor, unemployment, and civil liberties are to a large extent moral problems. The teacher should trace the consequences of social action on problems like these and bring out the responsibility of each individual to apply his moral principles to their solution.

The student should get actual experience in tracing the consequences of moral behavior in a great variety of situations, common and uncommon. He should also be taught to apply general moral principles in many situations, especially the situations in which there is conflict of values.

The following examples of the critical application of moral principles in a variety of high-school situations will show how the extracurricular life of the school may encourage the development of and application of moral principles.

The time came to choose the junior-class play. Ordinarily this was handled by one of the teachers in consultation with three or four juniors whose talent assured them leading parts; and they would choose a play that suited their particular abilities. This year the coach for the play, a new teacher, asked for a meeting of the entire junior class. At this meeting she called for a discussion of the purposes the play was to serve. After a lengthy discussion, the class decided that they wanted a play which would do two things: first, give a great many people a chance to participate; and second, teach some kind of lesson (a play of "social significance"). Then a committee was elected to select the play. All this consumed valuable time—time which might have gone into rehearsal. Many teachers would have lost patience and taken the situation into their own hands, fearing that there would not be time for adequate play practice, but this teacher believed that the decisions by the class, both of which were moral decisions, were worth more than the extra practice.

The school had an honor society, to which a person might be elected as a junior or a senior, though only the most outstanding juniors were elected. There grew up a good deal of criticism of the idea of having an honor society which distinguished people mainly for the possession of superior intelligence or talent, both of which were gifts. Eventually the students making up the society decided to change their criteria for selection to the society by adding "citizenship." A certain girl in the junior class was a brilliant student. She wrote better stories and poems than anyone else and was a good athlete and a good dancer, but she was unwilling to do humble things. When drudgery was necessary, she absented herself or stood around as if her presence alone was boon enough to the people who had to do the ordinary work. The honor society refused to elect her. It was a great blow to the girl, and she was bitter about it. One of the teachers whom she trusted tried to explain to her, but she became angry and would not listen. Nevertheless, the fall of her senior year saw a subtle change in her attitudes, a change which became more visible as the year went on. She began to do some of the necessary little things, without calling attention to them. When she was elected to the honor society at the close of her senior year she had become quite a different person.

This school is located in a manufacturing city and draws students from a working-class area, which includes an expanding Negro population. Tension has risen in the city, and there have been some ugly racial incidents. Foreseeing difficulty in the high school, the faculty formed a student committee on race relations. This committee has taken the lead in formulating a race-relations policy for the school and has succeeded in settling all difficulties as they have arisen. Complaints are brought before the committee and usually ironed out without reference to the faculty. Recently members of the student committee have attended an adult conference on race relations as official representatives of their organization.

The senior class decided to hold a fair, to raise money for books for the school library. After the date had been set and publicity had been sent out, the country club decided to hold a party on the same night, which would draw a number of the students and their parents away from the fair. Several of the boys and girls of country-club families shrugged their shoulders and said: "Who wants to go to the fair anyway? It will be a bore. A lot of people will be there that we don't know and don't want to know, and the entertainment will be tame compared with what we will have at the club." But two of the members of this group thought otherwise. They talked with the principal and on his advice got the country-club group together and said this to them: "We all want the school to have a better library, and we all agreed that we should try to raise some money for books. Now this fair has been decided on as the way to raise money. If we don't help to plan the entertainment at the fair and if we don't bring our parents, other students will become discouraged and stay away too, and the whole affair will be a failure. We have an obligation to the school that is more important than our having a good time that particular evening."

After some argument they won their point. The country-club group went to work on the fair, induced their parents to come, and helped to make the fair a success.

Finally there should be a conscious attempt to *humanize* the moral character of students—to help them build up broad sympathies and tolerance for differences of morality among different social classes and different cultures. It would be bad indeed if one effect of moral training was to give boys and girls a holier-than-thou attitude toward the mores of other social groups. They should learn to make distinctions between the lesser mores of eating, drinking, amusement, clothing, and marriage customs, which differ from one social group to another, and the more basic moral qualities, such as honesty, loyalty, kindliness, and courage, which are very nearly universal.

This humanizing of moral character, if combined with the rational analysis of moral principles and moral behavior and if carried on under teachers who themselves possess good character, would be in no danger of degenerating into moral relativism. It would help, instead, to give the compassion and humility which are needed to temper the vigor and rigidity of American middle-class morality.

Character Education for Various Personality Types

If the school can obtain sufficient data on its students to classify them into the personality types that have been described in Part

3, it could plan somewhat different approaches to character education for the several groups.

The Self-Directive Person is the type best adapted to the typical American high school. He wants from school and college just what school and college can best give him—a theater for the exercise and development of his abilities, and countless opportunities for achievement. At the same time, the ordinary high school tends to encourage some of the less-desirable traits of the Self-Directive Person—it encourages his competitive, self-assertive, self-seeking tendencies.

The high school can be of special service to this type of person if it can offer him the emotional security which will allay some of his anxiety over moral issues and some of his self-doubt, and if it can help him in formulating his moral principles by giving him experience in applying principles critically to a variety of concrete situations.

Although the Adaptive Person is a delight to school teachers, the school is usually of very little assistance in the character development of such a person. Since these persons are generally regarded as well adjusted, their good character is usually taken for granted. As has already been suggested, the good character of an Adaptive Person in a middle-class environment is fairly well insured.

But in view of the many shifts of social environment to which young people are subject in a changing world, and in view of the need faced by society to think through complicated problems and apply moral principles intelligently and fearlessly, it seems desirable to help the Adaptive Person become somewhat more reflective and critical on moral issues. This should be done, as in the case of the Self-Directive Person, by encouraging the study of moral principles and their application, through experience in making moral decisions concerning the life of the school, as well as through the vicarious experience gained in the study of moral problems through literature, history, and other studies.

The Submissive Person is usually approved by teachers because he is quiet and creates no problems. He will never cause trouble for other people; he will be a good citizen and a good neighbor as long as his world keeps its balance.

However, he is a poor risk in a world of shifting and conflicting values. If the school proposes to help this person become a more independent moral being, it must give him opportunity to participate with his peers in making moral decisions and in fashioning rules and principles of conduct. Above all things, he needs the experience of standing on his own feet and sharing equally with others in the solution of moral problems. He has had too much authority in his life, and he should be helped to develop a more autonomous conscience. The school should find opportunities for this type of person to assume leadership in areas where his talents and abilities will assure him of success. Failure would only confirm the tendency which is already too strong within him to leave the initiative to others.

The Defiant Person is such a trial to the average school that it usually gets rid of him as early as possible. Normally the school contributes little to the making of character, good or bad, in this person. His maladjustment to society usually has its source elsewhere in his life, and the school either confirms it or palliates it to slight degree.

Improvement of the character of a Defiant Person is essentially a matter of improving his personality, that is, of mental hygiene. Unless the school is equipped with guidance specialists there is little it can do for the Defiant Person that will more than gloss over the surface of his difficulties. The best procedure, once a Defiant Person has been identified, is to get the help of a psychiatrist or a child-guidance specialist.[2]

Failing to get help in this way, the school would be wise in adjusting the environment so as to give the Defiant Person as much sympathy, security, and chance to win social approval as is possible, without interfering too much with the school's program for other students. In other words, the school will not go wrong by treating the Defiant Person as an Unadjusted Person, though in most cases this will do little good.

The Unadjusted Person presents the greatest challenge to the school, as well as the greatest opportunity for the improvement of

[2] To repeat a point made earlier, it is not meant to imply that the Defiant Person is the only individual who needs the help of a psychiatrist. It is true that individuals of other personality types may become mentally ill. The extremely anxious, timid Submissive Person or the overconscientious, perfectionistic person of the Self-Directive group may also need psychiatric help. But only a few persons of these types become seriously maladjusted, whereas all Defiant Persons are seriously maladjusted.

character. This person has a poor moral reputation largely because he is not well adjusted to the school situation. Furthermore, he is capable of better adjustment through relatively easy manipulation of the school as a social environment—for example, through adding work experience to the school program, or developing a wider range of extra-curricular activities, or teaching certain elementary social skills, or making the curriculum more relevant to his needs.

The school should undertake to identify and study its Unadjusted Persons, find out what changes in the program—academic or extra-curricular—will promote a better adjustment of these persons to the school environment, and then make as many of those changes as possible. In rare cases, the school may decide that a person of this type will do better if transferred to another environment—another type of school, a job, or something else. But if the school is convinced that its job is to promote the social adjustment, and thereby the character, of all its boys and girls, it will not shirk its responsibility to the Unadjusted Person, but will try to make changes within its own framework to help this type of person.

A realistic examination of these suggestions for character education through the high school will disclose the fact that they are much more easily talked about than put into effect. In communities like Prairie City such a program would involve a very considerable reorganization of community attitudes about the functions of the high school, and a substantially greater commitment of community support for the school.

If Prairie City is serious about wanting better character education in the high school, it must revise its ideas of what a high-school program is; it must pay out more money; and it must be prepared to take the disturbing consequences in its own civic morality of active young minds wrestling with the moral problems of their society.

PART 5

Methods of Studying
Character and Personality

19

Methods of Studying
Character Reputation

As was pointed out in the Introduction, the character of the sixteen-year-olds in Prairie City was determined by investigating the degree to which the individuals in question manifested the traits of honesty, moral courage, responsibility, loyalty, and friendliness. On the basis of the results obtained in the Character Education Inquiry,[1] it was decided that the most practical way to determine the extent to which each individual manifested these traits was to study his reputation among the members of the community.

Since it was known that an individual behaves differently in different situations and with different people, and since it was also known that a rater's judgment may be influenced by more or less irrelevant factors, the attempt was made to get judgments about each individual from a variety of people—from his school teachers, his school principal, his Sunday-school teacher, his Scout leader, and his employer, as well as from his age mates. By pooling these ratings it was possible to get a more reliable estimate of the general reputation for character than by using any one person's judgment.

These judgments were obtained by means of four specially designed instruments, two of which were used with an adult group in the community and two with the age-mate group. Although the four instruments differed in form and detail of content, they were similar in that they described the same general type of behavior manifestations for each trait. Hence, the administration

[1] Hugh Hartshorne and Mark A. May, *Studies in the Nature of Character: III. Studies in the Organization of Character*, p. 369. New York: The Macmillan Co., 1930.

of two different instruments to the same group of people was not
for the purpose of increasing the range of behavior to be judged
but rather for the purpose of checking on the stability or consistency of the judges' opinions.

By comparing the results obtained from the instruments administered to adults with those administered to age mates, it was
possible to get some idea of the consistency of the sixteen-year-old's
reputation. If there was no agreement between the judgments
made by adults and those made by age mates, there would be little
basis for using reputation as an index of character.

THE CHECK LIST FOR ADULTS

The reputation of the sixteen-year-olds among the adult members
of the community was estimated, first of all, by means of a scaled
check list. This check list in its final form consisted of 126 descriptions of behavioral situations in which varying degrees of honesty,
moral courage, loyalty, responsibility, or friendliness were manifested. There were approximately 25 items for each trait. These
items were selected from a much larger number after the five traits
had been carefully defined in terms of the types of behavior likely
to be observed in sixteen-year-olds attending school.

In order to determine the degree of the trait expressed by each
statement, about thirty people were asked to serve as judges.
Working with one trait at a time, they distributed the experimental
statements into eleven groups, the first group including the items
each judge thought indicated the lowest degree of the trait; the
eleventh, those indicating the highest degree of the trait; and the
remaining statements, into the nine intervening groups. Numerical values were assigned to each statement by applying the
Thurstone Method of Equal Appearing Intervals.[2] Those statements on which the judges disagreed most, as well as those which
turned out to duplicate others in meaning and numerical value,
were eliminated. The range of scale values for each trait is from
0 to 100. The final list of items with their scale values is given
here for the trait of responsibility.

[2] L. L. Thurstone, "Attitudes Can Be Measured," *American Journal of
Sociology*, 33, pp. 529–554, 1928, and "Fechner's Law and the Method of
Equal Appearing Intervals," *Journal of Experimental Psychology*, 12, pp. 214–
224, 1929.

69 Keeps appointments.

27 Dawdles at his work.

86 Is very conscientious.

24 Is usually late for appointments.

71 Takes good care of school property.

47 Occasionally forgets an appointment.

11 Always forgets to do assigned homework.

5 Can never be depended on to complete a job.

20 Must be continually prompted to finish a task.

94 Takes the initiative in assuming responsibility.

70 Gets down to work without being prodded by others.

23 Is careless about employer's and school's property.

67 Is quite responsible for a boy (or girl) of his age.

82 Finishes assigned work whether checked up on or not.

34 When assigned homework, does only part of the assignment.

74 Does helpful things at home such as cleaning up before a party.

92 Sees jobs to be done and does them without waiting to be asked.

93 Feels a strong obligation to finish well whatever he undertakes.

16 Never feels any need to care for his room or possessions at home.

18 Lets others do the work he has agreed to do for his class or club.

56 Carries through an undertaking about as well as others of his age.

83 Takes his share of the burdens in planning as well as in executing plans.

31 Quits work as soon as the "whistle blows," even in the middle of a job.

41 Finishes most assignments promptly but in a careless, slap-dash fashion.

76 Works steadily and does not bother other people while teacher is out of room.

74 When left in charge of a younger child, does not neglect it for something more interesting.

13 People soon learn it is useless to assign him important tasks even if he is willing to accept them.

47 Will carry out a task entrusted to him if it does not interfere too much with something he would rather do.

14 Likely to drop or neglect a difficult responsibility without bothering to notify anyone or find a substitute.

xx I do not have sufficient basis for judgment.

The check list without scale values was mimeographed and presented to those teachers, Sunday-school teachers, employers, and youth-group leaders who were acquainted with one or more of the sixteen-year-old members of the community. Using a separate blank for each subject, the rater was asked to check those items which seemed to him descriptive of the subject's behavior.

Attempts were made to have all of the sixteen-year-olds in the community rated by five or more adults. Actually, however, the number of ratings for each individual varied from 0 to 8, the median number of ratings being 2. The majority of those who were rated by less than two people were either out of school or had only recently moved to Prairie City.

A score for each individual was obtained for each of the five traits by computing the median scale value of the items checked for him by the rater. When an individual was rated by more than one person, the average of the median score values was used to indicate his reputation in each of the five traits.

The following table shows the means and standard deviations for the group on each of the five traits.

TABLE 23   MEANS AND STANDARD DEVIATIONS OF THE RAW
SCORES OBTAINED FROM THE CHECK LIST

Trait	Mean	S.D.
Honesty	69	19.5
Loyalty	61	20.4
Friendliness	58	20.5
Responsibility	58	19.8
Moral courage	57	20.0

In order to make the reputation scores obtained from this instrument comparable to scores obtained from the other three instruments, the scores were converted into standard scores (called D-scores) with a mean of 20 and a standard deviation of 4. Figure 1 shows the distribution of standard scores obtained from the check list on each of the five traits.

Although the distributions show that the check list differentiated the individuals in the group on the basis of the qualities being measured, there is a piling up of scores at the high end of the distributions. This means that considerably more than half the sixteen-year-olds have a high reputation for honesty, responsibility, and so on. There may be several reasons for such skewed distributions. It might be the result of faulty construction of the test. For instance, it is possible that the items which have low scale values do not describe behavioral situations characteristic of sixteen-year-olds whose character is below the average.

Other explanations, however, seem to be more likely. When asked to judge qualities on which society places positive and negative values, the rater tends to give the ratee the benefit of any doubt he may feel in making judgments. It is also more than likely that, when a society sets up certain moral standards of

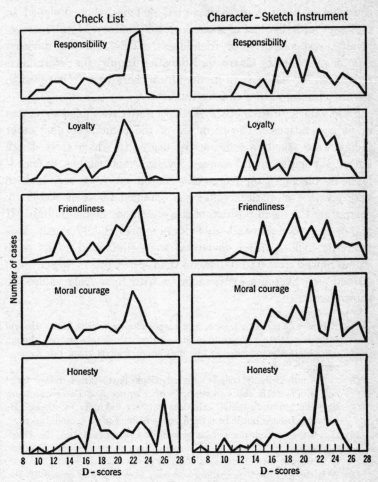

FIG. 1. Distributions of character-reputation scores from instruments administered to adults.

behavior, there is a greater tendency among the individuals in that society to conform to these standards than not. Hence, one would expect to find more people with high character reputations than with low character reputations.

THE CHARACTER-SKETCH INSTRUMENT

The second instrument administered to adults in the community consisted of a series of short verbal sketches, each designed to represent an individual of some degree of honesty, moral courage, loyalty, responsibility, or friendliness. This test was modeled after one used in the Character Education Inquiry for determining reputation for service. In its final form there were from seven to ten sketches for each character trait.

Scale values for each of the sketches were determined by means of judges' ratings. The members of the committee plus other judges were asked to indicate the degree to which each sketch indicated honesty, moral courage, loyalty, responsibility, or friendliness by placing it on a ten-point continuum, from very high to very low. A numerical value was obtained for each sketch by computing the mean position of the sketch on the continuum. If two or more sketches had scale values approximately equal, those with the highest mean deviations were eliminated. The scale values ranged from 0 to 100, the median scale value falling between 40 and 50. Sketches for friendliness with their scale values are shown here.

74   *Y* is a very pleasant person, and people like to be with him. He will come more than halfway in most social relationships. Indeed, though not outstandingly popular, he has more friends than the average person.

48   *D* has not as many friends as some people have. He is rather quiet and does not talk easily to strangers or older people. Those who know him like him very much. He does not talk unkindly to others. He helps his friends but is backward about helping mere acquaintances.

12   *O* is a very withdrawn person in manner and appearance. He seldom smiles, and he seems to avoid people. Since he never speaks to people or associates with them, he is almost without friends.

95   *N* is the sort of person whom everyone likes and who likes everyone. Boys and girls, young and old, are his friends. Wherever he goes, he is smiling and greeting people, often stopping to do something to help them.

5   *G* is habitually grouchy. When greeted, he either ignores the greeting, replies grudgingly, or seems to be suspicious. He is interested only in his own affairs and seems contemptuous of group activities.

45   *Z* is often smiling, although he is occasionally cross or depressed. He has friends of his own age and also some who are younger children and

adults. He often tries to be helpful, especially if it does not inconvenience him too much.

86 *W* is a very popular person who has many friends. He is always ready to help people without being asked. He does not talk about people or do things which would make them unhappy.

9 *S* is sometimes quarrelsome and selfish and likes to have his own way. When in a good mood, he is pleasant and cooperative and attracts people. But this happens too infrequently, and therefore he has few permanent friends.

These sketches were submitted to the same group of raters who filled out the Check List. The rater was asked to match the sketches with the names of sixteen-year-olds in the community with whom he was acquainted.

A score was computed for each individual by the same method as that used with the Check List. Table 24 shows the means and standard deviations of the scores for each trait.

TABLE 24 MEANS AND STANDARD DEVIATIONS OF RAW SCORES OBTAINED FROM THE CHARACTER-SKETCH SCALE

Trait	Mean	S.D.
Honesty	74	16.0
Loyalty	56	25.8
Friendliness	55	22.0
Responsibility	54	23.5
Moral courage	47	25.1

These scores were also translated into D-scores and were thus made comparable to the scores obtained from the other instruments. As shown in Figure 1, the distributions of scores were, in general, less skewed than those obtained from the Check List.

The smaller number of items on the Character-Sketch Scale might account for this difference in distribution. If the raters had a large number of persons to rate and a small number of items upon which to rate them, they might easily tend to spread their cases over the range of items. Thus, a greater proportion of those rated would get low scores. In the Check List, the large number of items provided a variety of ways in which many persons might get approximately the same score.

THE GUESS-WHO TEST FOR AGE MATES

The first instrument designed to get a measure of character reputation from age mates was a variation of the guess-who technique, first used in the Character Education Inquiry. The test consisted of forty-four word pictures, approximately ten pictures for each trait. These word pictures fell into pairs of opposites, one of each pair indicating a high degree, the other a low degree, of the trait in question. The items dealing with honesty are given here as examples:

1. Here is someone who goes out of his way to return anything he finds.
2. Here is someone who will keep anything he finds.
3. Here is someone who always tells the exact truth, even when it works to his disadvantage.
4. Here is someone who lies about things.
5. Here is someone who takes things from stores when he has a chance.
6. Here is someone who would never take anything from a store even if he had a good chance to do so.
7. Here is someone who never cheats in games.
8. Here is someone who often cheats in games.

The test was filled in by all the juniors and seniors in the high school of Prairie City in one testing period. The students were given a test blank and a list of the names of all sixteen-year-old persons in the community. They were asked to match each word picture with as many people from the list as they thought fitted the description. They were told that the tests were to be anonymous and they were not to sign their names to the papers (since it has been found in other studies that the number of unfavorable mentions is increased when test blanks are left unsigned).

In scoring the results, the word picture indicating a high degree of the trait in question was regarded as positive; its opposite was regarded as negative. A score for each sixteen-year-old on each of the five traits was found by computing the ratio of positive mentions to the total number of times his name was mentioned on the trait. Each ratio was then multiplied by 100 to eliminate decimals. Thus, individuals who were mentioned only positively received a score of 100; those mentioned only negatively received a score of 0. Those who were mentioned as many times positively as negatively would receive a score of 50. The formula for this score, which is referred to as the PPM score (proportion of positive mention), is:

$$\frac{100 \times \text{Frequency of positive mention}}{\text{Frequency of total mention}}.$$

This scoring procedure disregards the total number of votes. An individual who receives only one positive mention and no negative mentions receives the same score as another individual who receives fifty positive mentions and no negative ones. This was felt to be the main advantage of the scoring method, because it yielded a measure of character which would not be affected by

TABLE 25 MEANS AND STANDARD DEVIATIONS OF PPM SCORES OBTAINED FROM THE GUESS-WHO SCALE

Trait	Mean	S.D.
Honesty	61	34.0
Loyalty	51	33.0
Friendliness	57	24.3
Responsibility	54	36.8
Moral courage	56	26.3

popularity. The person who is mentioned fifty times as being honest may be no more honest than the person who is mentioned only once—he may simply be more popular.

The chief danger in this procedure is that, if a person is mentioned only once or twice on a positive or negative statement, his resulting score on that trait is less trustworthy than is the score of somebody who is mentioned ten, twenty, or thirty times. To overcome this danger, information was collected from other sources about the individuals who received only one or two mentions. On the basis of this additional information, two judges decided whether or not the guess-who scores characterized these people. If both judges agreed that the scores were justified, the scores were left in. If they disagreed, or both decided in the negative, the scores were omitted. As a result of this procedure, 23 of the 57 doubtful cases were included, and 34 were omitted. All self-mentions were omitted in the scoring.

The means and standard deviations of the scores on the five traits are presented in Table 25.

It will be noticed that the standard deviations are higher than those found on the other two instruments and that they are higher

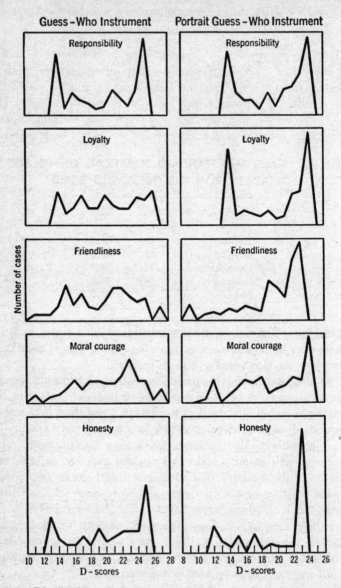

Fig. 2. Distributions of character-reputation scores from instruments administered to age mates.

for honesty, responsibility, and loyalty than they are for moral courage and friendliness.

The distribution of D-scores is presented in Figure 2. The figure shows that there is a greater piling up of scores at the extremes for honesty and responsibility than for the other traits. Also, the range of D-scores is less for these traits than for the others. The piling up of scores at the extremes indicates that an individual's reputation is consistent among his age mates.

The fact that the scores for friendliness did not show such a distribution may be accounted for largely by the presence of cliques among sixteen-year-olds. Members of any one clique tend to rate each other as friendly, while those outside the clique tend to rate the members as unfriendly.

The inconsistency of the ratings for moral courage resulted from the item "Here is someone who will stand up for his rights against teachers and others in authority." It is probable that there is ambiguity about the moral sanctions for the behavior characterized by this statement—some individuals considering the behavior desirable, others considering it undesirable.

When there is a piling up of scores at the extremes of a distribution, the standard deviation of the distribution is necessarily high. When the scores making up such a distribution have been translated into D-scores, thus making the unit of measurement one standard deviation, the differences between scores are diminished and the degree of variability among individuals in respect to the trait appears less than it would if there were more cases in the middle of the distribution. This fact accounts for the smaller range of D-scores for the traits of honesty, responsibility, and loyalty than for moral courage and friendliness.

PORTRAIT GUESS-WHO FOR AGE MATES

The second instrument designed to get a measure of the sixteen-year-olds' reputations among their age mates was a variation on the guess-who technique, adapted from a test constructed by Raths and his coworkers at Ohio State University.[3] The test con-

[3] The Ohio Recognition Scale, "Who's Who in My Group?" Developed by the Euclid Elementary Teachers in cooperation with the College of Education, Ohio State University. Issued by Ohio Scholarship Tests and Elementary Supervision, Ohio State Department of Education.

sisted of two short paragraphs for each trait, one paragraph describing a person who showed a high degree of the trait, the other describing a person who lacked the trait. It differed from the guess-who in that each portrait combined several manifestations of a trait, as they might be found in a hypothetical individual. Sample portraits from this instrument are given below; the first two represent responsibility; the second two, moral courage.

Suppose you were going to choose boys and girls to plan a party, or to organize a campaign to sell savings stamps. You want boys and girls who have some good ideas, who will work hard, and who will stick to the job until it is finished. They know how to plan and they do careful work. They try to do their very best.

Some boys and girls do not do their share. They are careless and do not take very good care of things. They do not do good work on a committee. They cannot be counted on to do what they say they will do. They let other people do all the hard work.

Some boys and girls always let other people make up their minds for them. They will do things they know are wrong if other people do these things. They are afraid of what other people will say. They will not stick up for the right if their friends are against them.

Some boys and girls always do what they think is right, no matter what other people think. They are not afraid to be unpopular. They look out for the rights of other people. They help everybody who needs help. They will speak up against teachers and other grown-up people if necessary.

The test was given to all juniors and those sixteen-year-olds who were not juniors, about three months after the first guess-who was given. The subjects were given a list of the sixteen-year-olds and were asked to put the letter of each paragraph before the name of each boy or girl on the list whom they thought the paragraph described. They were asked not to rate themselves.

The scoring procedure was the same as that used on the other guess-who test, that is,

$$\frac{100 \times \text{Frequency of positive mention}}{\text{Frequency of total mention}}.$$

Since the scoring procedure was the same, the standard deviations shown in Table 26 are likewise high, and again they are highest on honesty, loyalty, and responsibility.

As shown in Figure 2, the range of D-scores is lowest on the three traits, honesty, loyalty, and responsibility. The distributions for loyalty and responsibility reveal a high percentage of the cases falling at both extremes, whereas the distributions for the other three traits show a high percentage only at the upper end of the distribution. This difference in distribution as compared with the Guess-Who Test may result from a difference in the quality of the paragraph portraits intended to show lack of the trait in ques-

TABLE 26 MEANS AND STANDARD DEVIATIONS OF PPM SCORES OBTAINED FROM THE PORTRAIT GUESS-WHO SCALE

Trait	Mean	S.D.
Honesty	76	37.3
Loyalty	62	40.3
Friendliness	74	27.5
Responsibility	60	38.6
Moral courage	66	33.0

tion. For instance, the clique factor is not likely to cause negative mentions on the friendliness trait, because an unfriendly person in this test is described as one who has no friends.

COMBINING THE TEST SCORES

In order to get a single measure of the reputation of each sixteen-year-old for honesty, moral courage, friendliness, loyalty, and responsibility, the mean of his scores on the four instruments was computed. The distributions of these mean scores are shown in Figure 3. Since each raw score was converted into a D-score before being averaged, all instruments received equal weight in the final score. This final score was regarded, for purposes of the study, as the criterion of character reputation and was the one to which other data were related. When the mean score or criterion score is used, however, it covers up possible discrepancies among the four scores from which the mean is computed.

Of the total group of sixteen-year-olds in Prairie City, numbering 147, there was insufficient information on 30 cases to permit a criterion score for character reputation.

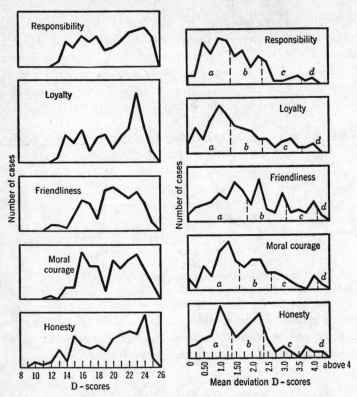

FIG. 3. Distributions of means of scores on four instruments.

FIG. 4. Distributions of mean deviations of means of scores on four instruments.

RELIABILITY OF THE INSTRUMENTS

The authors used several methods for studying the reliability or consistency of the instruments used in measuring character reputation.

The first method was to study the variability of the four scores received by each individual. The distributions of the mean deviations of the scores for all subjects on each of the five traits is shown in Figure 4. The distributions are characteristically skewed, with most of the deviations falling at the low end of the distribution, indicating that for most of the subjects there was high agreement among the four scores. In other words, the four ratings obtained by the individual are not the result of prejudice or chance factors; in general, there is something about the individual rated that leads him to be judged similarly on different tests and by different raters.

The second method of studying reliability was to correlate scores obtained from the various instruments. Because there were four different instruments used to determine reputation and because there were two different groups from whom judgments were obtained (adults and age mates), this problem was broken up into several subproblems, namely (1) What was the extent of relationship between the scores from the instruments administered to adults? (2) What was the extent of relationship between the scores from the two instruments administered to age mates? (3) What was the extent of agreement between the scores obtained from adults and those obtained from age mates? and (4) What was the extent of relationship between scores when difference in raters were ignored, that is, when scores from one adult and one age-mate instrument were averaged and compared with the averaged scores from the other adult and the other age-mate instruments?

In order to answer these questions, product-moment correlations were computed between (1) scores on the Check List and on the Character Sketch; (2) scores on the Guess-Who and the Portrait Guess-Who; (3) average scores of the two instruments given to adults and average scores of the two instruments given to age mates; (4) average scores of the Check List and the Portrait Guess-Who, and average scores of the Character Sketch and the Guess-Who. The coefficients of correlation are listed in Table 27. The number of cases involved in each correlation was approximately 100, the number varying slightly because the scores for each individual were not always complete.[4]

The coefficients range from 0.46 to 0.86. On the whole, they tend to be lower than coefficients generally thought necessary to indicate a highly reliable measuring device. There are, however, several reasons for these low coefficients. First of all, reliability

[4] In computing the correlations for the average of the five traits (the last entries in Table 27), all individuals were included who had scores on at least three of the five traits. This procedure was used because most of the persons with incomplete scores fell at the low end of the distribution, and it was desirable to include as many of these as possible.

coefficients for rating scales tend to be lower than those obtained for more objective instruments. Moreover, the present coefficients were not obtained in the manner usually used for determining the reliability of rating scales. In the latter case, the same scale is presented to two different, but comparable, groups of raters. Thus, the only variable is that of the rater. In the present study, two different scales were presented to the same group of raters; then two different scales were presented to two different groups of raters. Hence not only was there a rater variable, but there was also an instrument variable.

TABLE 27   PRODUCT-MOMENT CORRELATIONS BETWEEN
CHARACTER-REPUTATION INSTRUMENTS

Trait	Check List and Character Sketch	Guess-Who and Portrait Guess-Who	Average Adult and Average Age Mates	Check List plus Portrait Guess-Who and Character Sketch plus Guess-Who
Honesty	0.51 ± 0.05	0.80 ± 0.03	0.78 ± 0.02	0.74 ± 0.03
Moral courage	0.63 ± 0.04	0.68 ± 0.04	0.47 ± 0.05	0.69 ± 0.03
Friendliness	0.57 ± 0.04	0.46 ± 0.05	0.47 ± 0.05	0.66 ± 0.04
Loyalty	0.67 ± 0.04	0.72 ± 0.03	0.67 ± 0.04	0.74 ± 0.03
Responsibility	0.86 ± 0.02	0.70 ± 0.03	0.73 ± 0.03	0.80 ± 0.02
Average of five trait scores	0.80 ± 0.02	0.76 ± 0.03	0.79 ± 0.02	0.86 ± 0.02

In addition, there was a time variable, since the four tests were not filled in at the same time; and there is a possibility that the behavior of the ratee within the time interval elapsing may have affected one or more of the raters' opinions of him. Another factor possibly contributing to the lowering of the reliability coefficients in the present study is the fact that the distributions of scores on the four tests were not normal. Non-normal distributions in general tend to lower correlation coefficients, especially if the two sets of scores involved have different distribution curves.

In spite of the factors mentioned above, the coefficients obtained are sufficiently high to indicate considerable consistency in the character reputations of the sixteen-year-olds in Prairie City.

On the whole, the lowest relationships exist between the instruments filled in by adults and those filled in by age mates. This lower relationship may result either from differences in the behavior of sixteen-year-olds observed by adults and that observed by their age mates, or from differences in the standards of judgment used by the two groups. The highest coefficients tend to occur between the average scores of one adult and one age-mate test, and average scores of the other adult and other age-mate test. The fact that these coefficients are higher than the others incidates that the four tests combined give more reliable estimates of reputation than do any of the tests taken individually or in pairs. As a matter of fact, the reliability coefficient of 0.86 between these two halves of the total reputation score is as high as are the reliability coefficients of most well-established rating scales.

RELATIONS BETWEEN THE FIVE TRAITS

It will be seen in Table 27 that average scores for all five traits show higher correlations between test instruments than do scores for single traits. This result suggests the presence of a general factor that influences the judges' ratings on all five traits. What this general factor is cannot be definitely stated on the basis of the evidence now available, but two hypotheses suggest themselves. One is that it is an unanalyzed and undefined "halo," favorable or unfavorable, possibly an effect of the individual's relative geniality, courtesy, and general likeability. "He is a nice boy; therefore he must be honest, reliable, loyal, morally courageous, and friendly." This explanation seems untenable, however, since the ratings on friendliness, the trait most nearly resembling geniality, show (in Table 28, p. 224) the lowest average correlation (0.70) with the other four traits of any of the five.

The second hypothesis is that the factor actually being rated on all five traits is the individual's degree of conformity to the middle-class standards of the school and community. This hypothesis, stated in earlier chapters, seems borne out here by the fact that, of the intercorrelations shown in Table 28, the highest are those involving the trait of loyalty. Of the five traits studied, loyalty is the most closely related to conformity; it is, in a sense, a reflection of conformity.

If the correlations in Table 27 and 28 are compared, the correlations between traits are seen to be higher, on the whole, than the correlations between instruments for the same trait. This means

that there is a very general tendency for individuals who are rated
high on one trait to be rated high on all traits and for individuals
who are rated low on one trait to be rated low on all the others.
There is a suggestion that this tendency is greater than is the
tendency for different observers to obtain the same impression of
an individual's character.

Although the intertrait correlations are generally high, it is
worth noting that the correlations between friendliness and the
other traits are significantly lower than the others (Table 28).

TABLE 28   TETRACHORIC CORRELATIONS BETWEEN TRAIT RATINGS

	H	MC	F	L
Moral courage	0.73 *	—		
Friendliness	0.68	0.82	—	
Loyalty	0.86	0.78	0.74	—
Responsibility	0.82	0.78	0.55	0.80

* Based on average scores for each trait, computed from scores on all four
instruments. *N* is 77.

Also, the correlations between instruments for the friendliness trait
are generally lower than the correlations for the other traits
(Table 27).

These results concerning the friendliness trait may be because
the trait is less homogeneous than the other four traits. As described by the check-list items, it seems to consist of two things,
which may be called respectively "sociability" and "kindliness."
Although these two are positively correlated, they are far from
being identical. A person may be very gregarious but not very
kind and self-sacrificing; or he may be rather reserved socially,
yet within his range of contacts be thoughtful and considerate of
others.[5]

A second factor is that an individual's effect upon others in
respect to friendliness may be more variable than in respect to
other traits. The rater judges a subject's honesty in terms of
all he knows about that subject's honesty; but he tends to rate a

[5] Because the friendliness trait was found to be so ambiguous, it was replaced,
in the studies made on a younger age group, by two traits, "sociability" and
"kindness." A third trait, "self-control," was also added.

subject's friendliness more in terms of his friendliness to the rater himself. Thus an individual may be regarded as friendly by the members of his clique and as unfriendly by non-members of the clique. If this factor is important, it would cause disagreement among peers and between peers and adults.

The correlations between instruments for moral courage, although generally higher than those for friendliness, are not as high as those for honesty, responsibility, and loyalty. They are lower perhaps because it is difficult for the rater to know whether the conduct described in several items, those expressing nonconformity to popular opinion, is really a matter of the subject's high moral principles, or whether he wants to get attention by being different, or whether it is merely an expression of habitual negativism. If his raters think well of him and hence tend to interpret his motives favorably, they are likely to check those items which will give him a high rating; whereas a less-complimentary interpretation of the same acts might easily result in a lower rating.

As has been pointed out above, there is a high positive relationship between the five traits that we selected for particular study. These traits were not originally selected because they were thought to be generally associated; and it is very likely that, if other character traits had been selected, the relationships among those and the ones studied here would also be positive. Hence there is a certain justification for considering the mean of the scores on the five traits as an estimate of the individual's general character reputation.

20

Methods of Determining Social Status

The existence of a social hierarchy in our society is readily recognized by the majority of its citizens. The members of every community are aware that they have a place in the social scale—above certain people, below certain others. Some people belong to "the country-club crowd"; others live on "the wrong side of the tracks"; but the great majority are "the solid, hard-working citizens." The groups thus differentiated are often labeled upper, lower, and middle classes, respectively.

One of the tasks of the social scientist has been the clarification of these distinctions that are made often only semiconsciously by the people themselves. This process of clarification involves both more precise differentiation of the groups that are ranked in socially superior and inferior positions and a more searching analysis of the factors that determine this differential placement.

In one of the most comprehensive studies that has been made on the social relationships of members of a modern American community, Warner and his coworkers [1] found that more social classes could be distinguished than most people are commonly aware of. Within each of the so-called "upper," "middle," and "lower" classes, hierarchical distinctions were discovered that justified the breaking down of these categories into smaller subdivisions.

These investigators also found that the determinants of class membership were more complex than is generally supposed. The consensus had been that differential placement in the social hierarchy was directly traceable to differences in economic status; the extent of a man's wealth determined his position in society. But Warner and Lunt found that, although comparative wealth did

[1] W. Lloyd Warner and Paul S. Lunt, Yankee City Series: I. *The Social Life of a Modern Community;* II. *The Status System of a Modern Community.* New Haven: Yale University Press, 1941, 1942.

contribute greatly to an individual's rank status in the community, other factors not directly correlated with wealth were also important.

For instance, they found that a white-collar worker enjoyed higher status in the community than a skilled laborer, even though the wages of the skilled laborer might be higher. They also discovered that individuals within a given occupational field and income range were ranked differently. Some doctors, for example, enjoyed the highest social status in the community; others were ranked beneath them in spite of the fact that some of the latter were admittedly better physicians. Similar inequalities of status were found among ministers, lawyers, and other professional men.

People were ranked by other members of the community on the bases of manners, speech form, outward behavior in general, and the people with whom they associated. These factors were by no means always correlated with the more generally recognized economic factors; hence they had to be taken into consideration before an individual's social status could be accurately determined.

It seemed likely that similar non-economic factors might be important in determining the social status of the members of the Prairie City community. Hence, efforts were made to collect the following types of information about the individual before assigning him to a particular social class:

1. His social participation with others in the community. With whom does he go around? To what clubs, organizations, and church does he belong? Since differences in social participation are the essence of class differences, information of this kind is of primary importance.

2. His reputation in the community and the way in which he is described by others. Such statements as "He's a big shot," "He's one of our class," or "When you mention the X family, you scrape the bottom of the pile," place the individual in relation to the informant.

3. His personal behavior and personal appearance, as, for example, his manner of speech and the neatness and style of his clothing.

4. His socio-economic and educational status. Included in these categories are such data as the individual's income and occupation, the type and location of his house, and the type and level of his education.

SOURCES OF DATA

The most important technique for acquiring the necessary information for "class typing" individuals is the interview. By means of the interview, the investigators can learn about the par-

ticipation of the informant in the social life of the community, as
well as his opinions about others.   Other valuable sources of information include actual observation of social behavior in various
situations, questionnaires, and documentary material, such as
lists of members in various community organizations, directories,
and the local newspaper.   The social pages of the newspaper are a
very useful means of learning about membership in informal social
groups or cliques.

All these techniques were used by the six trained investigators
who were studying the social structure of Prairie City.   Their
first step was to discover through interviews the reputation of
various easily differentiated groups in the community.   It was a
relatively easy matter to discover individuals or groups who were
regarded as the "aristocracy," or "upper crust," of Prairie City
and to determine other individuals or groups who were regarded
as "the river rats."   Between these two extremes were "the community leaders," or "the people you go to, to get anything done
in the community," and the "sober, hard-working class who never
give anybody any trouble."   In these early interviews information
was also obtained concerning the relation between certain groups
of people and certain geographical areas in the community, such
as the "upper crust" with "Main Street" or "the West Side"; the
"river rats" with the area "north of the tracks" or "over by the
coal chute"; the "community leaders" with "around the park";
and the "working class" with "the new development" or "the little
new houses by the foundry."

Clique Participation

The next step was to secure, by means of interview, observations,
and clique and association analysis,[2] fairly complete information
about a group of Prairie City residents who represented a cross
section of the total social hierarchy.   Since Warner had found that
social participation is the most important single criterion of class
membership, the investigators concentrated their first efforts on
securing information about this factor.   Moreover, since it had
been found that the more informal participation in cliques was
restricted to a narrower class range than was participation in the

---

[2] A clique is an informal social group of people—a group who "go around
together."   An association is a more formal organization with rules or regulations concerning membership, ritual, and so on.

more highly organized groups or associations, the primary emphasis was on clique participation.

Various key people were interviewed for the purpose of finding out not only who the people were whom they regarded as their friends but also what their attitudes were towards other cliques of which they themselves were not members. Having once identified the relative class position of one or more of the members of each clique, it was possible to identify the class position of the remaining members. For instance, the investigators in Prairie City readily found out that families *A* and *B* were always mentioned as "the best people in town"; that is, they were regarded as being at the top of the social hierarchy. By means of interviews it was possible to find out with whom the members of these families associated in intimate social gatherings. These other people could then also be placed at the highest social level.

The investigators also found out about other small groups, none of whom associated intimately with the first group of people. In fact, the members of these cliques admitted the existence of a social gap between themselves and the so-called "upper crust" of the community. But on the basis of the other criteria for class memberships, such as participation in the more formal organizations, personal behavior and appearance, occupation, house type and location, these second groups differed very little from the first group. Therefore they were placed at the level in the social scale just below the first group.

This procedure was carried out for a wide variety of people. In placing this sample of the Prairie City population in the social hierarchy it was found possible to distinguish five different social classes to which the symbols U (upper), UM (upper-middle), LM (lower-middle), UL (upper-lower), and LL (lower-lower) have been assigned. The U or upper class consists of those people who occupy the highest social position in Prairie City; class UM or upper-middle, the next highest, and so on, class LL or lower-lower consisting of those who occupy the lowest social position.

To get complete information about the clique participation of everybody in Prairie City was too long a task to be practicable. Hence, two other procedures were used for estimating the class position of the rest of the Prairie City population—procedures which did not involve the tedious process of interviewing. It should be emphasized at the start that neither of these methods is sufficiently accurate by itself. But, since fairly complete information had already been obtained on a representative sample of the population and since the characteristics of each of the social classes was known, it was possible to type the rest of the population by means of these shorter methods.

Associations

The first of these methods involved the use of association lists. Fairly complete membership lists were available for nearly all the important associations in town. These included lodges and social associations, such as the Moose, the Masons, and the Women's Club; church organizations; and service organizations, such as the Rotary and the Lions. Some of the people in each association had already been class typed, and in addition something was already known about the reputation of each of the associations. For instance, organization A was known to be made up of the "prominent men in town"; members of association B were "the poor folks and the misfits"; while the people in association C came from "higher up on the economic scale."

By analyzing the reputation of the association and the class position of its members who had already been placed, it was possible to assign limits to the possible class position of those members who had not yet been placed. If these members also belonged to other associations, more accurate class placements could be made.

It is a general characteristic of American society that not only do people choose their friends from their own social class but that they also belong to associations in which the members are more or less socially equivalent to themselves. The use of association lists, however, is somewhat less accurate than the use of participation in cliques, since associations have a larger number of members and in general have a wider class range than cliques. The class range is dependent on the nature of the association. Some are very "exclusive" and attempt to limit their membership, while others are interested in having as large a membership as possible. The former tend to be purely social organizations; the latter are more often service, commercial, or church associations. Thus the validity of association lists for class placements is dependent both on the size and the function of the organization.

Index of Social Characteristics

Somewhat later in the research another short method was devised for determining class position. This method consisted of getting an index of social characteristics [3] for any individual or family.

Fairly complete information was already available for the sample of the community that had been investigated through interviewing. Therefore, it was possible to find what pattern of characteristics—apart from participation in cliques and associations—the members of each class in the sample had in common. For example, it was found that members of the upper-middle class tended to live in big, well-kept homes in a distinctive part of town, to be professional or businessmen with good incomes, and to have had college or professional school educations. Those in the lower-middle class, on the other hand, tended to reside in "nice little homes" in the factory areas, to be small businessmen, white-collar or skilled workers with enough income to get along adequately, and to have had at least some high-school education. A similar patterning of characteristics was found for each of the other social classes.

No single factor in itself was sufficient to class type a family, but a placement could be made if several factors were known about the family. Seven different factors were finally used: (1) occupation, (2) amount of income, (3) source of income, (4) house type, (5) area of town lived in, (6) education, and (7) ethnic group. Each of these factors was classified and divided into seven categories which were ranked from one to seven. For example, occupation was classified as follows:

1. Professional and large proprietors (businesses worth over $5,000)
2. Small professional (nurses, teachers, etc.)
3. Clerks and kindred workers (white-collar workers)
4. Skilled workers
5. Small proprietors (businesses worth less than $5,000)
6. Semiskilled workers
7. Unskilled workers

The individual or family was given a numerical rating for each of the characteristics. The ratings were added, and the total was divided by the number of characteristics used. This gave a score called the Index of Social Characteristics.

[3] W. L. Warner, Marchia L. Meeker, and Kenneth Eells, *The Measurement of Social Status*. Chicago: Science Research Associates, 1948.

When the method had been used on a sufficient number of families, a range of scores was worked out for each class. The final score for any individual placed him within a certain range and hence within a certain social class. Since the Index was based upon a different sort of data, it served as a check on the class placements made from association lists. In addition, it gave a quantitative rating to the families in the community. The Index was tested in relation to social participation, and the two were found to be closely related, though not equivalent.

Since reputation and participation were not involved in determining a person's Index of Social Characteristics, there were a few cases in which the Index and the class assignment did not coincide. These were deviant cases, in which the reputation and participation of the individuals in question did not correspond with the status value of the other characteristics known about them. The number of such deviant cases was very small, and it was found that there were fewer discrepancies between the Index scores and the qualitative class ratings as more characteristics were included in the Index. It was found inadvisable to use the Index unless information on at least three characteristics was available.

As it was impossible to obtain sufficient pertinent information on all the families of the sixteen-year-olds in Prairie City, not all the subjects received a score on the Index of Social Characteristics.

Any one of the methods described in this chapter can be used singly. But if more than one method can be used on a given family, the final result will be more valid. By using one or more of these methods it has been possible to determine the class position of a large proportion of the people in Prairie City.

21

Methods of Studying Affectional Family Relationships

Character, as it has been defined in these studies, is a result of the interplay between the individual and his society. It is the compromise and balance which the individual must accept for himself if he is to be socially acceptable, effective, and personally satisfied. It is the relatively constant pattern of behavior he has learned to employ in order to cope with the interplay of forces from within and without.

Since his progress towards such a compromise and balance is largely dependent upon submission to forces already existing in the social system, his family must be the first potent influence upon the direction he takes and maintains throughout his life, for his family provides his first problem in social living. Within the family group the individual becomes sensitive for the first time to social necessities, and from the family group he takes his initial cues for action which develops into character.

The purpose of this part of the Prairie City investigation was to test one of the hypotheses set up by the Committee at the time the study was initiated, namely, that character development is influenced by the quality of affectional family relationships. As the study progressed, however, two purposes emerged: the first, to devise and validate an instrument for the measurement of affectional relationships within the family; and second, to determine the extent to which affectional family relationships influence personality and character development.

DEVELOPMENT OF THE FR QUESTIONNAIRE (1943)

Since it was impracticable to secure data on family relationships by studying the overt behavior within the family, a less-direct method had to be devised. Accordingly, a questionnaire was constructed for use with Prairie City subjects. The selection of items for the questionnaire was determined largely by an operational definition of affectional family relationships. The conditions believed necessary for good affectional relationships in the family are as follows:

1. The child exhibits a feeling of trust and security in the parents by sharing confidences with them and by going to them for advice and help on perplexing problems.
2. The child has an opportunity for self-expression.
3. The child is given recognition for his work and play activities.
4. There is mutual sharing in work and play, and in making decisions which involve the whole family.
5. Parents take pains to insure order and discipline in the home without resorting to force or regimentation, i.e., are willing to sacrifice some of their own interests, desires, and freedom for the welfare and security of their children.
6. The family possesses "solidarity" or mutual loyalty.

Using this operational definition of affectional family relationships, the Committee formulated a number of questions covering each of these areas. The items fell into three divisions which, although not significant in the scoring, proved useful in testing the internal consistency of the instrument. One section contained questions which were unemotional and pertained only to the routine aspects of the home situation, such as meals, bedtime, and so forth. The second section contained items which were highly toned emotionally; that is, their content pointed directly to emotional relationships of one kind or another, as, for example: "Do you feel your friends have happier homes than you?" The third division consisted of items which implied emotional relationships but which were not directly loaded with emotional tone. For example: "Do you talk to your parents about your problems and worries?"

The questionnaire in its 1943 form contained 55 items to be answered one of five ways: "very often," "fairly often," "occasionally," "very seldom," or "almost never." In order to correlate the results from the questionnaire with other quantitative data, it was necessary to assign a quantitative value to each response. Obviously the question of "right" and "wrong" or "desirable" and "undesirable" could not be avoided. The difficulty lay in deciding what degree and kind of affectional relationships are desirable in terms of present-day standards. To meet this problem, each item was considered by three experienced judges, and the five possible responses were assigned numerical values, ranging from one to five. In cases of disagreement among judges, majority opinion prevailed. In spite of the fact that no common frame of reference had been set up in advance, there was surprising unanimity among the judges' evaluations.

A method for evaluating the items other than the one used had been suggested, namely, that of letting the subjects themselves decide the relative desirability of each item by majority response. This method, however, would have been based on an untenable assumption—that what is done by the majority in Prairie City constitutes the "best" or most desirable. Moreover, if this method has been used, the questionnaire would have had less value when applied to other situations. New values for the items would have to be determined for each new group of subjects.

A section of the questionnaire is reproduced below:

The FR Questionnaire

Directions:

Below are a number of statements about which there is no general agreement. People differ in the way they do things and in the way they feel about them; and there are no right or wrong answers. We are trying to find out why people are different, and you can help us by answering each question as honestly and carefully as you can.

Read each question. If it is almost always true, or happens *very often*, put a check in the *V.O.* column; if it is frequently true, or happens *quite often*, put a check in the *F.* column; if it is only occasionally true, put a check in the *O.* column; if it is rarely true, or happens *very seldom*, put a check in the *V.S.* column; or if it is *almost never* true, or *never* happens, put a check in the *A.N.* column.

Remember: *V.O.* stands for very often or almost always

F stands for frequently or quite often

O stands for occasionally

V.S. stands for very seldom or rarely

A.N. stands for almost never or never

	V.O.	F.	O.	V.S.	A.N.
1. Do you go to bed at a regular hour during the school week?	5	4	3	2	1
2. Do you go to the movies with your parents?	3	5	4	2	1
3. Do you fool around uptown with your friends after supper on school nights?	1	2	3	4	5
4. Do you have your meals at regular hours?	5	4	3	2	1
5. Do you go to games (football, baseball) with your father?	5	5	5	3	2
6. Are you worried about what your parents think of you?	1	2	3	4	5
7. Do your parents praise you when you do your work well?	5	4	3	2	1
8. Do your parents ever whip you?	1	2	3	4	5
9. Do your parents mistrust you?	1	2	3	4	5
10. Are your parents cheerful and happy when together?	5	4	3	2	1
11. Do you feel your parents are pleased with you?	5	4	3	2	1
12. Do your parents compare you unfavorably with other children?	1	2	3	4	5
13. Do you feel your parents try to understand your problems and worries?	5	4	3	2	1
14. Do you feel your friends have happier homes than you do?	1	2	3	4	5

The questionnaire was presented to 61 ten-year-olds and 65 sixteen-year-olds on an ordinary school day with classroom conditions prevailing. The tester, who was well known to the subjects,

TABLE 29   CORRELATIONS BETWEEN SECTIONS OF THE FR QUESTIONNAIRE

Sections	Sixteen-Year-Olds	Ten-Year-Olds
Emotional vs. unemotional	0.67	0.38
Indirectly emotional vs. unemotional	0.90	0.43
Emotional vs. indirectly emotional	0.71	0.72

explained as much about the questionnaire and why it was being used as she thought would ensure cooperation. Questions concerning words and meanings were answered, but every effort was made to avoid suggestion. There was no time limit for the test, and subjects were assured that no one but the investigator would see their responses.

Questions in all three divisions received the same weight in scoring, and total scores were obtained by adding up the numerical values for the responses. Scores ranged from 137 to 235 in the ten-year-old group and from 130 to 237 in the sixteen-year-old group, with 209 and 219 as the respective medians.

Coefficients of correlation were computed between each pair of the three sections of the questionnaire. These coefficients are much higher for sixteen-year-olds than for ten-year-olds, as is seen in Table 29.

REVISION OF THE FR QUESTIONNAIRE (1946)

In 1946 the questionnaire was considerably revised. Ten areas of family life were selected for study:

1. Common participation in work and play
2. Degree of approval-disapproval
3. Regularity in the home
4. Confidences shared
5. Sharing in family decisions
6. Child's acceptance of home standards
7. Trust and faith in child by parents
8. Parental attitude toward peer activitie
9. Interparental relations
10. Signs of tension

Items concerning family relationships in each of these areas were selected from the old questionnaire, and new questions were added, to make a minimum of five items per area. The questions were again to be answered on a five-point scale.

The ten areas were not given equal weight in the scoring of the questionnaire but were weighted according to what the authors thought was the importance of each area in character development. Those areas concerned with regularity in the home, interparental relations, and signs of tension were considered to have the least relation to affectional family relations as far as the child was concerned and consequently were given a weighting of 1. Six areas were given a weighting of 2: common participation in work and play, confidences shared, trust and faith in child by parents, sharing in family decisions, child's acceptance of home standards, and parental attitude toward peer activities. One area was considered to have the strongest relation to affectional family relations and was given a rating of 3. This was the area, degree of approval-disapproval.

The questionnaire was scored by computing the average scores for each of the ten areas, and then combining the ten scores according to their relative weights of 1, 2, or 3. With this method of scoring, the highest possible score for the test as a whole was 90, and the lowest possible score, 18.

This revised questionnaire was administered in the same way as the earlier form, in the school situation. The group born in 1932, now aged thirteen, were the subjects. The range of scores was from 45.6 to 81.6.

Reliability

A test of reliability was made on the 1946 FR Questionnaire. Items in each of the ten areas were divided by the odd-even method, and the resulting scores were added to give two sets of scores for the group. When the two sets of scores were correlated, the coefficient obtained was 0.87.

Validity

The validity of subjects' responses to the FR Questionnaire (1946) was checked in two ways. The first method was to compare the child's estimate of affectional family relations, as determined by his responses on the FR Questionnaire, with ratings made by an adult judge who worked from interview material obtained from the child's mother.

These interviews were made by a field worker during a visit to the child's home. The questions of the FR instrument were used in the interview but were framed in the third person rather than the second person. For example, "Do you go to the movies with your parents?" was changed to "Does the child go to the movies with his parents?" The interviewer had a copy of this transformed questionnaire and was instructed to obtain answers to as many questions as possible without making the interview too formal or stereotyped. Those questions which could not be answered specifically by reviewing this interview with the mother were left blank, the total score for each area being computed from the average score on the specific items answered in that area.

The FR ratings obtained from the interviews correlated with the subjects' own responses on the FR Questionnaire to the extent of 0.39. This is probably as high as can be expected when it is considered that the interview ratings were the result of family relationships seen third hand (the mother to the interviewer to the judge), while the child's FR score was the first-hand evaluation of the family relationships as they appeared to the child.

The second method of checking validity was the one upon which more reliance was placed. A correlation was made between the child's scores on the various areas of the FR Questionnaire, and ratings made by the research group after an intensive case study of each child. The results of such instruments as the Thematic Apperception Test, the Rorschach, the California Personality Inventory, the Interest Inventory, the Emotional Response Test, as well as interviews with the parents and teachers, were studied before these ratings were made. The resulting coefficient of correlation was 0.46.

The results obtained from these studies of validity indicate that the child's responses on the FR Questionnaire present a reasonably valid picture of the type of affectional family relations which exist within his home.

RESULTS OBTAINED FROM THE FR QUESTIONNAIRE

Character Reputation and Total FR Scores

Correlations were computed between the FR scores and character reputation scores for the three age groups and are presented in Table 30.[1] It must be remembered that these correlations are based on two different forms of the FR Questionnaire—the 1943 form for the ten- and sixteen-year-olds and the 1946 form for the thirteen-year-olds.

For all age groups there is a positive correlation between FR scores and character reputation. The correlation decreases with increasing age, being greater for ten-year-olds than for thirteen-year-olds and greater for thirteen-year-olds than for sixteen-year-olds.

[1] See Andrew W. Brown, Gertrude B. Couch, and Joan W. Morrison, "The Influence of Affectional Family Relations on Personality and Character Development," *Journal of Social and Abnormal Psychology*, Vol. 42, No. 4, pp. 422–428, October, 1947.

FR scores are more closely associated with some traits than with others. For example, responsibility shows a significantly higher

TABLE 30   CORRELATIONS BETWEEN FR SCORES AND CHARACTER REPUTATION FOR THREE AGE GROUPS

Trait	Ten Years	Thirteen Years	Sixteen Years
Honesty	0.65	0.40	0.24
Moral courage	0.51	0.22	0.25
Friendliness	0.71	0.35	0.20
Loyalty	0.69	0.36	0.24
Responsibility	0.79	0.43	0.34

correlation with FR scores for all three age groups than do any of the other character traits.

Character Reputation and Scores on Various FR Areas

Correlations were computed between character-reputation scores and scores from the various areas of the FR Questionnaire (1946) to determine which of the areas were most closely related to character reputation. These correlations are presented in Table 31.[2]

TABLE 31   CORRELATIONS BETWEEN CHARACTER REPUTATION AND VARIOUS AREAS OF THE FR QUESTIONNAIRE

FR Area	r
Common participation	0.31
Degree of approval-disapproval	0.31
Regularity in the home	0.24
Confidences shared	0.35
Sharing in family decisions	0.45
Trust and faith in child by parents	0.26
Child's acceptance of home standards	0.34
Parental attitude toward peer activities	0.42
Interparental relations	0.42
Signs of tension	0.14
Total score	0.45

[2] Subjects are thirteen-year-olds, for whom character ratings were obtained within a few months of the FR testing.

It is interesting to note that the area of family relationships which seems to be most closely associated with character reputation is the area, sharing in family decisions, i.e., that area which concerns itself with the degree to which democratic standards prevail in the home.

Another area which shows relatively high relationship to the character-reputation scores is the area of interparental relations. Illustrative items in this area are:

Are your parents cheerful and happy when together?	5	4	3	2	1
Do your parents usually agree about punishing you?	4	5	3	2	1
Does either parent seem to like you better than he (or she) likes the other parent?	1	2	3	4	5

These questions are designed to reveal the degree of affection existing between the parents. Although the correlation of 0.42 shown in Table 31 is not high, it indicates a substantial relationship between the attitudes of the parents toward each other and the character reputation of the child.

As previously stated, the original weighting of the ten areas was arbitrarily decided by members of the research group. One of the areas, interparental relations, which was given the lowest rating, proved to have a comparatively high correlation with the reputation scores. Similarly, some areas that were weighted high by the research group proved to have a low correlation with the reputation scores.

In the light of these correlations, the areas were reweighted. The areas, regularity in the home, and signs of tension, were given a weighting of 1; common participation in work and play, degree of approval-disapproval, confidences shared, child's acceptance of home standards, and trust and faith in child by parents were given a weighting of 2; and the three remaining areas, sharing in family decisions, parental attitude toward peer activities, and interparental relations, were given a weighting of 3.

When the total FR scores, recomputed according to these new weights, were correlated with character reputation, the coefficient of correlation rose from 0.45 to 0.54 (the last entry in Table 31).

FR Scores and Social Adjustment

In the process of the research on Prairie City subjects, the California Personality Inventory had been used. This test is designed to reveal the extent to which the individual is adjusting to the problems which confront him and is developing a normal, happy, and socially effective personality.[3]

The correlation between scores on this test and total scores on the FR Questionnaire (1946) was 0.51.[4] Although not high, this correlation implies a definite association between degree of affectional family relations and personal and social adjustment as determined by the California Personality Inventory.

CONCLUSIONS

The correlations reported here between affectional family relations and character reputation are positive but not high. This may be explained by both of two facts.

1. The instrument could not get at all the facts of the home situation. Boys and girls either did not know, or were unwilling to give true answers to, all items having to do with affectional family relations. Thus the scores do not present a completely accurate account of home conditions.

2. Many other environmental factors besides affectional family relations contribute to the child's character development. Thus a one-to-one relation between character reputation and affectional family relations could not be expected, even if the latter were accurately measured.

[3] See Chapter 10 for a more detailed description of this instrument.

[4] Subjects who had taken the California Personality Inventory, Intermediate Form, were thirteen-year-olds.

22

Methods of Studying the Role of Adults

Outside the Family

In studying the influence of adults outside the family the research was exploratory. The data suggested, but did not prove, that certain adults were influencing the boys and girls of Prairie City. The research methods were aimed at finding out which adults are admirable and visible to the subjects, on the inference that the adults who are both admirable and visible enter into the image of an "ideal self" which a boy or girl forms.

There were two methods for obtaining data, both of which consisted essentially in asking the subjects to name adults whom he admired and would like to be like. One method was called the Adult Guess-Who Test, and the other was an essay method.

THE ADULT GUESS-WHO TEST

The Adult Guess-Who Test is shown here. This form was adopted after a longer form had been tried out with eleventh- and twelfth-grade students in two other high schools. The items which drew the most general response were retained in the final form.

Adult Guess-Who Test

Name_____ Date_____

Here are a number of word pictures of men and women in this community. Write in the names of all the people you think of who seem to fit the descriptions. They may be young or old, just so they are past high-school age. Write in only the names of people who live (or whose families live) in Prairie City or Prairie County.

Remember: Write as many names as you can think of that fit the descriptions.
Write the names of people who are past high-school age.
Write the names of people who live (or whose families live) in Prairie City or Prairie County.
You may write the name of a person more than once if he fits more than one description.

1. Here is someone who always has a ready smile for everyone.
2. Here is someone who is very good looking. I wish I could look like him or her.
3. Here is someone who does a lot of things for the good of the community.
4. Here is someone whom I admire very much. I want to be like him (her).
5. Here is someone who always holds responsible positions. People have great confidence in him (her).
6. These are the people whom I would not like to trust with money and other valuables.
7. These are the people who pay a lot of attention to boys and girls and do many things for them.
8. I am really a great deal like this person.
9. These people are loyal to the high school and support it in every way they can.
10. These people dress very well.
11. Here is a person who works hard to make a success of any organization he belongs to.
12. These are the men and women who can always be counted on to help people when they need help.

The test was given during the high-school homeroom period in such a way that nearly all subjects took the test at the same time. It was made clear to the subjects that the data would not be seen by anyone outside the research group.

The results were tabulated for each item, and the items grouped together into the following five categories:

1. Friendly and makes a good appearance (items 1 and 10)
2. People to be admired and imitated (items 2 and 4)
3. Helpful to boys and girls (item 7)
4. "I am really a great deal like this person" (item 8)
5. Respected, responsible citizens (items 3, 5, 9, 11, and 12)

Item 6, "These are people I would not like to trust with money and other valuables," elicited responses which were difficult to interpret. Two or three of the community's notorious characters were mentioned often, as well as two or three of the "leading citizens" who had incurred some criticism of their methods of doing business and securing power. The total number of responses to this item was small, and many subjects left it blank. The data for this item were not used.

Item 8, "I am really a great deal like this person," drew relatively few responses, most of which were names of family members.

It was stated in Chapter 7, "The Role of Adults Outside the Family in Character Formation," that a small number of persons, probably not exceeding 1 per cent of the adult population, exert considerable influence on the character development of Prairie City adolescents. This statement must be interpreted in the light of the nature of the Adult Guess-Who as a test instrument. There were no items, except number 6, which described unfavorable traits or which asked for negative mentions. As a result, that group of adults in the community who enjoy a particularly bad reputation were not mentioned.

It is probable that in Prairie City, as in other communities, such adults also influence the character development of young people. These persons are pointed out as "bad examples," and boys and girls are exhorted to refrain from certain types of behavior ascribed to these people.

Were the instrument differently designed, it might be found that two small groups of adults outside the family play a role in character formation—one group, a positive role; the other, a negative role.

On the whole, the instrument seems to yield valuable information and seems to warrant further development. One improvement would be a more carefully differentiated statement of items, so as to make the various categories more distinct. Another improvement would be a better balance of the number of items included in each category.

THE ESSAYS

The essays assigned to sixteen-year-olds, the methods of administration, and the method of treating the data are reported in a later chapter.[1]

Of the three essays, "Where Do I Get My Ideals?" "The Person I Would Like to Be Like," and "My Heroes—Three People I Admire," the second proved to be the most useful in discovering

---

[1] Chapter 24, "Methods of Studying Values."

persons who are admirable and visible to adolescent subjects. This topic more than the others seems to leave the subject free to express himself in his own way. The first, "Where Do I Get My Ideals?" leads the more-verbal boys and girls into a discussion of the propriety of imitating others and often into some interesting introspection; but the less-verbal people find little to write about. The third, "My Heroes," suggests that outstanding people of current or past history should be mentioned. Thus the subjects' choice is more limited than it is in the case of "The Person I Would Like to Be Like."

The authors were uncertain about the consistency of response on essay assignments such as these. It is conceivable that the responses of boys and girls are so variable from one day to the next that the results obtained from a single testing would not be reliable.

To study consistency of response, a group of thirteen- and fourteen-year-olds in another school were asked to write an essay on this topic, and, after an interval of two months, were asked to do so again. The distribution of persons mentioned into categories, as shown in Table 10, Chapter 7, did not change significantly over the two-month interval.[2]

These facts support the conclusion that the results on the essay "The Person I Would Like to Be Like" are fairly reliable.[3]

[2] Further discussion of the consistency of essay data is given in Chapter 24.

[3] More-careful studies of the reliability of the essay method are reported in Robert J. Havighurst, Myra Z. Robinson, and Mildred Dorr, "The Development of the Ideal Self in Childhood and Adolescence," *Journal of Educational Research*, pp. 241–257, December, 1946.

23

Methods of Studying Moral Beliefs

There are not many studies of the moral beliefs of adolescents; neither instruments nor methods for study have been highly developed. For this reason the committee was forced to develop two new instruments, as well as to explore the ways in which the data from these instruments could be interpreted most meaningfully.

Chapter 8 contains the analysis of the data on moral beliefs. This chapter undertakes a more detailed discussion of the genesis of these two instruments and of the methods used in analyzing and interpreting the data.

STUDENT BELIEFS

Development of the Questionnaire

One of the instruments developed was a general questionnaire consisting of statements related to the character traits which were being studied.

The first step in the development of this questionnaire was to establish operational definitions of the five traits. It seemed clear that these definitions should describe concretely the behavior reactions to be considered, as well as the situations in which these reactions are likely to occur. For example, responsibility was defined in the following ways:

The individual who shows responsibility fulfills tasks expected of him. He accepts duties voluntarily and seeks out opportunities for service. He shows initiative in solving any difficulties that he may encounter. He is punctual and willing to face difficulties in carrying out what is expected of him. He is independent in carrying on his tasks and in fulfilling his promises. He is not dependent either on his fellow students or on adults. He shows these qualities at home, in school, in his relationship to peers, and to employers.

A tentative list of statements for the questionnaire was drawn up, based upon such operational definitions. This tentative form was examined by all committee members and revised in the light of their criticisms. Committee members also helped in deciding which statements represented positive or desirable beliefs and which were to be considered undesirable. This tentative questionnaire was then tried out on a group of students in a public high school. An item analysis of these results led to further revision— ambiguous statements were clarified and indiscriminating items sharpened.

The final draft of the questionnaire is reproduced here. It consists of 109 statements distributed among the five traits as follows: [1]

Honesty	20
Friendliness	21
Loyalty	20
Moral courage	19
Responsibility	25

Under each of the five traits, different types of behavior and different situations were sampled. For example, items on honesty dealt with lying, stealing, keeping promises, and returning lost articles; they also dealt with situations relating to family, to school, to friends, and to employers.

Student Beliefs

Directions:

You have a list of statements and an answer sheet. Fill in the blanks at the top of the answer sheet, and in the space marked "Test" write "Student Beliefs."

There are no right or wrong answers to these statements. They express what people believe. Each statement is numbered. The numbers in the booklet correspond to the numbers on the answer sheet. There are three spaces marked A U D.

---

[1] Eight statements were classified under two headings. For example, agreement with item number 35 was classified for loyalty; disagreement, for friendliness. The actual count of classified items thus adds up to 105. The questionnaire includes 12 items on family relations (21, 27, 37, 42, 56, 65, 73, 76, 90, 93, 95, 100) which were not used in this analysis.

Mark the answer sheet the following way:

<u>A</u> U D   If you agree with what the statement says, blacken the space opposite its number under *A*.

A <u>U</u> D   If you are uncertain as to how you feel about the statement, blacken the space opposite its number under *U*.

A U <u>D</u>   If you disagree with what the statement says, blacken the space opposite its number under *D*.

There should be only one mark for each statement.

Answer *every statement.*

Do not pause long on any one statement.   Mark the answer sheet right after you have read the statement.

It should take you about thirty or forty minutes to finish this.

1. You should not say unkind things to another person, even if he greatly irritates you.

2. You cannot be expected to always consider whether what you say or do will hurt the feelings of others.

3. Young people can be forgiven for doing some things they know are wrong if other people are doing them too.

4. When things need to be done it is priggish of persons in a group to keep on raising questions about the rightness or the wrongness of proposed acts.

5. "Honesty is the best policy" may be a good motto, but in real life one cannot be successful by being completely honest.

6. No one is an honest person unless his statements can always be relied upon.

7. You should support all the actions of a chosen leader, even if you sometimes disagree with his ideas or ways of doing things.

8. Students should not be expected to turn out to their school games when they are very tired or busy or when they have something else important to do.

9. When assigned a somewhat difficult task at school or by your employer you should be expected to work it out yourself, without the aid of adults.

10. When a school has rules they should be obeyed, regardless of how stupid or unnecessary you believe them to be.

11. It is all right to be late to a meeting if you know that other people are going to be late also.

12. Some persons are naturally carefree and forgetful, and so they must be excused when they fail to complete assigned duties.

13. Students who do not attend the school games, plays, and parties are poor citizens.

14. When you accept a job you should complete it, regardless of what happens to make it difficult to do so.

15. A person should not feel obliged to be friendly or attentive to persons who have few friends, because they do not know how to get along with people.

16. People who are busy cannot be expected to go out of their way to be friendly to others who do not matter to them.

17. Even though you may be called "preachy" for doing it, you should not hesitate to tell others when certain of their acts are wrong.

18. It is not really wrong to exaggerate stories of what you have done.

19. People who have put off completing their school work should not be given extra time by their teachers to get their work in.

20. A person who has stolen only a few times is not really a dishonest person.

21. When the family goes on a vacation trip high-school-age children should have a part in planning the trip.

22. When an adult tells you to do something which is more difficult than you thought it would be it is best to let him take over the task.

23. If you find an article of little value it is foolish to spend time searching for the owner.

24. When it is "quitting time" you should feel free to leave your job, even if the task on which you are working is not quite finished.

25. Regardless of what happens to you as a result of it you should challenge untrue accounts about another person when you hear them.

26. It is usually wise not to uphold the minority.

27. Parents should not expect sixteen-year-olds to come home at a set time from parties and dates.

28. Students who are not interested in school parties or dances should not be expected to attend.

29. People will regard you as a more sincere person if you are not trying to be friendly with all kinds of people.

30. It is foolish for a busy person to take time to cheer up someone who is unhappy because of his own fault.

31. Borrowing things without permission and then forgetting to return them to the owner is no better than stealing.

32. Some matters in life are so important that it would be foolish not to cheat a little to gain them.

33. Students should not insist that a teacher explain to them why they were given a low grade even though they believe the low grade to be undeserved.

34. A person who tries to win many friends cannot be a very true friend.

35. You should not tell your friends about things which go wrong in your club or on your committee.

36. When you have not the time to keep up your lessons and your friendships, it is better to neglect your lessons than your friends.

37. After having warned them, parents should not protect children who get into serious trouble.

38. You should not risk being regarded as a bore or pest by urging others to support a club or organization to which you belong.

39. When the school is run in such a way that student rights are disregarded, or an injustice is done to certain students, you should protest against such practices, even though you may suffer from doing so.

40. It is all right to copy an answer from a neighbor's paper if you knew the answer but cannot remember it at the moment.

41. You should report people who make a habit of taking other students' property.

42. Young people should be allowed to have the family car when they want it, even though the family has only an A card.

43. In case of important decisions one should not choose ways which are easier, pleasanter, or will get him farther if these ways are not also morally right.

44. Some matters in life are so important that it would be foolish not to lie a little in order to gain them.

45. You are justified in refusing to go to Sunday school if only a few persons of your age attend.

46. A club should not expect you to do tasks which you are not willing to do.

47. A busy person has the right to refuse to do a job which will benefit a club to which he belongs but which will not benefit himself.

48. Students who know the required subject matter should be given high grades even if they haven't completed all the required work, such as reports, notebooks, etc.

49. A student need not feel that he should straighten up a disorderly room at school if he was not responsible for the disorder.

50. When you see another student misusing school materials you should not interfere in what is his own affair by trying to stop him.

51. You should stop going around with friends whose beliefs of right and wrong and whose standards of behavior differ greatly from yours.

52. You need not feel obliged to keep a promise if you had to make it hurriedly or thoughtlessly.

53. You need not feel under any obligation to do things at school which have not been especially assigned to you by a teacher or a student officer.

54. Students who are not willing to do the minor and somewhat-boring tasks to help the school and teachers are not really good citizens of the school.

55. Stars in athletics and other school activities should not be expected to be punctual about other school work.

56. It is all right for boys and girls to enjoy being in a friend's home more than being in their own home.

57. Friendliness is all right with persons whom you like, but many people are too boring to bother to be friendly with them.

58. It is all right to use without permission small sums of money (fifteen or twenty cents) belonging to your family.

59. You should drop a friendship if your reputation is endangered because of it, even though that friend has been a loyal one.

60. You should never have anyone telephone your employer saying you are ill when you cannot come to work for another reason.

61. You should not hesitate to express your beliefs before friends who may not agree with your convictions.

62. There is nothing wrong in telling your parents that you were in on time when you really came in about an hour late.

63. It is all right to listen to dirty stories, even if you believe that it is not right to tell them.

64. Since it is not normal that parents always agree, it is all right for them to disagree about matters of discipline in the child's presence.

65. It is wrong to try to avoid a subject where you know your honest opinion differs from that of others and discussion on this subject would cause you to have to express a contrary opinion.

66. A really fine person should avoid an unpopular political or social group.

67. When traveling you should take time to write to your friends, even if the time it takes causes you to miss visiting some points of interest.

68. When conversing with a friend you should remember to say pleasant and complimentary things to him.

69. At a party you should try to make strangers feel at home, even though that causes you to have to neglect some of your friends.

70. It is best to let others tell you when they want to do things with you and not suggest them yourself, since they may prefer being alone.

71. You should not invite newcomers in your school to a party at your home unless you are sure your crowd will want them.

72. Members of a committee should expect club members not assigned to that committee to help them, if additional help is needed.

73. Parents who grew up in an earlier generation when times were different cannot advise the children of this generation.

74. One should not stick with an organization, no matter how worth while, whose members often do not come to meetings and where, in general, there seems to be little enthusiasm for the organization.

75. If your home room or class decides to do something which they know you do not care to support, you have the right to refuse to help them.

76. High-school students should make their own decisions on important matters without troubling their parents.

77. One should never criticize or talk about a friend to other people.

78. If you see things which should be done at home or around your place of work it would be foolish to do them unless you were asked to do so.

79. Students who give much of their time to the school's activities should still be expected to work hard at their studies and not expect special allowances from their teachers.

80. You need not feel obliged to be faithful to a friend who has done something bad to you.

81. Talented people should not be expected to do the simple and uninteresting jobs of the school or of an organization.

82. It is unforgivable to refuse to help a friend in difficulty, regardless of how much trouble it causes you to render such aid.

83. One should work hard for the school when needed, even if this means giving up an after-school job which is not a necessity but which would help ease the family financial affairs.

84. It would not be fair to speak against a candidate who very much wants the office, even though he would not make a good officer.

85. Your family should not expect you to give them any money which you earn.

86. A good father is one who places emphasis on the financial support of his family, rather than on the character development of the children.

87. Everyone should belong to several friendship groups, "gangs," or clubs.

88. High-school-age people cannot be expected to show much interest in the affairs of their parents or other adult members of their family.

89. Although everyone should stand by the right when forced to express an opinion, the best thing to do is to keep out of situations which call for the expression of an opinion.

90. The mother should make the decisions about the home and children, while the father should put his time and energy on being the breadwinner of the family.

91. You should defend the rights of all people, even people whom you dislike.

92. It is wrong to take candy, cookies, or other food at home if you are sure that your mother would not approve of your taking it.

93. High-school students should never talk back to their parents, however much they are provoked by them.

94. If an employer asks you to do a job you think is wrong you should refuse to do it, regardless of how good a job it is.

95. Families should plan to spend some time together as a group in recreational activities.

96. If you had to skip some of the things your employer asked you to do, it is all right for you to pretend that you did them.

97. You should defend your family against criticism, even if you know that such criticism is true.

98. To keep a family happy and to avoid arguments it is best to tell your family only that part of what you do which will not upset them.

99. Since the running of a business is not the responsibility of an employee, you need not be concerned with the shady business practices of your employer.

100. A sixteen-year-old is justified in complaining to his mother when he has been unable to keep an appointment because his meal was not ready on time.

101. When at home you should put yourself out to be friendly with members of your family, even those who are not always too friendly with you.

102. When it interferes with your job you should not talk in a friendly way with the customers on whom you are waiting.

103. It is all right to tell slightly exaggerated stories about your family if that is necessary to make them appear in a better light.

104. You should not tell even a close friend about family quarrels or difficulties.

105. You should tell a referee that the other side should be given the basketball if you were the one who knocked it out of bounds, when the referee did not know who last touched it.

106. You should be willing to drop out of school to help earn money for your family if your support is needed.
107. If someone has "fallen down" on a responsibility he should not again be entrusted with a responsible job.
108. Boys or girls should not be expected to help around the home if they are busy and if a maid or another adult is there to help.
109. When the father is finding it difficult to get along on his wages, a high-school student should voluntarily help provide for the family, even if he is prominent in school and must give up school activities to do this.

The students were asked to respond to each statement by indicating whether they agreed with it, disagreed with it, or were uncertain about it. Each item was keyed to indicate whether agreement or disagreement represented the desirable response. This key, shown in Table 32, was first made by the members of the committee; it was checked and revised by examining the item analysis, also given in Table 32.

Three scores were obtained for each of the five traits: a plus (desirable) score, a minus (undesirable) score, and a score on uncertainty.

Later, a score on "superitems" was added. "Superitems" were judged to be statements which expressed extreme positions regarding a trait—positions which are unrealistic, even unreasonable. In selecting "superitems," statements with which 75 per cent or more of our subjects agreed were not included, on the assumption that these statements represented commonly accepted stereotypes rather than extreme positions.[2]

Item Analysis

The results from this questionnaire raised several questions which could not be answered directly from scores. For example, it seemed evident that some items were more popular than others; that is, a large proportion of students answered them in the desirable way. These were items on which, obviously, there was little difference of opinion and which were part of the common code of the sixteen-year-olds in Prairie City. Others drew frequent undesirable and uncertain responses, suggesting division of opinion or difficulty in taking a position. An item count was made, therefore, to determine the frequency of desirable, undesirable, and uncertain answers to each item.

[2] The total of the "superitems" is 35; the number varies from 5 to 9 for each trait.

TABLE 32 STUDENT BELIEFS: ITEM ANALYSIS AND KEY

Item Number	Key	Item Analysis—Number of Subjects Who		
		Agree	Uncertain	Disagree
Friendliness 21 Items				
1 *	Agree	60	14	6
2	Disagree	26	25	29
15 †	Disagree	8	33	39
16	Disagree	9	15	56
29	Disagree	15	22	43
30 *	Disagree	4	15	61
34 *	Disagree	3	11	66
35 †	Disagree	28	30	22
36 ‡	Agree	10	30	40
51 ‡	Disagree	32	27	20
57	Disagree	13	25	42
67	Agree	39	26	15
68	Agree	51	19	10
69 *	Agree	73	6	1
70	Disagree	31	23	26
71	Disagree	20	19	41
87	Agree	52	19	9
88	Disagree	9	17	54
101	Agree	59	14	7
102	Disagree	25	17	38
104 ‡	Disagree	56	17	7
Honesty 20 Items				
5	Disagree	13	15	52
6	Agree	40	16	24
18	Disagree	11	18	51
20	Disagree	6	16	58
23	Disagree	10	21	49
31 *	Agree	67	9	4
32	Disagree	8	23	49
40	Disagree	10	19	50
41	Agree	44	23	13
44	Disagree	12	20	48
51	Agree	32	27	20
52	Disagree	1	21	58
58 *	Disagree	6	12	62
60 *	Agree	67	10	3
62	Disagree	4	18	58
92 *	Agree	66	10	4
96 *	Disagree	1	5	74
98	Disagree	23	28	39
103	Disagree	8	25	47
105	Agree	44	17	18

TABLE 32   STUDENT BELIEFS: ITEM ANALYSIS AND KEY (Continued)

Item Number	Key	Item Analysis—Number of Subjects Who		
		Agree	Uncertain	Disagree
Loyalty 20 Items				
7 ‡	Agree	22	23	35
8 ‡	Disagree	37	16	27
10 *	Agree	73	4	3
13 ‡	Agree	23	25	32
28 ‡	Disagree	53	15	12
35 †	Agree	28	30	22
38 ‡	Disagree	30	13	19
46	Disagree	26	23	31
47	Disagree	16	20	44
59 †	Disagree	15	32	33
72	Agree	54	15	11
74	Disagree	11	24	44
75	Disagree	23	25	32
77	Agree	58	14	8
80 †	Disagree	19	31	30
82	Agree	46	26	8
85	Disagree	18	25	37
97 †	Agree	38	33	9
103 ‡	Agree	8	25	47
104	Agree	56	17	7
Moral Courage 19 Items				
3 ‡	Disagree	30	9	41
4 † ‡	Disagree	34	35	11
17 †	Agree	27	30	23
25	Agree	43	28	9
26 †	Disagree	5	49	26
33	Disagree	9	14	57
39 *	Agree	65	11	4
43	Agree	54	21	5
45 *	Disagree	6	9	65
59 †	Disagree	15	32	33
61	Agree	52	17	11
63	Disagree	9	28	43
65 ‡	Agree	17	23	40
66	Disagree	25	24	31
84	Disagree	9	25	46
89	Disagree	8	28	44
91 *	Agree	67	10	3
94	Agree	43	29	8
99	Disagree	8	28	43

TABLE 32   STUDENT BELIEFS: ITEM ANALYSIS AND KEY (Continued)

Item Number	Key	Item Analysis—Number of Subjects Who		
		Agree	Uncertain	Disagree
Responsibility 25 Items				
9	Agree	44	19	17
11 *	Disagree	3	12	65
12 *	Disagree	6	11	63
14 *	Agree	71	7	2
19	Agree	51	11	18
22	Disagree	9	29	42
24 *	Disagree	8	12	60
36 †	Disagree	10	30	40
48	Disagree	7	15	58
49	Disagree	18	12	50
50	Disagree	15	23	42
53	Disagree	15	19	46
54 *	Agree	64	11	5
55 *	Disagree	3	7	70
72	Agree	54	15	11
78 *	Disagree	2	2	76
79 *	Agree	68	7	5
81	Disagree	12	8	59
83 ‡	Disagree	5	27	48
84	Disagree	9	25	46
102 ‡	Agree	27	17	38
106	Agree	45	22	12
107 † ‡	Agree	6	30	43
108	Disagree	28	23	38
109 *	Agree	62	15	2

* More than 75 per cent of subjects gave the desirable response to this item.
† More than 37½ per cent of subjects were uncertain about this item.
‡ More than 37½ per cent of subjects gave the undesirable response to this item.

Three groups of statements were isolated: the items on which 75 per cent or more of our subjects gave the desirable response, items on which 37½ per cent or more were uncertain, and items on which 37½ per cent or more gave the undesirable response. These items are shown in Table 32. They are marked *, †, and ‡, respectively.

The item analysis was useful in two ways. A survey of the frequency of desirable and undesirable answers suggested certain general characteristics of moral beliefs common to the whole group of subjects. Isolating the items with a high frequency of desirable, undesirable, and uncertain responses was useful in interpreting the scores of individual subjects. For example, a different meaning was assigned to two identical scores on honesty if one was composed largely of popular items and the other of items which drew frequent uncertain or undesirable responses.

Scoring Pattern and Distribution of Scores

Each item was classified under one of the traits. For example, item 1, "You should not say unkind things to another person, even if he greatly irritates you," was classified under friendliness; agree-

TABLE 33   STUDENT BELIEFS: SCORES ON CHARACTER TRAITS

Trait	Number of Items	Desirable			Uncertain		Undesirable	
		Range	Median	S.D.*	Range	Median	Range	Median
Friendliness	21	2–18	11.8	3.2	0–14	5.2	0–10	5.1
Honesty	20	1–19	14.5	3.9	0–13	4.2	0– 8	2.4
Loyalty	20	2–15	9.2	3.1	0–14	6.1	1–12	5.8
Moral courage	19	3–17	11.1	3.3	0–14	5.6	0– 8	3.6
Responsibility	25	4–24	16.5	3.7	0–16	4.7	0–15	4.3
Total		18–87	61		6–44	19	1–68	22
Total superitems	35	6–29	17	4.8				

* Standard deviations have been computed only for the desirable scores, since all computations in the analysis of data are based on desirable scores.

ment with the key was scored as a desirable score on friendliness and disagreement as an undesirable score.[3] Uncertainty was also scored. Thus three scores were obtained for each character trait. Table 33 gives the ranges, medians, and standard deviations of these scores.

Focusing attention upon desirable scores, it will be seen that the scores are fairly evenly distributed over the whole range. The greatest spread is on responsibility and the narrowest on loyalty. There is only a slight concentration of scores toward the upper end of the scale, most marked on the traits responsibility and

[3] Although, strictly speaking, a score is not "desirable" or "undesirable," these terms are used to avoid the confusion which would result from introducing a third set of terms. The reader should bear in mind that a "desirable" response may be either agreement or disagreement.

honesty. The median on responsibility is the highest. Moral courage and friendship are subject to a larger number of undesirable or uncertain responses. This difference among the traits seems consistent with the observational evidence—in Prairie City, responsibility is emphasized both at home and in school.

The range of desirable scores on each trait is at least four times the standard deviation. Consequently, it is possible to group scores into four quartile groups without overlap. These quartile groups have been used in the comparisons discussed in Chapter 8.

Reliability

Reliability was assessed only on the desirable scores on each trait and for the total. Results are shown in Table 34.

TABLE 34 STUDENT BELIEFS: RELIABILITIES OF DESIRABLE SCORES *

Honesty	0.76
Responsibility -	0.71
Moral courage	0.66
Friendliness	0.62
Loyalty	0.59
Superitems	0.73
Total desirable	0.89

* These computations were made by the formula developed by Kuder and Richardson. See G. E. Kuder and M. W. Richardson, "The Theory of the Estimation of Test Reliability," *Psychometrica*, Vol. II, No. 3, pp. 151–160, 1937.

The reliability coefficients are within the range common to most attitude scales. Although the scores are not extremely dependable, the reliability is high enough to use the questionnaire in ways described here and in Chapter 8.

Intertrait Relationships

One important question in the study was the degree of generality in moral beliefs. It was assumed that behaviors as well as beliefs would form clusters which for convenience could be called traits. It was therefore important to check to what extent there was a variation in beliefs from one trait to another and to what extent there was a general undifferentiated acceptance or rejection of all conduct values. To study this question correlations were calculated for each pair of traits. Coefficients of correlation are shown in Table 35.

As can be seen from this table, the correlations are fairly high, ranging from 0.41 between friendliness and responsibility to 0.66 between friendliness and loyalty. This would suggest that beliefs about conduct are highly generalized; acceptance of values pertaining to one trait involves the acceptance of values pertaining to all others. If the expression of moral beliefs according to the specific content of the values involved is considered a sign of maturity, the conclusion seems warranted that these students have not yet reached a level of understanding which permits discriminating judgment.

Going further into the relation between immaturity and lack of discrimination, the coefficient of correlation was calculated be-

TABLE 35   STUDENT BELIEFS: INTERTRAIT CORRELATIONS

	Honesty	Loyalty	Moral Courage	Responsibility
Friendliness	0.48 ± 0.06	0.66 ± 0.05	0.54 ± 0.06	0.41 ± 0.07
Honesty		0.58 ± 0.05	0.52 ± 0.06	0.60 ± 0.05
Loyalty			0.51 ± 0.06	0.52 ± 0.06
Moral courage				0.47 ± 0.06

tween the score on "superitems" and the total score on Student Beliefs. This coefficient was 0.85. Evidently the subjects did not discriminate between the moderate and extreme positions on these values. For example, of the eighteen persons in the highest quartile on desirable scores, ten were also in the highest quartile on "superitems." Of the nineteen people with desirable scores in the lowest quartile, twelve were also in the lowest quartile on "superitems." No cases were found of a person standing in the highest quartile on the total score and in the lowest quartile on "superitems," or vice versa.

The examination of the case-study materials, however, suggested that subjects were discriminating to a greater degree than these correlations suggest. It seemed important, therefore, to temper this conclusion with certain qualifying considerations.

One important consideration was that those subjects with lower scores may have had a general tendency to agree with all statements in the questionnaire. To check this, a comparison was made of the frequency with which the students in the highest and lowest quartiles on desirable scores earned these scores by agreeing or disagreeing with the statements.

This comparison was made in the following way: A separate item count was made of the responses of students with total desirable scores in the highest quartile and of students with total desirable score in the lowest quartile, to see how many students responded to each item by "agree," "disagree," or "uncertain." For each item the number of responses given by the lowest-quartile group was subtracted from the number given by the highest-quartile group. These differences were then averaged separately

TABLE 36   STUDENT BELIEFS—DIFFERENCES BETWEEN HIGHEST-
AND LOWEST-QUARTILE GROUPS

Type of Response	Desirable		Undesirable		Uncertain
	Agree	Disagree	Agree	Disagree	
Friendliness	3.1	8.5	−3.1	1.3	−6.0
Honesty	7.6	13.5	−3.3	0.7	−7.5
Loyalty	5.5	7.4	−2.2	−1.2	−5.8
Moral courage	8.9	9.2	−0.4	0.5	−7.0
Responsibility	6.2	9.1	−1.9	−0.3	−4.7

for agreement, disagreement, and uncertainty and were grouped separately for desirable, undesirable, and uncertain scores. Table 36 shows these average differences between the groups in the highest and lowest quartiles.

As might be expected, the highest-quartile group exceeded the lowest-quartile group in agreeing with items for which agreement was the desirable response. However, this group also exceeded the lowest-quartile group in disagreeing with items for which disagreement was the desirable response. The lowest-quartile group exceeded the highest-quartile group in the number of uncertain responses. Thus the lowest-quartile group showed more of a tendency to agree or to be uncertain than the highest-quartile group.

A second consideration was that some statements requiring disagreement for a desirable answer were stated in a negative form; that is, they involved a "not." It seemed quite possible that this double negative constituted an extraneous difficulty for students with low verbal intelligence. Upon analysis, however, this did not seem to be the case. First, the mistakes made on these items on the several traits were not in proportion to their number. Second, the correlation between IQ and the total desirable score was also quite low (0.29). Apparently, this particular factor was not an influential one in determining the differences between high and low scores.

Relation to Reputation

One of the hypotheses in this study was that moral beliefs influence conduct. One way of checking this hypothesis was to examine the relationship between the scores on reputation and the scores on

TABLE 37   CORRELATIONS BETWEEN STUDENT BELIEFS AND REPUTATION

Moral courage	0.29 ± 0.08
Friendliness	0.28 ± 0.08
Responsibility	0.27 ± 0.08
Honesty	0.22 ± 0.08
Loyalty	0.18 ± 0.08
Total score	0.34

Student Beliefs. The formal comparison was made by correlating the desirable scores on Student Beliefs with the criterion scores on reputation.

It seemed evident that the formal correlations, as given in Table 37, understated the actual relationship. Several factors contributed to this. In the first place, although an attempt was made to follow the same operational definitions, those actually used in the reputational instruments differed in considerable detail from those used in Student Beliefs.

In addition, only the desirable scores on Student Beliefs were used in computing coefficients of correlation. Since the desirable score is only one of three interdependent scores, it is not in itself an accurate description of the subject's position. For example, the same desirable score may have two different meanings, depending on whether it is accompanied by a high undesirable score or by high uncertainty. High uncertainty in verbal expression can very well be accompanied by desirable overt conduct and high reputation, whereas marked negativism in moral beliefs tends to produce undesirable overt conduct and low reputation.

Certain difficulties also existed in using the average criterion scores for reputation. These scores have a narrow spread and are highly skewed towards the upper end of the scale.[4]

[4] See Chapter 19 for discussion of these points.

LIFE PROBLEMS TEST

Development of the Test

The specific function of the Life Problems Test was to measure the ability to apply general moral beliefs to concrete life situations.

Several problems were faced in devising this instrument. First, because only a few problems could be presented in a short test, it was very important to choose situations most representative of the moral values being studied. This was a difficult task because it involved not only a careful selection of particular values but also an accurate prediction as to what meaning or emotional effect each situation had for different individuals. It was difficult to determine, for example, whether honesty was to be represented by stealing or some other behavior, and whether the situation should involve the family or the school.

Second, to obtain even moderately valid results, it was important to have situations which were concrete and challenging and which at the same time would not arouse such highly individualized reactions to the details of the situation as to obscure the main issues. In other words, it was necessary to make the problems real to the student while avoiding deviate emotional responses.

The field worker was therefore asked to assemble suggestions for the appropriate types of situations from her observations in the school. Tentative formulations of these situations were then presented to students in another community. The tentative instrument included only the statement of the problem and alternative courses of action. The students were asked to choose the best course of action and to give in writing their reasons for the choice. The resulting material was used in the final formulation of the test as it appears below.

The test consists of eight situations presenting problems of conduct in school, at home, with friends, and in school activities. Each problem introduces a conflict of values, such as a conflict between friendship and responsibility, loyalty and self-interest, and so on. Courses of action presenting desirable and undesirable alternatives follow each problem.

A list of reasons is then given, from which the student chooses those which support his choices. These reasons usually represent both positive and negative values, such as telling the truth and lying. Most exercises introduce values related to several traits. Reasons expressing selfish personal interest are also included. The directions leave the student free to choose any number of reasons. This is done to get an estimate of the inclusiveness of his reasoning.

The key for the test was made in the following way: For each course of action, there were a certain number of logically related reasons. For example, in Problem I, reason number 1 logically supports course of action *B*. For the course of action *B*, reason number 1 would be scored as consistency, while its use for either *A* or *C* would be scored as inconsistency.

Each reason was also classified as to the values it expressed, both positive and negative. Thus reason number 1 in Problem I is scored minus on honesty, while reason number 6 is scored plus on honesty. This key made it possible to assign the following scores, illustrated in Table 38.

1. The total number of reasons marked.

2. Percentage inconsistency; that is, the proportion of reasons used which did not logically support a chosen course of action.

3. Three scores on values for each trait: (*a*) a plus score for the number of desirable reasons; (*b*) a minus score for the number of undesirable reasons; and (*c*) a percentage-plus score indicating the proportion of desirable values among all reasons used. The percentage-plus score was computed in order to neutralize the effect of the differences in the numbers of reasons used.

Life Problems

Name_____ School_____

Grade_____ Date_____

Directions:

This is not a test. There are no right and wrong answers to the problems which you will find described in this booklet. Each person should decide what is best to do in each situation. He should mark only those reasons which express his own feelings.

Please read the problems carefully enough to be sure you understand them.

Problem I

Bill was one of the key players on the football team which was scheduled for an important game. In order to play he had to pass examinations in all his courses. Because of extra football practice, he did not know the answers to several questions on the monthly English test, though usually he was a good student. He asked Glen who sat next to him to give him some of the answers. The teacher suspected Bill had gotten help and asked Glen about it. Glen knew that the teacher would not forgive Bill and that Bill could not play if it were known that he had gotten help on the English test.

What should Glen do? (Check which statement you think is best.)

_____ A. Tell her the truth.

_____ B. Say he knew nothing about it.

_____ C. Suggest that the teacher had better ask Bill.

Why? (Check in the spaces below the reasons that express *why you believe* the action which you have checked is best.)

Key*		Reasons
H –	B	_____ 1.† Everybody at one time or another does something dishonest and is forced to tell a white lie.
H –	BC	_____ 2. Not even the most honest person likes a tattler.
F– L– H+	A	_____ 3.† Having cheated, Bill is not a good sportsman anyway and not worth protecting.
H –	B	_____ 4.† Some things are so important that it would be foolish not to lie a little to gain them.
F+ L+ H–	BC	_____ 5. One should never talk against a friend.
H+	A	_____ 6. Dishonesty in this case would be worse than the risk of losing the game.
		_____ 7. Glen was a partner to cheating and should be man enough to stick it out.
PB	BC	_____ 8. The best policy is to avoid trouble with the teacher as well as with Bill.
H+	A	_____ 9. Honesty is the best policy in all cases.
F+ L+	B	_____10. One should not go back on a friend who trusted you, when he needs help.
F+ L+ H+	C	_____11. One should avoid lying as well as being a stool pigeon.
H+	A	_____12. Telling the truth is the best policy even at the expense of losing the game.
F+ L+ H–	B	_____13.† Under the circumstances it is Glen's duty to protect Bill.
PB F+ L+ H+	A	_____14. Not telling the truth would put both Glen and Bill in bad with the teacher.
H+	BC	_____15.‡ The person who did the cheating should be the one to tell the teacher.

* H, R, MC, L, F, PB refer to the values honesty, responsibility, moral courage, loyalty, friendliness, and personal benefit. The plus sign indicates that the item is given a positive score for the particular value; the minus sign, that the item is given a negative score for that value. A, B, C, D refer to consistency. A means the reason is consistent with course of action A.

† Less than 15 per cent of subjects checked this reason.

‡ More than 50 per cent of subjects checked this reason.

Problem II

Earl is carrying a heavy study schedule and takes part in many interests and activities. He also works on Saturdays for spending money. Well towards the middle of the year the photography editor of the yearbook is found to be unable to manage the job, and Earl is asked to take his job as he is best qualified. Earl knows that if he accepts this job, he will either have to drop his hobbies, drop a subject, or run the risk of getting poorer grades.

What should Earl do? (Check which statement you think is best.)

____ A. Under the circumstances he is justified in refusing the job.
____ B. He should accept the job.

Why? (Check in the spaces below the reasons that express *why you believe* the action which you have checked is best.)

Key		Reasons
R + L +	B	____ 1.† Students in a school have the responsibility of helping with school affairs.
R −	A	____ 2. No job on the yearbook is more important than grades and subjects.
PB R −	A	____ 3.‡ One does most for the school by keeping up one's work and interests.
R +	B	____ 4.† Personal inconveniences, such as having no time for hobbies, are less important than the success of the yearbook.
PB	A	____ 5.‡ Hobbies and interests help him during his whole life, while his work on the yearbook will only make the yearbook better for one year.
R + L +	B	____ 6. It means a lot to the school to have a good yearbook.
PB R −	A	____ 7. A student should not be expected to work on school affairs unless he can conveniently spare the time.
PB R −	A	____ 8.† Since he was the second choice, Earl should not give up anything that is important to him for this job on the yearbook.
R + L +	B	____ 9.† Good citizens of a school should be willing to do the hard jobs for the school.
PB R −	A	____10. A student's first duty is to do the things he either likes or which help him in his life career.
PB R +	B	____11. The experience as editor may be helpful for him in later life.
PB R −	A	____12.† High-school students go to school to educate themselves and not to help out the school.
PB	B	____13. Editing a yearbook will give Earl a chance to become more popular.

Problem III

A committee was appointed to take care of the scrap collection in the school. Bob was a member of the committee. His task was that of weighing the scrap. The chairman who was popular was careless in his work. Bob found it difficult to do his share well without also doing some of the work the chairman was supposed to do. He spoke about it to the chairman, but the chairman did nothing about it. Many other students defended the chairman because he was so well liked.

What should Bob do? (Check which statement you think is the best.)

_____ A. Do the things that the chairman was supposed to do, and say nothing about it.

_____ B. Propose that someone else be appointed as chairman.

_____ C. Do his own job well enough to get by and not worry about the rest.

_____ D. Resign from his job quietly.

Why? (Check in the spaces below the reasons that express *why you believe* the action which you have checked is best.)

Key		Reasons
R+ MC+	B	___ 1. This job is important enough for Bob to reveal the inefficiency of the chairman, even if that makes Bob unpopular.
R− MC−	C	___ 2. Bob's duty is to act as a committee member; he will not be thanked for butting into affairs which are not his business.
PB MC−	AC	___ 3. People who complain about how things are run are not well liked.
R+	D	___ 4.† If Bob resigns, the scrap activities are likely to be organized better.
R+ MC−	D	___ 5.† Under the circumstances there is nothing Bob can do about poor leadership except to get out.
MC−	C	___ 6. Bob has done his duty by doing his own part as well as he can.
R+	A	___ 7. Responsible people do the work that needs to be done, even if it includes things other people should be doing.
PB R− MC−	C	___ 8.† Bob would save himself trouble with the chairman and other students by doing his part and not trying to oust the chairman or to take over the chairman's duties.
R− MC−	AC	___ 9.† As a member of the committee, Bob should avoid causing hard feelings on the part of the chairman.

Key		Reasons
R+ MC+	B	____10. Important work should be done right, and it is the duty of Bob to see to it that it is done under efficient leadership.
R+	A	____11. It's all for a good cause, and so it really doesn't matter who does the work or who gets the credit for it.
PB R−	CD	____12.† Why work hard on something for which another gets the credit?
R− MC+	CD	____13. There is no sense in a person doing all the work to cover up another person's inadequacy.
PB MC−	ACD	____14.† If Bob criticizes the chairman, it will look as if he wants to be appointed chairman.
PB	ABD	____15. Poor work by the committee would not be Bob's fault, but it would still reflect on Bob if the committee made a poor showing.
PB MC−	D	____16.† By resigning, Bob will avoid being party to a failure.
R+ MC+	B	____17. A careless and inefficient chairman does not deserve the honor or privilege of his position.
R+ MC+	D	____18.† Bob's resigning would make the chairman face his responsibility.

Problem IV

Carl and Jim were friends and kept their books and coats in the same locker. Both boys were interested in reading a great deal and took out books from the school library. Carl had a job helping to check books out in the library. One day a new and interesting book for which there was a long waiting list disappeared. The librarian asked Carl to find out where the book was. Carl asked Jim about it, but Jim said he knew nothing about the book. Three days later Carl was cleaning out the locker and saw the book among Jim's things.

What should Carl do? (Check which statement you think is best.)

____ A. Take up the problem with both Jim and the librarian.
____ B. Give Jim a chance to return the book unnoticed.
____ C. Let the matter pass.

Why? (Check in the spaces below the reasons that express *why you believe* the action which you have checked is best.)

Key		Reasons
L– H–	A	_____ 1.‡ Both boys would have a clear conscience by clearing the matter with the librarian.
F+ MC– L+ H–	BC	_____ 2. By keeping quiet about having found the book, Carl would avoid telling a lie as well as embarrassing a friend.
R+ MC+ H+	A	_____ 3. Carl's duty as a helper in the library is to see to it that irregularities about borrowing books are reported.
F+ MC– L+ H–	BC	_____ 4.† One should not tell on a friend, even if it involves untruth.
F+ L+	BC	_____ 5. One does not break up a friendship because of a book.
F+ L+ H–	B	_____ 6. Taking books out of the library is a small matter, and Jim could be saved the embarrassment of returning the book to the librarian.
F+ MC– L+ H–	BC	_____ 7.† Carl should not run the risk of impairing his friendship with Jim.
R– H–	C	_____ 8.† It is not Carl's duty to report things he has found out accidentally outside the library.
F– L– H+	A	_____ 9. In this case, honesty is a better policy than protecting a friend.
F+ L+ H–	B	_____10.† Jim's friendship with Carl obligates Carl to help Jim.
F– L– H+	A	_____11. If Jim disobeyed the rules, he should face the consequences for doing it.
R– H–	C	_____12.† It is no affair of Carl's if Jim wishes to break library rules.
F– L– H+	A	_____13. "Borrowing" books in the way Jim did is being unfair to other students and should not be overlooked.

Problem V

A high school was planning an entertainment to earn some money for their athletic equipment. The dramatic club which was in charge assigned all students something to do. Some had parts in the skit; some arranged stage lighting; others sold tickets. All the members of the club could stay inside during the entertainment. One boy who was not a member of the dramatic club was asked to stand outside and keep youngsters from climbing up on the window ledges.

What should this boy do? (Check which statement you think is best.)

_____ A. This boy should accept this task without questioning.
_____ B. He should refuse to do it.
_____ C. He should agree to watch only part of the time.

Why? (Check in the spaces below the reasons that express *why you believe* the action you have checked is best.)

Key		Reasons
PB R+	*AC*	____ 1.‡ He would probably be liked much better for doing his job.
PB R−	*B*	____ 2. He should not be expected to play stooge while others were having fun.
	AC	____ 3. Since he probably was going to use the athletic equipment, he could put in a little time watching.
R− L−	*B*	____ 4.† Since the entertainment was in the hands of the club, its members should be responsible for the worst job.
R+ F+	*AC*	____ 5. No one else would like this responsibility any better than he did.
PB R−	*B*	____ 6.† Those who get the credit should take the responsibility for the unpleasant jobs.
PB R+	*A*	____ 7. By asking him, other people showed they had confidence in him and he should be proud.
R−	*B*	____ 8.† The dramatic club had no right to ask him in the first place.
PB L+	*AC*	____ 9. To refuse altogether would show him up as a person who cares nothing for the school.
R+	*AC*	____10.‡ In life there are always unpleasant things to be done, and one should train oneself for them.
R+	*C*	____11.† By working part of the time this boy has done all that can be expected of him.
R+	*A*	____12. Everyone should contribute all they can to making the show a success.
PB R−	*B*	____13. He should have an equal chance with others to watch the fun.
R+	*C*	____14. It is only fair that other students should share in this responsibility.
R+ L+	*AC*	____15.‡ The entertainment is for the benefit of the school, even though it was managed by the club.

Problem VI

Judy admires Helen very much and wants to belong to the group that is often invited to Helen's house. Once, while Judy is visiting Helen with some other girls, Helen makes some quite damaging remarks about Nancy. Judy knows Nancy only slightly, but she is sure the things Helen says are not true. She also knows that Helen gets angry easily when crossed and that Helen is not likely to invite her again if she offends her.

What should Judy do? (Check which statement you think is best.)

____ *A.* Keep quiet and ignore the remarks.

____ *B.* Defend Nancy.

Why? (Check in the spaces below the reasons that express *why you believe* the action which you have checked is best.)

Key		Reasons
F— MC—	A	___ 1. Such gossip and critical remarks are not serious enough to make a fuss over them.
F+ MC+	B	___ 2.‡ When someone's reputation is at stake, it is cowardly not to stand up for the truth.
PB F— MC—	A	___ 3.† Judy would be foolish to risk Helen's friendship and that of her group by defending a mere acquaintance.
F+ MC+	B	___ 4.‡ Judy's conscience would bother her if she failed to defend Nancy.
PB F— MC—	A	___ 5.† There is not much point in defending a person who does not matter to you.
MC+	B	___ 6.‡ If Judy wants friends, the best way to get them is to show that she is loyal and courageous in defending others.
F+ MC—	A	___ 7. One should avoid being impolite to a friend whose house one is visiting.
MC+	B	___ 8.‡ If Helen is offended by the truth, she is no friend worth having.
PB F— MC—	A	___ 9. In such a case a wise person will avoid the issue and will neither agree with Helen nor defend Nancy.
F+ MC+	B	___10. It is wrong to keep quiet when a person who cannot defend herself is being talked about.
F+ MC+	B	___11. Judy would be as bad as Helen if she listened to untruths about Nancy and did not try to defend her.

Problem VII

Mary, a junior in high school, has been invited to a party at Jean's home. Mary's best friends have also been invited and are all planning to attend. However, Mary's mother very much disapproves of Jean's family. Mary knows that her mother has such a strong feeling on this subject that if she knows that the party is at Jean's home she will be forbidden to attend. Mary herself wants very much to go to the party and is sure that she will have a good time. What should she do?

If you were this student, what do you think would be the best thing to do? (Check which statement you think is best.)

___ *A.* She should tell her mother about the party.

___ *B.* She should go to the party and tell her mother about it after it is over.

___ *C.* She should go to the party and say it is somewhere else.

Why? (Check in the spaces below the reasons that express *why you believe* the action which you have checked is best.)

Key		Reasons
H+	A	____ 1.‡ One should not deceive one's mother, even though one may suffer thereby.
H−	BC	____ 2.† What parents do not know does not hurt them.
H−	C	____ 3.† To keep a family happy and to avoid arguments, it is best to tell only that part of what you do which will not upset them.
H−	B	____ 4.† It is all right for the young people to do what their parents disapprove as long as they tell afterwards.
H+	A	____ 5.‡ Being honest with parents and having them trust you is more important than an evening of fun.
H−	C	____ 6.† As long as nothing wrong is done, it is better to tell an occasional untruth than to aggravate parents.
H+	A	____ 7.‡ Truth is always the best thing.
H−	B	____ 8.† By telling about the party later, Mary will not have lied.
H−	BC	____ 9.† One cannot be completely honest with parents when they have foolish ideas.
F+ H−	BC	____10.† For young people it is more important to keep their friends than to tell their parents everything they do.
H+	A	____11. If Mary wants to go, it would be better for her to disobey her mother than to tell her a lie.
F+ H−	C	____12.† Keeping friends is so important that it would be foolish not to tell a little fib to accomplish that.
H+	A	____13.‡ In life we have to sacrifice fun for the sake of honesty.
H−	B	____14.† It is better to keep quiet than to tell an outright lie.

Problem VIII

George had started a group in school, which had been trying to do something about keeping order in the halls and believed in what they were doing. Against George's advice some of the members used bossy methods and got into a scrap with some of the students. The result was that this group became unpopular and became known as a police squad. Members of this group were shunned by others, and several of George's friends made fun of him.

What should George do? (Check the statement you think is best.)

____ A. Stop working with the project.

____ B. Stay with the group and keep on working on the project.

____ C. Try to help the project along, but drop out of the group.

Why? (Check in the spaces below the reasons that express *why you believe* the action which you have checked is best.)

Key		Reasons
F+ L−	A	____ 1.† One's reputation with friends is worth more than sticking with an unsuccessful group project.
L+	B	____ 2.‡ It is not right to desert a group one has been working with, in time of trouble.
R+ L+	B	____ 3. If George gives up the project he will be regarded as a quitter.
F− MC+ L+	B	____ 4.‡ It is foolish to be influenced by the razzing of friends, if one knows one is right.
PB L−	A	____ 5.† George has a perfect right to stop working with the group because they did not follow his advice.
MC− L+	C	____ 6.† By dropping out without deserting the project, George might awaken the members of this group to their mistakes.
PB L−	AC	____ 7.† It is not wise to be associated with a group that has a bad name.
PB L+	B	____ 8. George could win a reputation for himself by influencing the group and making the project successful.
PB R+ L−	C	____ 9.† By working without belonging to the group, George can help the project without hurting himself.
R+ L+	B	____10.‡ One should always stick out the difficulties when working for a worth-while cause.
MC− L−	AC	____11.† A group that does not know how to get along with others does not deserve support.
R− L−	A	____12.† As long as there is difficulty in getting cooperation from other students, it is no use carrying on.
PB R− L−	AC	____13.† It is important to protect one's reputation by not belonging to an unpopular group.

This multiple scoring has its advantages and disadvantages. It is extremely difficult to include a sufficient sample of reasons for each type of score. Furthermore, since students are free to mark as many or as few reasons as they choose, the part scores are often extremely small and therefore undependable. On the other hand, for diagnosing value patterns and reasoning, a pattern of responses provides a more valid picture of an individual than does a single score, even if the single score has greater dependability.

In our case studies, the multiple scores proved valuable. The percentage-plus scores on values were used most consistently in interpretation. The plus and minus scores were used primarily to indicate the relative proportions of desirable and undesirable answers. The score on total reasons was considered only in cases of extremely few or many responses, and no independent conclusions

TABLE 38   SCORES FOR ONE INDIVIDUAL ON THE LIFE PROBLEMS TEST

	Plus	Minus	Plus Percentage of Total
Friendliness	5	6	45
Honesty	9	4	69
Loyalty	3	8	27
Moral courage	2	10	17
Responsibility	1	13	8
Personal benefit	13	34	20
Total	20	54	72

Total reasons checked	38
Number inconsistent	3
Percentage inconsistent	8

were drawn from it. The inconsistencies turned out to be relatively few; these scores were helpful only in a few cases of extreme consistency or inconsistency. The main conclusions were drawn from the relative frequency of negative and positive values and their consistency from situation to situation.

Item Analysis

An item count was made of the frequency of choice for the various courses of action and for the reasons supporting these choices. The former is not described here because these courses of action have little meaning apart from the situations. The results of this analysis were used, however, in getting impressions about the relative consistency between decisions on conduct and supporting reasoning. For example, some people showed better judgment in *what* should be done than in *why* it should be done.

The freedom to choose from among a wide range of reasons produced highly scattered frequencies in number of reasons. Although on the average two to four reasons were named in each exercise, some of the reasons were used by very few students. Because of this, an item count of all reasons seemed unnecessary. It was sufficient for our purposes to examine the reasons used by fewer than 15 per cent, and by more than 50 per cent, of the students. These have been marked † and ‡, respectively, on the sample instrument reproduced above.

The conclusions suggested by this analysis are similar to those suggested by the analysis of the Student Beliefs Test. They reveal a strong approval of the common code, especially with respect to honesty. They give further and sharper evidence of an individualistic and self-centered motivation for responsibility, while ambivalence, confusion, and immaturity are shown in regard to friendliness and moral courage. Loyalty to a group and to personal friends is expressed more often in this test than in Student Beliefs. Apparently loyalty is more meaningful as a concrete act in a concrete setting than as a general principle.

The impression is also reinforced that these young people have difficulty in making choices among values and tend to rely on adult stereotypes when faced with difficult choices.

Distribution of Scores

As can be seen from Table 39 the total number of reasons marked ranged from 9 to 58, with an average of 29. The average number of reasons used for each course of action was 3.6.

Consistency is quite high, with a median of 89 per cent and a range from 50 to 100. This high consistency may be somewhat spurious because many students marked sparingly and thereby had little opportunity to reveal inconsistencies. It is not clear whether marking few reasons is due to caution or to the single-answer tradition in test taking.

On all traits, the medians for positive reasons is higher than those for negative reasons. For the five traits the lowest medians for percentage-plus reasons occur on responsibility and friendliness; the highest, on honesty. Since responsibility stood highest on Student Beliefs and lowest on Life Problems, one would conclude that in this trait general beliefs are not in keeping with their application.

Judging from the percentage-plus scores, the variations from trait to trait are slight. About the same percentage of positive values occurs on all traits.

For plus scores, the standard deviations in relation to range permit grouping the scores into three or four groups, with no overlap.

TABLE 39   LIFE PROBLEMS: REASONS MARKED BY SUBJECTS

	Number of Items	Median	Range	Standard Deviation
Total reasons marked	112	29	9 – 58	
Average per course of action		3.6	1.9– 7.2	
Percentage consistent		89	50 –100	
Total plus	98	33	5 – 59	9.7
Total minus	112	19	6 – 46	12.8
Total percentage plus		62	29 – 85	
Friendliness plus	20	5	0 – 11	2.6
Friendliness minus	9	3	0 – 6	1.4
Friendliness percentage plus		67	0 –100	
Honesty plus	17	8	2 – 13	3.3
Honesty minus	21	2	0 – 5	2.4
Honesty percentage plus		79	0 –100	
Loyalty plus	22	8	1 – 13	3.1
Loyalty minus	13	2	0 – 8	2.0
Loyalty percentage plus		73	27 –100	
Moral courage plus	14	7	0 – 13	3.5
Moral courage minus	19	2	0 – 11	2.5
Moral courage percentage plus		73	0 –100	
Responsibility plus	25	8	1 – 15	3.7
Responsibility minus	20	4	0 – 11	2.7
Responsibility percentage plus		67	8 –100	
Personal benefit	30	7	2 – 14	3.4
Personal benefit percentage		20	7 – 45	

This, however, is not possible for the negative scores, where the standard deviations comprise from one-third to one-half the total range. Since they were not differentiating, except for extreme cases, the latter scores had to be used with great caution.

Reliability

Reliability was assessed for plus and minus scores by using the formula developed by Kuder and Richardson.[5] In computing these reliabilities all reasons were used without regard to the particular test problem in which they appeared. As can be seen from Table 40, reliabilities of the plus scores range from 0.58 to 0.81, the

TABLE 40   LIFE PROBLEMS: RELIABILITIES

Moral courage +	0.81
Moral courage −	0.65
Honesty +	0.75
Honesty −	0.68
Responsibility +	0.67
Responsibility −	0.70
Loyalty +	0.64
Loyalty −	0.62
Friendliness +	0.58
Friendliness −	0.28
Personal benefit	0.64

highest being on moral courage and the lowest on friendliness. Negative scores on all traits are less reliable than positive and markedly so on friendliness.

Since the Kuder and Richardson method usually underestimates actual reliability, the scores from this test can be considered dependable enough to be used both in analysis of individual cases and in group comparisons.

Intertrait Correlations

Two studies were made to check on the relationships between values.

First, the scores on each trait were correlated with scores on every other trait. As can be seen from Table 41, these correlations are quite low, and in several instances they are negative. The lowest relationship is between honesty and loyalty; the highest is between honesty and moral courage.

[5] G. E. Kuder and W. W. Richardson, "The Theory of the Estimation of Test Reliability," *Psychometrica*, Vol. II, No. 3, pp. 151–160, 1937.

It is quite evident that the traits are much more sharply differentiated when judgments are made with reference to concrete situations (as in Life Problems) than when they are made at a level of generality (as in Student Beliefs). Often the test problems were

TABLE 41   LIFE PROBLEMS: INTERTRAIT CORRELATIONS

	Honesty	Loyalty	Moral Courage	Responsibility
Friendliness	−0.38 *	0.30	0.14	−0.03
Honesty		−0.42	0.46	0.31
Loyalty			−0.28	0.09
Moral courage				0.47

* Probable errors range from ±0.05 to ±0.06.

such that expression of loyalty to friends conflicted with other values, such as moral courage. Over and over again students refrained from betraying personal friends or from criticizing committee chairmen for fear of getting themselves into trouble. Am-

TABLE 42   STUDENT BELIEFS AND LIFE PROBLEMS: QUARTILE STANDINGS AND QUARTILE DEVIATIONS

		Sum of Quartile Standings on Five Traits	Average Quartile Standing	Average Quartile Deviation
Student beliefs	Range	5–20	1.0–4.0	0.00–1.40
	Median	12	2.5	0.64
Life problems	Range	8–19	1.6–3.8	0.32–1.44
	Median	11	2.4	0.80

bivalence was also shown between responsibility and loyalty to group undertakings and loyalty to persons involved.

Second, a comparison was made of the average deviation of the quartile position on each trait and the average quartile position for the test as a whole.

For Life Problems, scores for each trait were grouped into four quartiles. A value of 1 was assigned to the lowest quartile; a value of 4, to the highest. Each student's quartile standings were averaged, yielding an "average quartile standing."

Each quartile standing was then compared to the "average quartile standing," and these deviations, in turn, were averaged, yielding an "average quartile deviation."

The same procedure was used with data from Student Beliefs. Results are shown in Table 42.

The table shows that, in general, students assume about the same position on all traits but show a sharper differentiation of values in concrete situations than at a general level. On Student Beliefs, the average variation is a little over half a quartile, while on Life Problems it is more than three-fourths of a quartile.

Although there is this slight tendency toward a greater differentiation of values in concrete situations, the fact still remains that the moral beliefs pertaining to character and conduct tend to be generalized rather than specific, at least as regards the traits studied here.

Relation to Reputation

For data on the relationship between overt conduct and the ability to intellectualize problems of conduct, coefficients of correlation were calculated between the criterion scores on reputation and the

TABLE 43   CORRELATIONS BETWEEN LIFE PROBLEMS TEST AND REPUTATION

Honesty	0.33 ± 0.07
Responsibility	0.17 ± 0.08
Loyalty	0.17 ± 0.08
Moral courage	0.01 ± 0.08
Friendliness	0.03 ± 0.08

percentage-plus scores of the Life Problems Test. Results are shown in Table 43.

These correlations are low, ranging from 0.005 on moral courage to 0.33 on honesty. These low correlations suggest that sixteen-year-olds conduct themselves largely in terms of remembered rules and that the relationship between their overt conduct and what they think about conduct is relatively slight.

At the same time, there is good reason to believe that the actual relationship is higher than is suggested by these correlations.

Shortcomings in both instruments should first be taken into account in interpreting these correlations.

Using the percentage-plus score introduces additional problems, inasmuch as high scores are earned by people who mark extremely few reasons, thus, in many cases, distorting relative standings on values. All in all, a score-by-score comparison probably is too refined a method to be used with these data.

A comparison of quartile standings probably gives a clearer picture of the actual relationships. This comparison has been shown in Chapter 8.

Almost half the students stand in the same quartile on reputation as on Life Problems. Extreme discrepancy, that is, standing in the highest quartile on reputation and the lowest on the percentage-plus scores, occurs only in four to six cases on each of the five traits. Slightly less than half the cases have a discrepancy of one quartile point. It seems evident, then, that there is some agreement between conduct and the value positions as expressed in concrete situations. That some extreme discrepancies exist is evident from the case studies. In most such cases there were reasonable explanations to be found—in the attitude toward the test itself, in a personal maladjustment, or in differences in behavior between school and out-of-school situations.

Relation to Student Beliefs

To determine the relationship between general moral beliefs and their application in concrete situations, the total desirable score on Student Beliefs was correlated with the percentage-plus score on Life Problems. The percentage-plus score was used in place of the raw plus score in order to neutralize the effect of differences in numbers of reasons marked. At the same time, this score has the disadvantage that the people who mark extremely few reasons can easily earn a 100 per cent score.

These correlations are low, as shown in Table 44. They range from -0.13 on friendliness to 0.29 on responsibility, with 0.34 for the total score.

High correlations were not expected for several reasons. There is a marked difference in the two tests. Student Beliefs deals with generalities and covers a wide range of values, while Life Problems deals with specific situations, includes very specific statements, and covers a narrow range of values. It is therefore possible that students who in general accept principles of honesty may not apply them when the same principles are involved in a specific situation at a very concrete level.

Moreover, the Life Problems Test forced students to choose between values so that a high score on one trait necessitates a lower score on other traits. Each situation in the Life Problems Test posed a direct choice between conflicting values, while in Student Beliefs different values were represented by separate items. A factor not present on the Student Beliefs Test is that of character values contrasted with personal interest. Those individuals who are immature or less capable of rational thinking might be expected

TABLE 44   CORRELATIONS BETWEEN STUDENT BELIEFS AND LIFE PROBLEMS

Responsibility	0.29 ± 0.07
Moral courage	0.27 ± 0.07
Honesty	0.26 ± 0.08
Loyalty	0.11 ± 0.08
Friendliness	-0.13 ± 0.08
Total test	0.34 ± 0.07

to show marked differences. All these factors tend to produce discrepancies in subjects' scores on the two tests.

There are also reasons for assuming that the correlation coefficients underestimated the relationship. As was pointed out earlier, the structure of the tests and the distribution of scores tend to lower the Pearson coefficient of correlation. Furthermore, the detailed examination of responses on both tests for nineteen special cases revealed a much higher consistency than these coefficients would lead one to assume. Such discrepancies as existed had reasonable explanations. Thus, for example, in several cases where the scores on Student Beliefs were markedly below the scores on Life Problems, the discrepancy was evidently due to the absence of generalized beliefs and to a habit of responding to concrete situations in terms of expediency rather than in terms of general principles.

USING THESE INSTRUMENTS IN CASE STUDIES

Moral values, like any other values, tend to be expressed in unique patterns in each individual. For this reason any scoring pattern, no matter how elaborate, cannot yield an adequate picture of an individual. In using these instruments in connection with case data, therefore, it was necessary to supplement the evidence secured from scores by a rather minute examination of the specific items, in order to discover any unique features that might have been obscured by the scores. Several approaches were used. It was quite rewarding, for example, to examine the desirable, undesirable, and uncertain responses for an individual. Referring to the item analysis made it possible to note any deviations from the majority pattern.

Deviations in responses according to specific situations were also noted. For example, if an individual gave few desirable responses on responsibility but gave desirable responses on every item dealing with employment, a strong identification with the employment situation was indicated. On the other hand, when a broad positive reaction to honesty was coupled with rejection of those honesty items to which most students reacted favorably, a unique case of conditioning seemed to be indicated.

Of particular interest was the shift of patterns from trait to trait. Examination was made of the consistency of responses involving family relations to honesty, responsibility, and so on, to note to what extent a particular cluster of values was related to a particular situation.

On the whole, this analysis followed a certain pattern. First scores were marked according to the extent of deviation from the median; scores in the highest quartile were circled, and undesirable scores checked. The student's answer sheet was then examined to note which particular items he marked positively, negatively, or with uncertainty. Individual response patterns were compared with group averages. Desirable, undesirable, and uncertain responses were examined for deviations in different aspects of the same trait (e.g., whether lying, stealing, or keeping promises were emphasized in honesty) or for consistent mentions or omissions of certain situations (e.g., whether responsibility in school was accepted while responsibility at home was not).

Such a minute analysis is a time-consuming process and could not be applied in all cases. It was done for nineteen individuals on whom case studies were made. In these cases it was found to be a highly valuable process. It yielded more insight on the individual's pattern of values and beliefs than could be gained from manipulation of scores. It also provided clues to the inner dynamics of moral beliefs, which were helpful in making generalizations. Often it was possible to glean information on aspects of behavior which were not dealt with directly in the instruments. For example, the data on Student Beliefs yielded information on adjustment, attitudes toward work, and affectional disposition. Although such information was not dependable enough to be used independently, it was useful when added to other available data.

The most important contribution of this detailed analysis was the added insight in interpreting the scores of individuals on whom it was impossible to obtain case study summaries.

CONCLUSIONS

Although these instruments were derived from techniques developed in the Eight-Year Study,[6] their application to the field of personal beliefs, where "right" and "wrong" is strongly emphasized, represented a new venture. In both types of instruments, the general questionnaire as well as the problems test, it is more difficult to produce test items because great indirection is needed to obtain valid results. The present instruments, particularly the Life Problems Test, were not entirely successful in that respect, and many improvements are indicated should they be used again, particularly if used independently of other data.

In spite of the limitations of these instruments, the results were highly gratifying and suggest that, with adequate care, it is possible to construct helpful objective instruments in this field. They provide a broader sampling of beliefs and attitudes than it is usually possible to obtain through interviews or observation. They also represent a necessary supplement to the "projective" tests which require a specially trained interpreter and which do not provide systematic sampling of a wide variety of reactions.

It is very important, however, to point out that the data from such instruments cannot be treated mechanically, even though objective scores are provided. A certain flexibility must be maintained in interpreting individual patterns.

[6] Eugene R. Smith and R. W. Tyler, *Appraising and Recording Student Progress*, Chap. 3. New York: Harper & Brothers, 1942.

24

Methods of Studying Values

In an attempt to get data on the moral values of sixteen-year-olds, one of the methods used was the analysis of essays written on topics designed to elicit indirect expressions of moral ideology.

A series of compositions were assigned and written in the last twenty-five to thirty-five minutes of the English class period. The facts that this was not regular classwork to be handed in and graded, and that class time was taken up and the subjects' own free time not infringed upon, made for a favorable set toward the task. Though asked to sign their names, students knew that the material would not be evaluated in relation to their academic records, since the entire procedure was administered by the research worker with whom they were already acquainted and with whom they had already cooperated in other aspects of the character studies.

The essays were written on three different days. The following directions were given:

1. "The Person I Would Like to Be Like"

Describe in a page or less the person you would most like to be like when you grow up. This may be a real person or an imaginary person. He or she may be a combination of several people. Tell something about this person's age, character, appearance, occupation, and recreations. If he is a real person, say so. You need not give his real name if you do not want to.

2. "Where Do I Get My Ideals?"

Is there someone whose ideals and ideas you follow? Are you choosing a life work because someone you respect and admire is successful in that particular occupation? Do you admire someone for his or her home life? Do you walk and talk like this person? Think about questions like these, and then write a brief essay telling about this person, if there is such a person in your life.

3. "My Heroes"

Write a paragraph on each of three to five people who are your heroes. They may be living or dead. They may be men or women. Tell what you like about each one. If they are living, give their age as nearly as you know it.

The first day all subjects seemed able to write fairly easily. The second day several students said they had written everything which pertained to this subject before; they were asked to write it again if necessary. By the third day there was considerable resistance to the task.

The first essay proved to give the best coverage on all the areas. On the essay "Where Do I Get My Ideals?" it was impossible to determine the moral values held by the students because in many cases the student merely listed a parent or another person and gave no indication of the qualities or the characteristics for which this person was admired. The lack of interest manifested by the third day was reflected in the response on "My Heroes." It was decided therefore to use only the essay "The Person I Would Like to Be Like" in analyzing values.

METHODOLOGICAL PROBLEMS

A scale was devised for rating the essays on moral values. There was no effort to make fine philosophical discriminations. Typical responses were formed into a scale ranging from the selfish and materialistic to the altruistic and spiritual,[1] and numerical weights were assigned to each scale unit.

Three judges, working independently, then rated typewritten copies of the essays from which the name of the writer had been deleted. The range of numerical scores proved to be small, and there were many papers with the same score.

Consequently, the papers were reranked by each judge in order of merit according to his qualitative judgment. This resulted in placing all the papers in a rank order. The average of the three rank-order scores was used as the measure of the values expressed in an essay. These average scores were used in comparisons of the essay material with other data.

Agreement among Judges

Agreement among the three judges was checked by finding the rank-order correlation coefficients for the various pairs of judges. The coefficients were 0.58, 0.61, and 0.68.

[1] The scale reproduced in the following section is a refined form of the scale actually used in the study.

Consistency of Judgments

Two judges rerated the essays after an interval of two months. The rank-order correlation between the first and second ratings was 0.79 for each judge.

When agreement among judges and consistency of judgments had been computed, as described, scores on values were assigned to each subject, and these scores were correlated with reputation ratings, IQ, school achievement, and social-class position. These data have been described in Chapter 9.

Refinements of the Scale

The use of written essays and a scale for rating values expressed in essays seemed at this point sufficiently profitable to warrant further refinement of the method. Although the data on Prairie City sixteen-year-olds had already been analyzed, the method was to be applied to other subjects. For the sake of the reader who is especially interested in methodology, a description of further refinements is included here.

Conferences were held by the three judges who rated the essays written by sixteen-year-olds, to discuss those essays on which there were the greatest disagreements. These conferences resulted in a revised form of the scale as reproduced here. It does not differ greatly from the earlier form actually used in this study, but categories have been more finely drawn.[2]

Rating Scale for Essay "The Person I Would Like to Be Like"

	Score
I. Character and personality traits	
Material values: money, property, clothes.	0
Good looks, good appearance, neat, clean.	1
Good personality: stereotypes, popular.	1
Friendly, lots of friends, courteous, polite, can take a joke.	2
Honest, responsible, industrious, church goer, kind, patient.	3
Cooperative, helpful.	4
Self-sacrificing, working for social justice, peace, human brotherhood; altruistic.	5

[2] Had this second form of the scale been used with the essays written by sixteen-year-olds, the data presented in Chapter 9 would remain unchanged. This is because all comparisons made in Chapter 9 are based on rank-order scores. The numerical scores which are available from the revised scale do not affect rankings to any appreciable extent.

Score

II. *A.* Occupation—type

    Glamorous occupations: movie star, airplane pilot, singer, comic strip character, baseball player.   0

    Ordinary occupations: secretary, farmer, housewife, lawyer, filling-station attendant, teacher, also high-order but "glamorous" occupations, such as author, inventor.   1

    Occupations involving service and altruism: nurse, doctor, minister, social worker.   2

    B. Occupation—values

    Money reward, fame, excitement.   0

    Enjoyment, happiness, adjustment.   1

    Achievement, self-support (pulling own weight).   2

    Contribution to society through service, creativity, occupation as a carefully thought-out part of a design for living.   3

III. Recreation

    Ordinary recreations, merely listed.   0

    Creativity in recreation, and recreation as part of a design for living.   1

IV. Abstraction

    Imaginary person or combination of qualities from several people.   1

The new form of the scale made the rating procedure more objective. The following rank-order coefficients were obtained from the ratings of four different judges on several different sets of essays: 0.88, 0.83, 0.77, 0.76, and 0.73. Approximately the same agreement was found when the scale was used by untrained judges.

Number of Judges Necessary

The question had arisen in treating the data on sixteen-year-olds: How many judges are necessary to yield an average ranking for each subject which will be reliable? It was decided that an average of the ratings of three judges on a given essay gave a score sufficiently objective for the purposes of the study. This decision was based on a calculation of the predicted correlation between the average ratings of three judges and the average ratings to be expected from an infinite number of judges. Using the average correlation coefficient for any pair of the judges as 0.80, the predicted correlation with the average of an infinite number of judges is 0.96. Hence very little could be gained in objectivity of scoring by using more than three judges. In fact, the average of two judges' ratings has a predicted correlation of 0.94 with the average of an infinite number of judges.

Reliability of the Essays

There was one further methodological problem. After it had been demonstrated that a judge's ratings were self-consistent and that two different judges agreed fairly well in their ratings, there remained the question of the consistency of values as expressed by an individual in verbal statements. That is, how closely does a given boy or girl repeat himself when he writes on the topic of values at two different times? This was the problem of determining the reliability of the essay as a test of values.

This question was approached in two ways. First, the Prairie City group was asked to repeat the essay after an interval of one year. Only 44 of the original 78 individuals wrote the essay both times. Three judges, two of whom had been involved in the original ratings, ranked the 44 essays. An average of all three judges' ranks was then assigned to each essay. The correlation for the average rank for the first and second writing of the essays was 0.37. Upon investigation it was found that 5 of the 44 cases deviated so greatly as to account in large proportion for the low correlation.

The second check on the consistency of values stated by the individual at different times was made by comparing the papers of children who wrote the essays with a two-month interval between the two writings. These groups were thirteen and fourteen years old, not in Prairie City but in other midwestern communities. Their first assignment was as nearly as possible the same as that given the Prairie City group. After a period of two months they were asked to repeat the process and were given the following directions:

Write on the subject "The Person I Would Like to Be Like." You will probably remember you were asked to write on this same subject some time ago. Just write anything you like, and do the best you can.

The instructions regarding the essay itself and the leading questions were then repeated, and a note to the administrator of the essay was attached as follows:

Note: If pupils ask whether it is all right to repeat what they wrote before, say "yes" and go on to say that it is also all right to change what they said before, and vice versa. Be sure to include both possibilities with equal stress whichever way the question may be asked.

Three judges ranked each essay, as before. For one group (the fourteen-year-olds) the rank-order correlation between the first and second essays was 0.51. For the other group (the thirteen-year-olds) the correlation was 0.60.

On the basis of these correlations, it was concluded that the average test-retest correlation for the essay is about 0.55. This seemed the soundest conclusion in spite of the possible hypothesis that the reliability of the test decreased with age. The thirteen-year-old group was more heterogeneous than the fourteen-year-old group and hence might be expected to show a higher reliability coefficient. The correlation for Prairie City was omitted in calculating this average, on the ground that a year is too long an interval for test-retest. Considerable development in values and ideals occurs within a year, and this development may proceed at different rates in different persons. A two-month interval seems about right, since the memory of the preceding essay is probably dim, and yet not much time has been allowed for the development of values due to added maturation and experience.

Comments on the Method

It has often been questioned whether an individual will discuss his "private" beliefs and problems with any degree of frankness or whether he could tell much, even if he were willing to divulge this aspect of his life. The essays seemed to ask for that part of the value pattern which is in the foreground of consciousness and can be rather readily expressed because relatively free of emotion.

It has also been questioned whether such material is "warm" enough to get anything but superficialities. Perusal of the essays seemed to show that an official ideology, common to all members of the school group and probably representing that which the community has emphasized and rewarded, was expressed in some of the papers. This is what the individual can and is willing to express—an official ideology, as distinguished from a private ideology.

This set of official values may be different from those values which actually guide the individual's behavior; or perhaps, although they serve as a guide, they are difficult to carry through and exemplify. It is a truism that what one believes one should do is different from what one really does do.

The criticism is also made that the individual, when asked to reveal his feelings and beliefs, will feel under pressure to conform to social expectations.

Granting the worth of such criticisms, the essay is a method of getting at those values which, of all the values to which he has been "exposed," the individual feels are important enough to warrant at least outward or seeming conformity.

RELATIONS BETWEEN VALUES AND OTHER FACTORS

As stated in Chapter 9, the relationships between values as expressed in the essays and character reputation, between values and IQ, values and school achievement, and values and social class

TABLE 45   CORRELATIONS BETWEEN VALUES SCORE AND OTHER SCORES

	Reliability Coefficient	Correlation with Values Score	Correlation with Values Score Corrected for Attenuation
Values score	0.55		
Reputation score	0.86	0.42	0.61
School achievement	0.70	0.41	0.66
Stanford-Binet IQ	0.90	0.34	0.48

position, all proved to be positive but low. This generalization should be qualified in the light of certain statistical considerations.

The correlations of value scores with other scores are all reduced artificially because the essay test has low reliability. Scores on a test with low reliability cannot correlate highly with scores on other tests, even though there may actually be a very high correlation between the factors which the tests are supposed to measure.

The reliability coefficient of the essay test as described above is about 0.55. Knowing the correlation coefficient between values scores and other sets of scores, such as reputation, intelligence quotient, or school achievement, and knowing the reliability coefficients of these other measures, we can apply the usual formula to get the correction for attenuation. This formula gives the estimated correlation between two variables, if the measures of the two variables have been completely reliable.

In Table 45 are given the correlation coefficients actually found for values scores and scores on other factors, the reliability coefficients of the various tests, and the hypothetical correlation coefficients corrected for attenuation. In this table the reliability coefficients for school achievement and Stanford-Binet IQ are conservative estimates from other studies. The correlation coefficients given in the second column are the product-moment coefficients corresponding to the rank-order coefficients cited in Chapter 9.

The corrected correlation coefficients may be taken as estimates of the results which would have been obtained if measures of values and the other factors had been completely reliable. Although an estimated coefficient of correlation must be used with caution, it is probably safe to say that the relation of values to reputation is actually considerably higher than is indicated by a correlation of 0.42 and may be as high as 0.6 or more.

Thus it seems a sound conclusion to say that, of all the factors positively related to high character reputation, verbal statements of ideals, when obtained in an essay of the type used here, have a relatively high relationship with reputation.

25

Methods of Studying Personal-Social Adjustment

In endeavoring to trace in such a population as the Prairie City sixteen-year-olds the relationships that exist between traits of personal adjustment and reputation ratings, either of two methods of approach may be used.

1. The patterns of personal adjustment in selected individuals may be examined, in order to discover how different configurations of personal characteristics are reflected in the different character-trait ratings, i.e., the "case-history" approach. This method has been employed on a number of sixteen-year-olds, using data obtained from a variety of inventories, questionnaires, interviews, and other sources, and is described in Part III.

2. Using such techniques as correlation or group difference, statistical comparisons may be made between the performance of groups of individuals on whatever adjustment inventory is used (in this case the California Personality Inventory, Secondary Series) and their reputation ratings. The latter procedure is the subject matter of the present chapter.

The two methods are complementary, rather than competing, methods of inquiry; each makes its distinctive contribution to the understanding of the relationships and of the nature and course of the adjustment processes themselves. The statistical analysis here summarized shows general trends and contingencies, but these trends may be masked or compensated for in a variety of ways in individual cases.

CORRELATION METHODS

Table 46 shows coefficients of correlation between adjustment scores and character ratings for sixteen-year-olds. These coefficients are tetrachoric coefficients, computed with the aid of

TABLE 46   CORRELATIONS BETWEEN ADJUSTMENT SCORES AND CHARACTER RATINGS FOR SIXTEEN-YEAR-OLDS

	Self-Adjustment	Social Adjustment
Honesty	0.39	0.29
Moral courage	0.26	0.10
Friendliness	0.43	0.16
Loyalty	0.31	0.02
Responsibility	0.20	0.21
Average of five traits	0.32	0.16
Self-adjustment and social-adjustment scores		0.80

tables.[1] A number of the correlations have also been recomputed by the product-moment formula, with substantially the same results.

As stated in Chapter 10, the general relationship between adjustment and character reputation appears from these data to be positive, but low.

It might be asked in this connection whether the correlations obtained are low because responses to the adjustment inventory cannot be taken at their face value. One aspect of this problem has been discussed in Chapter 10. To go a step further, the correlations cited above can be compared with those obtained with similar data on Prairie City ten-year-olds.[2] Correlation coefficients for the ten-year-old subjects are shown in Table 47.

It will be seen, by comparing Tables 46 and 47, that the relationships are much higher at the ten-year-old level than at the sixteen-year-old level.

Correlations which decrease so much with six years' age difference call for some explanation. Although the data deal with

[1] L. Chesire, M. Saffir, and L. L. Thurstone, "Computing Diagrams for the Tetrachoric Correlation Coefficient," University of Chicago Bookstore, 1935.

[2] Ten-year-olds were given the California Personality Test, Elementary Series. The "Elementary Series" resembles the "Secondary Series" given to sixteen-year-olds, except that there are a total of 144 questions instead of 180.

two different groups of young people and are therefore not conclusive, certain possibilities suggest themselves.

The first is that between the ages of ten and sixteen years the naïveté and frankness of the ten-year-olds in admitting feelings of personal and social inferiority decrease, and many sixteen-year-olds hesitate to give replies which might arouse humiliating feelings or be open to social criticism. They have perhaps learned in six years to "cover up" and make superficial adjustments at certain points. To discover just where and how these adjustments are

TABLE 47   CORRELATIONS BETWEEN ADJUSTMENT SCORES AND CHARACTER RATINGS FOR TEN-YEAR-OLDS

	Self-Adjustment	Social Adjustment
Honesty	0.46	0.78
Moral courage	0.31	0.51
Friendliness	0.59	0.64
Loyalty	0.59	0.66
Responsibility	0.45	0.88
Average of five traits	0.48	0.69
Self-adjustment and social-adjustment scores		0.59

made in individual cases would require more searching clinical techniques than can be provided by a questionnaire.

Another possibility is that the more conscientious sixteen-year-olds have had six more years of practice in making their habits conform to family and community standards of conduct. At the same time they may not have achieved a corresponding increase in self-confidence and sense of effective social adaptability. Consequently, they have high reputation ratings but low adjustment scores. When some fifteen cases known to fit this description were omitted from the correlation table, the coefficients rose materially, in some cases as high as twenty points.

Still another possible reason for the lower correlation coefficients at the sixteen-year-old level lies in the fact that many of the sixteen-year-old subjects with the lowest reputations had dropped out of school and did not take the test. The effect of eliminating a group from the lower end of the character-score range is probably to reduce the size of the coefficients of correlation.

In general, the correlations reflect the fact that "adjustment" is a loose and comprehensive concept and is not very meaningful until it is broken down into the different kinds and directions of adjustive behavior represented by the twelve subscores and in still further detail by the item analyses. Although this gives a larger variety of comparisons, such subscores represent too narrow a range of individual variation to make correlation coefficients meaningful. Hence chief reliance has been placed on the group-difference method.

GROUP-DIFFERENCE METHODS

Scores on Self-Adjustment and Social Adjustment

Table 17 in Chapter 10 shows the average scores made by the high ratees and low ratees on each character trait for total "self-adjustment" and total "social adjustment."

The differences between high- and low-rated groups are not large, considering the fact that each of the two parts of the inventory contains ninety items.

It should be borne in mind, however, that the range of scores is much less than 90. On self-adjustment, individual scores range from 32 to 87, with a standard deviation of 11.6; on social adjustment, from 28 to 90, with a standard deviation of 9.16.

Reliabilities of the differences shown in Table 17, Chapter 10, are moderate and vary with the trait. A few sample critical ratios were computed; they ranged from 1.7 to 3.

Scores on the Twelve Subtests

The difference between high- and low-rating groups on the twelve subtests were shown in Table 18 of Chapter 10. In 59 out of 60 comparisons the higher average adjustment score was made by the high-ratee group. Although the differences do not look large, it must be borne in mind that each subtest contains only fifteen items; and seldom is the interindividual range of scores on any one subtest greater than eight or nine points.

The consistent picture presented by Table 18, Chapter 10, is more significant than statistical reliabilities of separate items. For larger differences on separate items, reliabilities were found to be significantly high.

Differences between high- and low-rated groups on both "total" adjustment scores (self-adjustment and social adjustment) and subscores must, furthermore, be interpreted in light of the composition of the groups themselves. It will be recalled that the "high" group consists of persons receiving D-scores on character ratings of 22 or above; the "low" group, persons rated 18 or lower. Since 1 D-score is defined as 0.25 sigma,[3] the "high" group, on the average, contains a little more than the highest one-third of the total distribution; while the "low" group contains a little more than the lowest one-third. The actual proportions vary from trait to trait.

Assuming that there is some positive relationship between trait ratings and test scores, the differences between ratee groups as defined above would not be as large as if the contrasting groups were more sharply differentiated. However, the larger samplings would compensate in increased reliability for the smaller score differences. These expectations were verified by the fact, mentioned in Chapter 10, that on a trial comparison using a "very high" group (D-score 23 or higher) and a "very low" group (17 or lower), 51 out of 60 group differences were increased on the average by one-third; or, to include "total" scores, 61 out of 70 differences were increased.

Differences on Individual Test Items

Although any subtest represents a group of test items all of which express in some fashion the general characteristic named by the subtest title, the grouping cannot be taken too literally for several reasons. There are numerous items which could equally well have been placed in some other subtest. Some items, doubtless, are less valid than others in the same subtest but were included to equalize the tests in length. Moreover, the names attached to the subtests are themselves general and variable in meaning. As a consequence, any subtest is somewhat arbitrary in make-up, and this fact might be expected to influence group differences. Individual items, representing more specific habits of adjustment, thus should be scrutinized.

In Table 48 below are listed by number those items in the inventory which show the largest "low-high percentage differences." As explained earlier, this unit of measurement of the differentiating value of items is somewhat crude; so the table gives for each item the percentage of the low-ratee group and the percentage of the high-ratee group who give an unfavorable response. The "low-high percentage difference" can be readily computed from these figures.

[3] See Chapter 19 for description of D-scores.

**TABLE 48   DIFFERENTIATING ITEMS OF PERSONAL-SOCIAL ADJUST-
MENT**

Item Number	Unfavorable Response	Item, and Percentage Frequencies of Unfavorable Responses in Low-Ratee and High-Ratee Groups on Reputation Traits
		1A Self-Reliance
2	No	Is it easy for you to introduce or be introduced to people? [F53-33.]
4	Yes	Is it hard for you to continue with your work when it becomes difficult? [F60-39, R62-47.]
5	No	Do you give considerable thought to your future work or career? [F47-12, L47-22, R38-22.]
7 *	Yes	Is it hard for you to go on with your work if you do not get enough encouragement? [H20-40, L21-39.]
8	No	Do you usually do things that are good for you even if you do not like them? [F73-27, R57-29, H55-30, MC52-28.]
9	Yes	Is it hard for you to admit it when you are in the wrong? [H55-23, F47-21, MC48-23, L47-24, R48-29.]
11 *	Yes	Do you feel uncomfortable when you are alone with important people? [L42-59, R48-63.]
13 *	Yes	Do you usually feel uneasy when you are around people you do not know? [R86-59, L42-57.]
14	Yes	Do you usually get discouraged when other people disagree with you? [MC28-5, L26-7, R29-11, H25-8.]
15	Yes	Is it natural for you to feel like crying or pitying yourself whenever you get hurt? [R38-17, L37-17, MC28-13.]
		1B Sense of Personal Worth
16	No	Are you usually considered brave or courageous? [F73-39.]
17	Yes	Do you feel that you are not very good at handling money? [H53-30, R48-28, L42-24, MC40-23.]
19	Yes	Do you feel that people often treat you rather badly? [F47-27.]
20	No	Are you often invited to mixed social parties? [F53-30.]
22	No	Do your folks seem to think that you are going to amount to something? [F40-9, R38-7, L37-9, MC32-8, H32-13.]
23	No	Do people seem to think well of your family's social standing? [H20-3, R19-4.]
24	No	Do your friends seem to think you have likeable traits? [F27-3, L21-4, R19-4.]
28	No	Do you feel that people recognize your social standing as they should? [MC44-15, H37-13, L37-17, F27-9.]
29	No	Are you usually given credit for the good judgment that you show? [F40-18.]

**TABLE 48   DIFFERENTIATING ITEMS OF PERSONAL-SOCIAL ADJUST-
MENT (Continued)**

Item Number	Unfavorable Response	Item, and Percentage Frequencies of Unfavorable Responses in Low-Ratee and High-Ratee Groups on Reputation Traits
30	Yes	Are you considered a failure in many of the things you do? [H37-15, R33-11.]

1C   Sense of Personal Freedom

34	No	Do your folks give you a reasonable amount of spending money? [H45-11, R33-11, F33-12.]
35	Yes	Are you scolded for many little things that do not amount to much? [F40-15, L37-15, R38-17.]
44	No	Are you encouraged to help plan your future vocation or career? [F33-6, L26-7.]

1D   Feeling of Belonging

46	No	Do you feel that you are an important part of your school? [F73-30, L56-35.]
49	Yes	Do your friends and acquaintances seem to have a better time at home than you do? [F33-12.]
60	No	Do you feel that people usually think well of you? [L21-2, R19-2.]

1E   Freedom from Withdrawing Tendencies

61	Yes	Are certain people so unreasonable that you can't help but hate them? [R90-43, F67-33, H60-40, MC60-43.]
64	Yes	Do you have many problems that cause you a great deal of worry? [H60-28, R62-31, L58-33.]
66	Yes	Are your responsibilities and problems such that you cannot help but get discouraged? [L58-31, H60-38.]
72 *	Yes	Do you find it difficult to associate with the opposite sex? [R0-24, H0-23.]
73	Yes	Does it seem to you that younger persons have an easier and more enjoyable life than you do? [F33-12.]
75	Yes	Are people frequently so unkind or unfair to you that you feel like crying? [L32-15, F27-12.]

1F   Freedom from Nervous Symptoms

76	Yes	Are you likely to stutter when you get worried or excited? [F33-12, MC32-13.]
78	Yes	Do you have the habit of biting your fingernails often? [L47-17, F47-21, R48-24, H40-18, MC44-25.]
79	Yes	Do you sometimes have nightmares? [L53-22, H45-20, F40-18, MC40-23.]

TABLE 48   DIFFERENTIATING ITEMS OF PERSONAL-SOCIAL ADJUST-
MENT (Continued)

Item Number	Unfavorable Response	Item, and Percentage Frequencies of Unfavorable Responses in Low-Ratee and High-Ratee Groups on Reputation Traits
81	Yes	Do you suffer often from annoying eyestrain? [MC60-25, H55-25, L47-22, R48-28.]
82	Yes	Is it hard for you to sit still? [F60-33.]
83	Yes	Are you more restless than most people? [L42-9, R33-11, F27-6, H35-15, MC28-13.]
84	Yes	Are you inclined to drum restlessly with your fingers on tables, desks, and chairs? [L47-26.]
85	Yes	Do people frequently speak so indistinctly that you have to ask them to repeat their questions? [R72-43, F67-52, L63-48.]
86	Yes	Do you frequently find that you read several sentences without realizing what they are about? [F100-75, R95-76, H90-73, MC92-75.]
87	Yes	Do you find that you are tired a great deal of the time? [F67-30, H45-28, R48-31.]
88	Yes	Do you often have considerable difficulty in going to sleep? [H40-18, R38-17, F33-15, L32-17.]
89	Yes	Do you have frequent headaches for which there seems to be no cause? [MC32-13, L32-13, F27-12.]

2A   Social Standards

91 *	Yes	Is it right to create a scene when parents refuse to let people of high-school age go to movies? [F40-12, H32-13, MC12-28.]
92 *	Yes	Is it all right to avoid responsibility or work if you are not required to do it? [MC16-40.]
95	No	Do high-school students need to follow their parents' instructions even though their friends advise them differently? [F27-6, L21-2, R20-4.]
96	No	Is it always necessary to express appreciation for help or favors? [MC20-3, F20-3, H21-5.]
98	Yes	Is it all right to disobey teachers if their requests appear to be unfair? [H58-25, R40-22.]
102	No	Should a person be courteous to disagreeable people? [H32-8, R30-7.]

2B   Social Skills

106 *	No	Do you often introduce people to each other? [MC20-43.]

TABLE 48   DIFFERENTIATING ITEMS OF PERSONAL-SOCIAL ADJUST-MENT (Continued)

Item Number	Unfavorable Response	Item, and Percentage Frequencies of Unfavorable Responses in Low-Ratee and High-Ratee Groups on Reputation Traits
107	Yes	Is it hard for you to lead in enlivening a dull party? [F73-42, MC68-53.]
108 *	No	Is it easy for you to talk with people as soon as you meet them? [L26-44, R25-43.]
109 .	Yes	Is it difficult for you to compliment people when they do something well? [L37-15, R35-13, F27-12.]
110	No	Do you often assist in planning parties? [H72-35, R55-35, L53-35.]
111 *	No	Do you usually remember the names of people you meet? [MC32-50, F40-55.]
112 *	No	Do you keep from letting people know when they irritate you? [H47-28, F13-33.]
113	Yes	Do you frequently find it necessary to interrupt a conversation? [R45-24, L42-24.]
118	No	Do you like to have parties at your home? [H37-13, R30-13, F40-24.]
120	Yes	Do you find that many people are easily offended by you? [L37-11, F33-12, R35-15.]

2C   Freedom from Anti-Social Tendencies

121 *	Yes	Are you justified in taking things that are denied you by unreasonable people? [H33-15, F7-30.]
123	Yes	Are you often forced to show some temper in order to get what is coming to you? [R80-50, H74-48, L68-52.]
125	Yes	Are people often so stubborn that you have to call them bad names? [MC28-5, H21-5.]
130 *	Yes	Are teachers and other people often so unfair that you do not obey them? [F0-15, L0-15.]
131	Yes	Do you often have to fight or quarrel in order to get your rights? [H58-10, R55-15, MC36-13, L37-17.]
133	Yes	Do little "kids" often get in your way so that you have to push or frighten them? [L26-2, R20-4.]
134	Yes	Are people at home or at school always bothering you so that you just have to quarrel? [F20-3, L21-4.]

2D   Family Relations

136	Yes	Are you troubled because your parents are not congenial? [L21-4, R20-4.]

TABLE 48   DIFFERENTIATING ITEMS OF PERSONAL-SOCIAL ADJUST-
MENT (Continued)

Item Number	Unfavorable Response	Item, and Percentage Frequencies of Unfavorable Responses in Low-Ratee and High-Ratee Groups on Reputation Traits
140	Yes	Are things difficult for you because your folks are usually short of money? [F20-0.]
142	Yes	Do your folks appear to doubt whether you will be successful? [F47-9, H37-15, R30-15.]
144	No	Do you like your parents about equally? [F27-6.]
146	Yes	Do you usually like to be somewhere else than at home? [H53-20, R50-17, MC36-15, L37-20, F40-24.]
150	Yes	Do you sometimes feel like leaving home for good? [F33-6.]

2E   School Relations

151	Yes	Are some of your subjects so difficult that you may be in danger of failing? [R52-15, MC40-10, L47-17, F40-12.]
153 *	Yes	Would you like to be chosen more often to take part in games and other activities? [L21-57, H32-58, R38-61.]
154	Yes	If it were right would you stay away from school as often as possible? [R43-7, L42-9, H40-8, F33-9, MC28-13.]
155	Yes	Would you and your classmates like school better if your teachers were not so strict? [H35-18, F40-24, R33-17.]
156 *	Yes	Would you be happier if your classmates liked you better? [F67-48, L42-57.]
158	Yes	Do many of the teachers seem to be unfair or unreasonable to their students? [H35-13, R33-15, L26-11.]
159	No	Do you like to go to school affairs with members of the opposite sex? [L42-17.]
164	Yes	Are many of your classmates so unkind or so unfriendly that you avoid them? [L32-7, R29-11.]

2F   Community Relations

166	Yes	Do you dislike to take responsibility for the welfare or safety of children or old persons? [H40-18.]
167	No	Do you like to take care of your own or some neighbor's pets? [H47-26, L47-28.]
169	Yes	Do you know people who are so annoying that you would like to molest them? [L58-35, R57-35, H50-30.]
170 *	No	Do you often play games with young folks in your neighborhood? [R19-50.]
173 *	Yes	Do you live in a rather uninteresting neighborhood? [L16-37, F20-36.]

TABLE 48   DIFFERENTIATING ITEMS OF PERSONAL-SOCIAL ADJUST-
MENT (Continued)

Item Number	Unfavorable Response	Item, and Percentage Frequencies of Unfavorable Responses in Low-Ratee and High-Ratee Groups on Reputation Traits
174	No	Are the police officers of such a character that you would like to help them? [H45-13, L42-13, R43-15, MC40-15, F33-12.]
175	No	Do you visit with several young men and women in your neighborhood? [F53-30.]
176	No	Do you sometimes go to neighborhood affairs with members of the opposite sex? [R86-41.]
177	No	Do you ever do anything to improve the appearance of your home surroundings? [L21-2, H20-5.]
180 *	Yes	Are most of the people in your community the kind you refrain from visiting? [H20-3, R19-4, F13-33.]

Only those items which show a percentage difference of twenty or more on at least one trait, or of fifteen or more on at least two traits, are shown here.   The initials H(onesty), M(oral) C(ourage), F(riendliness), L(oyalty), and R(esponsibility) indicate the traits showing the difference indicated; the first number is the low-ratee percentage, the second number, the high-ratee percentage; "yes" or "no" indicates the unfavorable response to the question.   Note that several items (marked *) show a higher percentage of unfavorable response among high ratees than among low ratees, on one or more traits.

26

Interviewing and Miscellaneous Methods

The various tests, questionnaires, rating scales, and observations used in these studies yielded a wide variety of data about the young people in Prairie City. In addition, at various points in the research program, subjects were interviewed for certain types of information not otherwise available. For example, one field worker interviewed systematically for information regarding friendship cliques and social participation in the high school.

INTERVIEWING

When the study of individual cases was begun, it became apparent that there were gaps in the data that could be filled only by further interview material. Consequently, a series of interviews was undertaken with each of these individuals to yield more personal types of information.

The first interview in the series was planned to provide an opportunity for the special field worker to get acquainted with the subject and to establish a friendly basis for later, more significant interviews. The information requested was objective and matter-of-fact: the subject was asked to bring up to date his employment record and his record of school and community activities. Occasionally this first interview yielded useful information with reference to attitudes toward employment and future vocational goals. In each case, it provided an opportunity for a second conference.

All the persons interviewed had previously taken various intelligence and aptitude tests, and almost without exception they asked if they might have their scores interpreted to them. The second interview, therefore, centered about these test results and about future educational and vocational plans. Although the field worker avoided giving specific advice, she encouraged discussion of these problems. Sometimes she gave help in individual cases by securing specific information about opportunities open to the young person in various army and navy programs, cadet nursing, and the like. This involved additional interviews with some of the subjects.

These preliminary interviews were not always particularly valuable from the standpoint of yielding information especially needed for the case studies, but they helped to promote a friendly, sympathetic relationship between the field worker and the subject—a relationship which proved highly important in eliciting more personal information in the final interview.

The final interview occurred a few months after the initial one. Five questions were used, to obtain information on the following aspects: the subject's estimate of himself as a person; his idea of other people's attitudes toward him; his conception of his personal problems; and his judgments as to the sources of difficulty and conflict in his life.[1]

The questions used were these:

1. Describe briefly any important or unimportant difficulties you have had at school, at home, or at work.

2. (a) Describe briefly some conditions or situations in which you had a lot of unpleasantness or disappointment. (b) Describe briefly some conditions or situations in which you had a lot of fun and enjoyed yourself.

3. If you could change your condition or situation—your school, your job, yourself, anything—what changes would you make?

4. What special abilities do you have? What abilities that you do not have would you like to possess?

5. How does what other people think of you differ from what you think of yourself?

Because of the highly personal nature of the questions asked, the technique used in handling this interview was somewhat different from that used in earlier interviews. It was felt that the subject might find it difficult and perhaps embarrassing to attempt an oral response, and consequently he was given a copy of the questions and asked to write his answers. Before he read the

[1] The authors wish to express their gratitude to Dr. Mandel Sherman, of the University of Chicago, under whose guidance these interviews were planned.

questions, however, he was given, in substance, the following explanation and instructions:

> As part of the study we are carrying on, we are interested in finding out how well people of your age are able to think objectively about themselves and their problems. The questions you are asked here have been planned with this specific purpose in mind. Read each question carefully, and write your answer in the space following the question. If any question is not clear to you, ask me about it and I shall explain further just what is wanted. After you have answered the questions I shall go over your paper with you. I may want to ask other questions to make sure that I know what you mean, and you may wish to make additional comments.

After the subject had written his answers to the questions, the field worker read the responses and used them as a basis for discussion. Additional questions were employed to encourage the subject to elaborate his answers and give additional information. Although the subjects varied in their ability to discuss the problems raised, each made a conscientious effort to do what was asked of him. Several expressed interest in attempting this kind of self-exploration and obviously welcomed the opportunity to discuss personal problems and attitudes.

Much of the most significant material was brought out in the discussion period and was promptly recorded by the field worker. Occasionally, however, the subject made comments which he obviously regarded as "off the record"; these could not be recorded until a convenient opportunity arose later in the interview or until the interview was over.

The frankness with which most of the subjects discussed their personal feelings and the wealth of material obtained seem ample reward for the care with which the whole series of interviews was planned; they also seem to warrant the conclusion that the interviews were highly successful in eliciting information which probably could not have been secured through other means.

MISCELLANEOUS METHODS

Other techniques or instruments used in the study are either so well known as to require no extended description or have been used only in a minor capacity.

Intelligence Test

The Revised Stanford-Binet Test, Form L, was given to nearly all members of the group during the school year of 1942–1943.

School Marks

As a measure of school achievement, the school grades for 1942–1943 were averaged for each student.

Interest Inventories

Two interest inventories were used—instruments that were prepared for the Eight-Year Study of the Progressive Education Association.[2] The PEA 8.2*a* Inventory was used to obtain information on subjects' interest in the school program and in various school subjects.

The PEA 8.2*b* Inventory proved more useful in these studies because it threw light on certain personality factors. This inventory gives a score on liking for aggressive activities, leadership activity, activities involving submission to authority, activities with the same sex and with the opposite sex, and several other categories. The pattern of likes and dislikes on this inventory yields information concerning the individual's self-adjustment.

Problem Check List

The Mooney Problem Check List [3] was useful as a measure of self-adjustment.

Stories from Pictures

A modified thematic apperception test [4] was designed for high-school boys and girls, consisting of pictures showing young men and women in a variety of situations. The subject was asked to tell a story to fit each picture. This test was found useful as a means of exploring the personality structures of the subjects studied by the Clinical Conference Group.

Sociometric Test

During the school year 1941–1942 all the high-school students took a combined sociometric-guess-who test.[5] This test gave informa-

[2] Eugene R. Smith and R. W. Tyler, *Appraising and Recording Student Progress*, Chaps. 5 and 6. New York: Harper & Brothers, 1942.

[3] Ross L. Mooney, "Problem Check List," High School Form, Bureau of Educational Research. Columbus, Ohio: The Ohio State University, 1941.

[4] Henry A. Murray et al., *Explorations in Personality*, pp. 530–545. New York: Oxford University Press, 1938.

[5] Bernice L. Neugarten, "Family Social Position and the Social Development of the Child," Ph.D. Dissertation, University of Chicago Library, 1943.

tion about the popularity of the subjects and about the various friendship groups in the school. It was especially useful in the case studies.

Rorschach Test

The Rorschach test was given individually to the nineteen boys and girls whom we studied intensively in our Clinical Conference Groups. It gave valuable insight into their personality structures.

Emotional-Response Test

This was a free-answer test in which the student was asked to write down three experiences which had made him happy; three which had made him sad; three, afraid; three, angry; and three, ashamed. He was then asked to tell what was the "best thing" and the "worst thing" that could happen to him.

Moral Ideology Test

This was a free-answer test in which the subject was asked to name nine examples of "good" behavior for a person his age; nine examples of "bad" behavior; and, in each case, to tell who would praise or blame the behavior.

27

Comparison of These Studies with the Character Education Inquiry

The authors were fortunate in having available the results of the Character Education Inquiry, completed some years earlier.[1] Since the studies reported here were concerned with the same type of problem, the authors had the advantage of Hartshorne and May's experience and of using their materials as a guide.

The Character Education Inquiry was especially helpful in describing methods for the study of character, particularly methods of studying character reputation. The primary emphasis in the Inquiry was on the development of standardized test situations which would provide measures of honesty, service, and self-control, as shown by children in their actual behavior, that is, measures of conduct. Although the tests themselves elicited behavior which could be labeled honest or dishonest, altruistic or selfish, persistent or non-persistent, inhibited or non-inhibited, the problem of how general these behavior tendencies were in the life of the individual could not be answered by the tests alone. Hence, measures of character reputation were devised, most of which were administered to teachers, and one was administered to the child's age mates. By comparing the results of reputation instruments with the results of their tests, Hartshorne and May were able to study the degree to which the conduct of the children on the tests was related to the general impression of character held by teachers and age mates.

[1] Hugh Hartshorne, Mark A. May, et al., *Studies in the Nature of Character:* I. *Studies in Deceit;* II. *Studies in Service and Self-Control;* III. *Studies in the Organization of Character.* New York: The Macmillan Co., 1930.

The following summary of their results provides the empirical justification for using reputation alone as the criterion of character. The results are based on the scores obtained by approximately 850 children in Grades 5 to 8, in three communities located near New York City.

The correlations between different tests for the same type of conduct were generally low. The coefficients between different tests for service ranged from 0.12 to 0.32 with an average correlation of 0.20; those between different tests for persistence ranged from 0.15 to 0.38 with an average of 0.16; the coefficients between different kinds of honesty tests ranged from 0.003 to 0.40. (These last figures are based on a larger population of cases.)

On the other hand the correlation coefficients between the different methods of measuring reputation ranged from 0.36 to 0.77. The correlation between the test administered to age mates and the combined tests administered to teachers was 0.48, while the average of the intercorrelations of the scores reporting teachers' judgments was 0.60.

Thus, more agreement was found between measures of reputation, even when measures were obtained from different groups of judges, than was found between different measures of actual conduct. Moreover, the coefficients between the reputation scores and the conduct scores tended to be slightly higher than the coefficients between the conduct scores themselves.

On the basis of these results there is a certain justification for saying that the measures of reputation yield as adequate a picture of character as do several measures of conduct in actual test situations. The explanation of this finding may be that each measure of conduct covers only a very limited range of behavior, and the type of behavior manifested is dependent upon the type of situation. Hence there is little relationship between conduct scores on different tests. On the other hand, the reputation scores are the result of observations by different people over a long period of time in meaningful situations of daily life.

In order to get an objective measure of general conduct tendencies, or character, one would need a much greater number and a wider variety of tests than were used in the Character Education Inquiry. But one would not need many more measures of reputation to get just as reliable and as valid a measure of character.

Since measures of reputation are easier to devise and administer than measures of actual conduct, there is additional reason for using reputation alone as an index of character.

These considerations led Hartshorne and May to the following conclusion already quoted in an earlier chapter:

> When enough opinions can be gathered with reasonable care and from contrasted sources—as from pupils, teachers, and parents—the resulting score becomes a fair substitute for an elaborate and expensive program of objective testing.[2]

As a result of their experiences and conclusions, reputation was used as the criterion of character in these studies. Effort was concentrated upon the careful preparation of instruments and upon the collection of judgments about the subjects from as wide a variety of people as possible. Three of the instruments used in these studies are adaptations of the instruments for measuring reputation used by the Character Education Inquiry: the Check List for adults is similar to their Conduct Record for teachers; the Character Sketch technique for adults is similar to their Portrait Matching device for teachers; and the Guess-Who Test for age mates is similar to their Guess-Who Test for age mates.

The instruments used here differ from Hartshorne and May's partly because the specific traits being studied were not the same as theirs and partly because the point of view and objectives were not identical with theirs.

The correlations obtained in these studies between the various reputation instruments are considerably higher than those reported by Hartshorne and May. The coefficient obtained between scores from adults and scores from age mates was 0.79, in contrast to the coefficient of 0.41 reported by them for the same two variables. Likewise the coefficients obtained between adult scores was 0.80, while the most comparable coefficient reported by them is 0.60, representing the average of the intercorrelations of three sets of teachers' opinions.

There are several differences between these studies and the Character Education Inquiry which might account for the higher correlations obtained here. For one thing, the instruments used with Prairie City subjects were more similar in content than were

[2] Hartshorne and May, *op. cit.*, III. *Studies in the Organization of Character*, p. 369.

theirs, and as a result the correlations might be expected to be higher.

Another important difference between the two studies is the difference in ages of subjects. Their subjects were in Grades 5 to 8, the mean age being between eleven and twelve. Prairie City subjects, on the other hand, were all sixteen years old, and almost all were in Grade 11. It is possible that, by the time an individual reaches sixteen years of age, his patterns of conduct have become more consistent, making it possible for different observers to form more similar opinions about him.

The higher correlation obtained here between the ratings of age mates and those of adults may be because the age mates in these studies were older than those in the Inquiry. As a result, their standards for evaluating people may be more similar to adult standards.

The authors have approached the problem of character formation from a somewhat different point of view than did the participants of the Character Education Inquiry and consequently have made a somewhat different use of data. The primary consideration of the earlier research was the construction of test situations which would elicit certain types of conduct. The main objective of these studies has been a better understanding of the individual in the light of his character reputation.

Although Hartshorne and May carried out extensive investigations into the variables which they thought might be related to conduct, they were seeking general trends in the population and expressed their results mainly in terms of correlation coefficients. The primary interest here has been in trying to understand how variables combine in any one individual to produce his character and reputation. Consequently, greater emphasis has been placed upon case studies.

These studies are similar to recent studies in personality which focus attention upon the dynamic patterning of traits within individuals. The attention here is upon those traits of personality which are subject to the moral sanctions of society, in other words upon traits of character.

Index

313

634